French Blues

French Blues

A Not-So Sentimental Journey Through Lives and Memories in Modern France

Paul Rambali

Heinemann : London

William Heinemann Ltd
Michelin House, 81 Fulham Road, London SW3 6RB
LONDON   MELBOURNE   AUCKLAND

First published in 1989
Copyright © Paul Rambali 1989

ISBN 0 434 62012 2

A CIP catalogue record for this book
is available from the British Library

Printed and bound in Great Britain by
Richard Clay Ltd, Bungay, Suffolk

This book is dedicated to Maria and Gustave

The grape and the grain

THE MARKET COMES to Vaison once a week, making Wednesday an important day. From before dawn, traders arrive to fill the narrow streets with stalls. There is the plump couple selling *charcuterie*, bursting from their white aprons, pink and happy as pigs. There is the woman selling honey, her nettle of wiry black hair tied back from a face pinched as a bee's. She is of indeterminate age and with a kind, almost drugged regard, as though nourished by some secret apicultural recipe. Her jars of white honey lie evenly spaced and surrounded by little bouquets of lavender. There is the old woman selling purple lettuce, ruddy as her produce. Cats become like their owners, they say, and owners become like their dogs. By the same quiet process, nurtured by contentment one with the other, the stall-holders in the market at Vaison had come to resemble their merchandise.

Traders used to gather in the old Roman town of Vasio, one of the richest of all southern Gaul, a walled enclave on the hill across the river Ouvèze. Beneath crumbling grey walls – all that remains of the château of the Count of Toulouse – the town continues to prosper, its rhythm and purpose little changed. Two centuries after the French Revolution, the tolling of the bell in the church of Our Lady still counts the hours in the nearby fields.

To the south lies the peak of Mont Ventoux, which saw Hannibal's passing latterday conqueror, in what is reckoned the most arduous leg of the Tour de France, is awarded the fabled blue jersey, symbol of 'the Goat', the best climber, for the final rounds through Paris of the 92-year-old bicycle race.

From the medieval windows of what are now three-star hotels, tourists peer at the blue-green countryside of the surrounding Vaucluse. Locals venture up the cobbled streets nowadays only for weddings at the church or to visit through low wooden doors the cool stone rooms transformed into showcases full of antiques.

It was in a house like this, made of earth and stone and perched on a hill, that my grandmother lived. It belonged to her second husband, a blacksmith who was often to be seen lying drunk and unconscious across his cart, being dragged slowly home by his horse, Bordeaux. Despite his name, Bordeaux lived in a village in the foothills of the Alps and, like his master, had never seen the Atlantic.

Leaving her husband to his thirsty labours, my grandmother walked the few kilometres down the hill to the nearby town to visit a market like the one at Vaison. Such markets pitch up once a week in most of the small towns in France. Competing with the local shops, the traders benefit from low over-heads: just the running costs of a Citroën panel van, the kind that still have lights on stalks and, because they are made of aluminium, almost never rust.

It is the first sunny day of spring, a day full of the warm promise of renewal. There are pink blossoms on the trees and thin young asparagus on sale in the market. The town square, a sandy patch shaded by beech trees that for most of the week is the domain of old men quietly playing *boules*, has been transformed for the day into a busy circus of bright awnings and cellophane-wrapped, fluorescent-lit foodstuffs: red hams hanging in bunches; rows of yellow corn-fed chickens; fresh white cheeses laid on leaves; coloured sweets under perspex lids; thick brown loaves and rich, glistening fruit tarts.

There is little to disturb the reverie of the small town. All the bounty of rural France is laid here in profusion. The God brought by the Romans is in his heaven and his chief enemy is far away: a cruel, bitter prophet busy feeding his children to the flames of martyrdom.

A presidential election is in progress but its machinations in the faraway capital draw only a provincial shrug. Everybody knows the probable outcome. The polls confirm the feelings of more than half the population; that the ship of state, though it might be rocked, must not be capsized. '*Ton-Ton*', or 'Uncle' Mitterrand to his supporters in the media – that corrupt Jewish-intellectual *combine* with the Marxists at the Elysée – is sure to be re-elected to a second term of office.

Vaison is a conservative town and it is clear to many of its citizens that polls don't tell the whole story and that, with unemployment rising, the main problem in France is the *clandestins*, the illegal immigrants who infest the country, usurping what jobs there are. At any rate, this is what the *fromager* tells me – though nobody in the media will admit it. His wife throws up her hands. 'No more politics. Don't start again! I don't want to hear anything more today.'

Manifesting the inevitable vertigo of small towns, forever fearing rupture with a changing world beyond, the grumbles of the people of Vaison in the market that day, nothing new in their character, are less disturbing than the feeling of atrophy. Returning to rural France after 20 years, I cannot feel the embrace of the timeless so much as the grip of a time that has stopped – a charming old grandfather clock like those once manufactured in the region, whose oak casing is crumbling, riddled with woodworm.

Scattered through the streets around the stalls, among the salad leaves and empty cartons, are handbills for a public meeting that evening. Printed large in Wild West woodblock letters like the name of a new sheriff is that of the deputy chief of the *Front National*, the patriotic league which over the last five years has upset the ballot box of French liberal democracy. No agenda is given, but it is clear from the posters that line the quiet roads of the region, stuck to lampposts and to the backs of roadsigns, that the subject will be the urgency of voting in the coming election for Front leader Jean-Marie Le Pen.

The cold spring sunshine holds only icy warmth. Traders have gathered as usual, but their customers are dwindling and the market has acquired a patina of inactivity. For centuries the weekly market has been the hub of life in the town, but the busiest stall is now the one selling slices of defrosted and warmed over pizza. Basic items like fruit and vegetables, knives and dishcloths are still cheap, drawing the thrifty and sometimes threadbare locals, but other stalls selling more expensive produce are little frequented, undercut by the nearby hypermarket. It is to the new complex on the outskirts of town that the busy young mothers drive to shop in their hatchbacks, the old community supplanted by six TV channels. The market is now the confine of the aged, the carless or the carefree, city dwellers down for a few days at their converted farmhouses, for which prices in the region are high.

A regrettable murder

THE POLITICAL MEETING takes place in the new civic centre, a gymnasium-style concert hall with floor-to-ceiling windows built in the early Seventies, a legacy of the drive towards the *aménagement du territoire*.

At the doors, burly young men in blue suits collect the 30fr admission fee. Whether locals or part of the visiting entourage, they make convincing ex-Paras, some carrying walkie-talkies. A range of *Front National* promotional items is on sale inside. Among the pamphlets, books, ties, key-rings and cassettes of speeches are bottles of FN wines and tins of FN *cassoulet*, the pork-and-bean stew that occupies a special place in the cosmology of French gastric satisfaction. My first impulse is to buy a tin, an example of political kitsch equal to the commercially short-lived *Popu*, an aperitif produced by the Communist Party in the Thirties in a frank bid for worker loyalties. For a further 100fr, a full dinner is offered later in the adjoining room, with a choice of FN chicken or beef, followed no doubt by FN cheese.

Also on sale is the manifesto of the *Front National* in the form of a French passport. It claims that last year more than 100,000 foreigners obtained French nationality; that 30 per cent of the population of French prisons are foreigners, principally Africans and Maghrébins; that half of the hospital beds in the Paris region are occupied by foreigners, few of them with official papers; that two-thirds of drug traffickers are foreign. These are worrying statistics whose truth nobody in the brightly lit hall tries to question.

On the seats are laid some pamphlets, including one about AIDS that traces the origins of the disease to Africa. Many of the people here tonight are easily persuaded that any kind of foreign arrival, other than a passing tourist, is a potentially lethal contamination – especially any from Africa.

The townspeople who have come, many clearly uncertain of how they should be dressed for a political rally, sit in awkward murmuring knots, conscious of their visibility from the roadside. They wear suits or jewellery, confusing it perhaps with a visit to the theatre or church. They glance up and down rows to see who else has come. On the stage in front of them a long table has been laid with a white sheet on which are set fresh flowers and bottles of Evian. *Tricolores* stand furled at each end.

There is something improper about the idea of a political rally in Britain. Political expression, like religious devotion, is a matter for discretion. The ballot box offers the privacy of a urinal. Alone with one's conscience, a childishly fat crayon and a slip of paper, the Briton makes a dutiful political gesture. No doubt since Cromwell there has been a good democratic reason for this. In France, the tradition of public meeting, with its implication of public upheaval, remains potent. Tens of thousands manifest on behalf of the major parties; solemn, stiff-backed demonstrators march down streets in their Sunday best in the name of different extremes. On public holidays in Paris, parades and rallies weave around each other as though on a board of snakes and ladders.

Public rallies were the foundry of the Republic, its smouldering embers always capable of being relit. This is the nostalgic hope of the Left, while the dream of the Right is that next time, they will seize the day. And as the 200th anniversary of the Revolution approaches, dreams and nostalgia make both sides restless. Left and Right: a dismemberment of the body politic occasioned when the Assembly returned from Versailles in 1790 and the radicals arranged themselves on the President's left while the conservatives sat on his right, giving political terminology a useful distinction but casting thenceforth a sinister shadow over Radicalism, for the left is a zone of uncertainty. The word sinister comes from the Latin *sinistra*, left; it was not so long ago that left-handed people were driven out of villages. And if the fears of the right-handed villagers were well-founded? What if some psychological predisposition to disturb made those radicals choose the benches on the left?

In the same way, conscious of tradition, speakers of both sides invoke the Revolution by careful allusion, as though in unconscious awe of the powers they disturb, like the name of some great deity too terrible to utter. France is after all an infant republic, not as old as the United States, nor even as old as Haiti.

More than 200 people have turned up for the rally from a town of some 5,000. Their average age is 40 to 50, reflecting the local demography. People look forward to retirement in Vaison where farming and tourism are the main businesses. The young leave for the cities if they can. A local reporter tells me that the year before in nearby Avignon, the *Front National* drew crowds of 5,000 to one of their rallies. He wants to know if we have anything like this in Britain. He has heard of the National Front, but doesn't know what happened to them. I tell him that while they were arguing about uniforms Mrs Thatcher pocketed their votes. During her first election campaign, she warned of Britain being 'swamped by an alien culture'. Perhaps she meant European culture.

In Britain, as in France, a discreet appeal to the xenophobe is not wasted. Half of France feels a deep shame about the existence of the *Front National*. The other half is quietly in agreement.

Around the makeshift bar at the back of the hall – wreathed in smoke and selling coffee, *pastis* and wine – the conversation is much as around the zinc counters of countless other bars. Here, though, the freemasonry of local politics is convening. The blue-overalled billposters lined against the bar are paid tribute for their energetic work by the first speaker, a local party official. They have spent their evenings diligently scraping off the new posters of rivals and pasting on the Front logo, a burning *tricolore* that flashes like fire on dry scrub in the surrounding countryside, burning with its declaration of the unspeakable: that the great nation is in decline, her values eroded by weak and licentious rulers, her way of life at stake.

Unused to intercity politics, the speaker, squinting through his glasses and addressing just the front rows, urges his fellow Le Pen-ists to turn out and show just how many votes their hero can call on. 'This is the beginning of the adventure,' he declares, modulating his voice to its usual tone of club secretary to recount what he calls the *affaire de Marseille*. Two Maghreb Leftists wanted to provoke a Front militant. According to the local party man, 'he fell into the hands of counter-demonstrators of the Left and died'.

For obvious reasons, this was not mentioned in the press. 'The media are our enemy!' he warns. 'Be careful about the provocations that might come.' He cites a case that occurred before the elections of '86. Without the outcry over the killing of a 'Beur' (a second-generation Arab, born in France) they would have had twice the number of seats in the Assembly, he says. For the first time, I hear murder mentioned as though it were just an extraordinary item in the campaign ledger. Next, death will be an everyday sanction. People, and with them problems, will simply disappear, to be found months later decaying in a ditch. I have to remind myself that I am not in Latin America but in modern France. In the bright, pine-floored civic hall, there is a quiet nodding of heads that signifies acceptance.

The guest speaker who has arrived by plane from Paris is not Le Pen but his second-in-command, Jean-Pierre Stirbois, a handsome, dark-haired man in his late forties who wears a blue jacket and casual shoes. He makes a suave lieutenant to the rough-hewn leader of the *Front National*. Gripping the lectern with both hands, he begins by announcing that according to his information, it's possible that Jean-Marie Le Pen could beat the leading right-wing candidate, Jacques Chirac, into second place. There is a rustle of excitement. A middle-aged man with dark rings round his eyes, barely filling his grey suit, jumps up and down in his seat chewing gum and waving a pennant. A local speed freak – not uncommon in a country with three times the European average of drug prescriptions – he grimaces at the description of the shifting policies of the other parties. They are all the same. Right or Left, they have hedged and compromised. The FN has been constant in its aims because it is fighting not just for a place, but for an idea.

The number of *clandestins* – a spectral word suggesting the surreptitious existence of an unseen virus – is difficult to estimate, admits Stirbois, but under the Socialists only 1 per cent was repatriated. 'So it will take 100 years to send them all back!' he clamours. 'We are not prepared to wait 100 years!' He equates the number of unemployed with the number of immigrant workers. And lifting his palms upwards, '*Voici le problème!*'

The FN does not attack the strong French Left – the enemy of everybody in the hall – but the weak Right which formerly represented them. Xenophobes, they are nevertheless *pro*-Europe. There are Italians and Spanish in the movement. There are even a few ex-Socialists, jokes Stirbois. He means himself. They are trying to capture the middle ground, squeezing out candidates Jacques Chirac and Raymond Barre, representatives of liberal, polite conservatism. Both former Prime Ministers, they are flawed by their histories of compromise. It is the tragedy of democrats that the best they can offer is an unsatisfactory reconciliation.

In the previous Assembly, *Front National* deputies demanded increased maternity benefits. This has always been an emotive issue for the French who went from being the most populous nation in Europe under Napoleon to losing huge numbers in the First World War, which a declining birth rate has done nothing to replenish. Now many French people too feel in danger of being swamped by an alien culture. The Front's proposals for generous state help with a third child – a veiled racist reply to the higher birth rate among immigrants – were ignored at the time, but, to the fury of those xenophobes who dared then to speak their name, they have been adopted by Chirac as his own, demonstrating his concern for family values.

Sweating a little under the lights, his speech a 50-minute piece that proceeds with practised shifts of gear, Stirbois turns now to a familiar enemy – International Socialism. From a speech by President Mitterrand, he describes the possible chromosome mix of the next European generation, its immigrant population partly assimilated. In front of me, a middle-aged woman with blue-rinsed hair, wearing pearls and a lilac dress, shivers with pleasurable distaste. 'No!' insists Stirbois. 'The next generation will be French because Jean-Marie Le Pen will be President!' The woman applauds encouragingly.

Leaning forward conspiratorially to recall a visit to a prison during his tenure as a deputy, Stirbois tells how a warden took him aside to confide that official statistics are false, and that immigrant crime levels are at least twice as high as the figures suggest. There is a wave of disquiet in the auditorium as people whisper to their neighbours. Stirbois finishes by recounting, to general contempt, a series of positive integration measures, designed by the Socialists to supposedly enrich French culture. 'French workers are happy to have their culture enriched,' sneers Stirbois, 'when they have no jobs!'

What is he offering these people? Better schools? Better housing? Nothing but hatred. And hatred is what they appear to want, evinced by the shudder of the middle-aged woman safely delivered from fear; or the plump *charcutier*, the same one I saw that morning, rocking back and forth in his seat with mounting excitement. They have been treated to a seasoned show of political pornography.

The terms are generally polite but the subtext is taboo, hence the spell that Stirbois is able to cast over an audience, tweaking and massaging their unspoken fears with rehearsed phrases of sarcastic contempt, and, as he gives vent to momentary furies, finally bringing his public to a climax of hatred. Raising his voice insistently, shaking with urgency, he says that theirs is a movement of hope. He compares Le Pen to de Gaulle, a saviour. 'The villages of France will never be *Maghrébin*!' he says.

Polite confessions

A FEW DAYS later, in a thronging brasserie, beneath a sparkling chandelier, a woman tells me, 'You can understand how they feel.' She is well dressed, aged about 35, dining with her aunt from the country. 'They hear about crime and unemployment. And you know its true that the streets aren't safe any more.'

She returns to her *petit salé aux lentilles*, her compassion hiding assent. She too would whiten to hear the local party secretary warn against acts of murder because of their high electoral cost – but she too is dismayed with what France has become.

Here in the oldest brasserie in Paris she is surrounded by mirrored walls reflecting assured smiles. Elsewhere, elegance has been replaced by asphalt and neon. But even here the gratuity is now added automatically to the bill. It is the small details that the woman notices, and the passing headlines. There are more and more beggars on the Métro. A young man has been arrested for the murders of 19 old women, robbing them to finance decadent parties for his chic socialite friends. He was of French Caribbean descent, a heroin addict and transsexual.

In another restaurant, another woman is staring at the prism of light in the crystal glass she holds in her hand. She is searching for a way to describe her lifelong fascination with France.

'It's the only "other" I know.'

The construction of the sentence – its inferences loaded on the vague word 'other' – reveals her exposure to modern French semantic theories. She has studied French history and read French literature. She lived in Paris for a while. There is a hotel in St-Michel where at the age of 19 she took a room for an afternoon with a man she had just met, a Tunisian with soft hands and dark eyes.

These days she practises her French mostly on waiters. In the restaurant, one of the better French restaurants in London, she orders, with a polished, correct accent, *œufs-en-cocotte avec truffes*, followed by *gujons de lotte*. She takes pride in her fluency and her continental manners.

'That's the best way I can think of to describe it,' she says. 'It's the only place I know that's different that I really feel comfortable with.'

As the hors-d'œuvre arrive, she tells me that the truffles she has ordered are a kind of secret currency in the French countryside, offered between people as tokens of honour. It is not just for their moist, sour taste of the autumn forest that they are prized. Their scarcity, the rituals of preparation (they must be stored next to the eggs before they are cooked) and the obscure potency attributed to them lend truffles the status of a kind of French country cocaine. In some regions, they are still given to newly-weds on wedding nights. She sucks on the black, shrivelled fungus. 'But these aren't fresh,' she confides. 'When they're fresh you can almost get high on them.'

She knows this because she once went to France with a TV crew to make a series of programmes. 'We got sidetracked by the first good restaurant we came to and ended up making a series about French food.'

First harvest

I CAN THINK of no odour as intoxicating as the smell of a cross-Channel car ferry; the combination of salt spray and diesel fumes, a heady mix of oxygen and pollution, rendered emotionally combustible by the promise of adventure.

The slamming of doors and clanging of mooring lines signal that the adventure is under way. The drivers get out of their cars, stretch their backs, and look around for someone to share a few words with. 'Where are you going?' they enquire. 'Is that good for towing?' They spread maps on roofs and study routes they have planned long before, making sure that all is on schedule. They wear socks and sandals, under-managers and clerks transformed into open-shirted vagabonds.

Their wives smooth down dresses crumpled from their journeys. They have come mostly from the south of England, a day's drive through familiar territory, green and reassuring, all its signs legible. They have left their semis in search of some mysterious 'other'.

As a boy crossing the Channel with my family, I was too excited myself to notice their excitement, though I noticed its symptoms in the uncommon rash of camaraderie. I think that, being British, they had no immediate way to express this excitement other than through snobbery. 'We went there last year,' they would say. 'It's getting so crowded.'

The 'other' was thus to some extent relieved of its dangers by a hierarchy of class. Two structures intersected: the established castes of British life and the *nouveau* condescensions of the continental holidaymaker, accumulating destination points like so many bullfight posters. The more accomplished traveller could thus look down on the novice, who in other circumstances might be his social superior.

I was thrilled by the strange atmosphere of the ferries, the sound of the engines juddering behind the bulkheads; a round-the-clock feat of engineering to deliver an endless stream of traffic. It was my task to navigate, while my father, pretending to obey my signals, drove. In fact he knew the route by heart and had no need of my careful instructions. He had been driving from London to his mother-in-law's house in the south of France since the Fifties.

In those days, cars were lifted by a crane onto the decks of the Channel ferries, mostly Rolls-Royces and Bentleys whose occupants were motoring down to the Riviera. My father and mother must have made an odd couple amidst this aristocratic company, he a Guyanese and she a dark-haired Frenchwoman, with their Morris Minor convertible.

My father had not long arrived in Europe after joining a cattle drive across the high plains of Boa Vista in emulation of his cowboy heroes, and becoming the pay clerk on an oil rig. My mother, escaping from a convent school upbringing, thought him very exotic, a dark Clark Gable. There is a photograph of the two of them, snapped by a tourist shark from below waist height, striding proudly along the Champs-Elysées. There are no billboards or neon signs lining the avenue, just a few cafés and the tall grey buildings not yet cleaned of decades of soot.

My mother never quite overcame her sadness at the damp, grey land she found herself in, surrounded by reticent, undemonstrative people. With an immigrant's paranoia, she took this trait to hide a treacherous cunning.

She never really forgave the British for their coldness. But she never ceased to pity them for their impoverished agriculture. It seemed to her a cruel act of nature that there were no ripe figs to be had by the trayful in Britain. Driving back through Picardie in early September, across the wheatfields rippling yellow-brown in the sun, she would always remark at how lucky the French were, and how wretched the British, in that the French could harvest two crops of wheat, while Britain, despite its proximity, could only manage one.

Contemplating this land of plenty, where peaches lay piled at the roadside and wheat defied the seasons by ripening twice, I felt sure she must have been nursing some jealous grudge against Britain, though in fact it was largely disappointment. As a girl, she imagined that the streets of Britain gleamed with pride, streets that had never been tramped by Nazi jackboots. She was marked by the war in ways that differed from my friends' parents. She remembered coming out of a cinema after hearing machine-gun fire and seeing fresh blood on the snow, the blood of villagers shot in reprisal.

In the photo taken in the Champs-Elysées my mother is wearing a diamond brooch. It was around this time that she was involved in a smuggling ring. A few of the girls who worked with her at the nursing home and met later at the foreign club were also nervous accomplices. She brought watches and jewellery from Switzerland, part of the general post-war redistribution of property. The method was simple. She hid the contraband in a large wedge of Roquefort. 'No Englishman,' she told me, 'will ever put his fingers into a piece of smelly cheese.'

Continental style

THE CHANNEL FERRIES had not yet been transformed into floating snack-bars on an expressway to the *soleil* – fast, frequent, duty-free motorist lounges. They preserved at sea the social divisions. They were liveried. The restaurants had linen tablecloths. There was a first and second-class deck, a purser who examined passports. Around the time of the Arc de Triomphe or when the seasons began in Antibes or Gstaad, it was impossible to get a booking.

Returning on a busy ferry in the late summer of 1953 was a young Englishman from Surrey. He was on his way back to a second year at the Central School of Art, to the workshop he shared with Eduardo Paolozzi. The Italian sculptor had been teaching him to cook spaghetti with *calamari*. Terence Conran couldn't wait to get back and try out some of the dishes he had eaten on his first trip abroad. He and his girlfriend had been motoring through France in an open-top Bentley Lagonda belonging to a friend who knew the country well. They had been away for six weeks, sleeping in ditches, eating huge tomatoes and drinking bottles of wine that cost pennies. To the young couple he met in the lounge, he enthused about the marvellous food he had sampled. My mother laughed to hear him complain about returning to Britain, where the food was so depressing and there were hardly any restaurants anyway. 'You could go into nice cafés and have a plate of *charcuterie* and a glass of wine. He was amazed at the abundance of food in provincial France. He was full of talk about the bizarre ingenuity of French designs, from eccentricities like the 2CV cars to practicalities like the red enamelled cookware.

He had been educated at Bryanston, a progressive school that had grown from the Arts & Crafts movement of the Twenties, and he appreciated the pleasures of simple, functional forms. He explained that his father had been in the import business, bringing in gum from Malaysia.

In his excitement, these two factors began to interplay. As the ferry drew near the chalk cliffs of Dover and he pulled on a sweater for the first time in weeks, his fate, though he didn't know it, was decided. Communicating his enthusiasm, he would bring his own refinements to continental living and market it in the British high street. The shops that sold the hardware to furnish this lifestyle he would eventually call Habitat.

For the moment, though, he had another idea. He wanted to open a café, an unpretentious restaurant like those he had dined in abroad, selling simple, cheap, tasty food. He would call it the Soup Kitchen. And from behind the counter, he himself would operate the second ever espresso machine imported from the Continent.

The Continent. That's what it was always called, a largely subdued but occasionally quarrelsome grouping of undifferentiated peoples, many with nauseating breath and without indoor sanitation, best ignored. In the Fifties, Italy was still known mainly for cowardice, though it has now overtaken Britain in wealth.

It is an attitude summed up by a headline in *The Times* of London from around the turn of the century, after several days of heavy fog over the English Channel: 'THE CONTINENT IS STILL ISOLATED.'

From this isolation emerged the first Chianti bottles, rescued from tables clothed in red check gingham after a long Tuscan summer. These straw totems held candles to Mediterranean memories, eventually replaced by the real thing: *vin de table* from the local supermarket. Cheap plonk. Why ever was it called that? Because it made a plonking sound as it splashed into the glass? Because the bottles plonked as you walked as nonchalantly as possible through Customs?

What else came back from the Continent? The smell, never quite recaptured, of the French country kitchen. That was imparted by Elizabeth David, whose *French Country Cooking* in 1954 introduced, with the delightful tone of a schoolmistress freshly seduced, the philosophy of good food and wine. More than most systems of experiencing reality, this one was flawed by empirical confusion. The drunker and more sated one became, the less objective. You eat therefore you are.

What else? Colour and sensuality. Young men on Lambrettas in bright sweaters, copied from their US idols in the Ivy League. An old London Mod once told me: 'You cannot imagine how outrageous it was to wear a yellow sweater in Britain in the early Sixties. It was something that not even homosexuals dared.' Latin men wore bright, sensual, feminine colours. They walked arm in arm along the seafront with no concern, at a pace profoundly disorienting in its lack of purpose. And if you were a woman, they approached you with predatory self-confidence, unafraid to look, a look as impudent as a caress.

Accustomed to parrying more polite advances, English women were ill-prepared. Powered no doubt by an equal libidinal drive, but deprived of spontaneity and imbued instead with rigour and patience, the English man was forced to stand by as shoals of English women shed their reserve and plunged into the Mediterranean, swimming with divine freedom (compared to their local counterparts), soon to be washed ashore and into the arms of first the French, then the Italians, then the Spanish, and then (by now topless and, according to Aegean legend, quite uninhibited) the Greeks. Of course it ended badly: the impetuous lover and his overweening mother left behind; the stoic hero of the piece, not as patient as we thought, having it away with someone else.

What was it like for those Britons coming to the Continent for the first time? Nowadays, jets disgorge new visitors into a vast unbuilt holiday isle in the scorching midday heat. The first smell of the 'other' is likely to be that of grisly hamburgers frying in burnt rapeseed oil; the first sign in bad English. Charter flights in the Seventies offered a short cut to the sun: the culture shock of sudden confrontation with Latin races in all their dark oily splendour. The slow drive southwards at least allowed for progressive acclimatisation.

For an older generation, the culture shock was at least as great at Dunkerque as at the Costa del Sol. And beyond the Channel ports, the sombre, industrialised lowlands; the shabby detached houses with unkempt gardens and – perhaps the greatest psychological blow to the British who strive always to define and preserve personal distance – the absence of fences. This was as unsettling in its way as the knowledge that when greeting one another Frenchmen kissed on the cheek.

Arriving in France in the Sixties, the smell of the drains and the Gauloises easily persuaded British voyagers that after sailing 30 miles they had disembarked in Arabia. The northernmost Arab town is not Algiers, nor even Marseille, but Dunkerque. With its peeling, unkempt walls and zinc roofs, it is here that Mediterranean civilisation begins.

The Belgian stigma

THE FINAL PERIMETER of Mediterranean culture lies, in fact, a few leagues
further north at the border of the old Roman Empire, which now dissects
that schizophrenic buffer zone, Belgium. Created by Louis Napoleon, the
Belgians are prime victims of the arrogant French. Not in Africa, the Caribbean, Indochina or the Pacific is there a French *département* more pathetic
than Belgium.

What is it like to live under the small but perfectly formed cultural heel of
the French, to try to grow strong on a diet of French contempt?

Here I must stop – as have, in the eyes of the French, the thought processes
of the Belgians themselves. The French tell all the well-known Irish/Polish
jokes about the Belgians. Here is a Belgian joke about the French: Why are
there no lights on French autoroutes? Because the French think they are
radiant enough themselves!

Alongside the Parc Leopold II in Brussels there is a museum dedicated to
the work of a self-proclaimed leading figure of the revival of Historicism,
Antoine Wiertz. After exhibiting a painting entitled *Patrocle* at the Salon de
Paris in 1839 without meeting the acclaim he had hoped for (the painting
ended up as the prize in a raffle), Wiertz asked the Belgian ministry to build
him a suitable atelier in return for consigning his significant *œuvre* to the state.
He did not hesitate to compare himself to Jacques-Louis David, recently

exiled in Brussels; but Wiertz had no revolutions or coronations of emperors to depict. In what is now his museum, he set about painting pompous pseudo-historical tableaux as well as smaller and often ghoulish depictions of contemporary *faits divers*. He also penned a curious tract in which he attempted to demonstrate, with diagrams and bits of dubious statistical extrapolation, how Paris was destined to become a suburb of Brussels. Sadly for Wiertz, this never happened. His life's work now languishes beside a new extension to the offices of the European Community. His grudge against the cultural imperialism of Paris and his overwrought style, adopting the manners of the salon painters of the time with a crippling vengeance, are symptomatic of the stigma that afflicts France's closest and most abject colony. Even nowadays, national figures in France try to hide their Belgian origins because of it.

Moving northwards from the Somme through Wallonie, the scrubby, ill-defined gardens of French houses give way to the walled, well-tended gardens of Flanders, resembling those of Britain, Holland or Germany. The houses themselves grow taller and huddle together, suddenly relieved of their individuality, replaced by ordered communities. The sky is greyer and the vegetation greener.

What is it about these lands that has proved so resistant to southern ideologies? In the early nineteenth century during a short period of direct rule, Napoleon established a legal structure and sent the sons of Flemish merchants to the Lycée Français to encounter the sons of French aristocrats and imbibe at the font of French cultural values. But ever since Roman times – and despite waves of conquest by the Spanish, the Austrians and finally the French – the provinces of Flanders and Wallonie have served as a hazy, bimorphous zone separating the two principle peoples of Europe, the Latins to the south and the Saxons to the north.

The two million bilingual citizens of Brussels, which aspires to be the new capital of Europe, live on the great divide of Europe, the frontier that runs through Ireland, Belgium, Alsace, over the Alps and through Bavaria, the frontier between Catholic and Protestant, between the grape and the grain.

In a famous painting, *The Empire of Light*, by the Belgian surrealist Magritte, there is a house shrouded in darkness and lit by a single streetlamp, but above, the sky is bright. Enigmatic, contradictory, it illustrates the dilemma of living two realities at once, the dilemma of the colonised and the immigrant. Between the two realities, there is a space that has no rules, an opaque, marshy region like the Zwyne to the west of Brussels, regularly flooded by the sea, in which strange fauna flourish, adapted to both air and water. The Zwyne gives its name to the Zwanze, the Brabançon dialect of French, an intercode, a mongrel language between languages, with a curious fondness for bilingual wordplay that opens nonsensical chasms of meaning.

Such chasms often made me dizzy as a child as, periodically surrounded by the language, I would wake up to find myself thinking in what sounded like French but wasn't. It was French governed by a mix of grammatical rules, disorienting but also intoxicating in its absurdity, like touching yourself and feeling someone else's skin. I amused myself by constructing feeble phrases in my head and wondered if my English would ever return. It did, and the experience left me with an abiding curiosity about the sex of objects. Mistakes of gender common among anglophones annoy and disturb the French, for whom a table, let us imagine – supine, stable, bounteous – cannot be anything other than female, probably their mother's. As I grew older, I would turn these concepts around in my head trying to mate gender and object, an irksome pair trying to find the most satisfying position.

The plan

DRIVING SOUTHWARDS, I recall a surge of elation as, after three hours of claustrophobic streets clogged with traffic, the grand buildings of Paris gave way to the strip of ribbon development towards Orly airport, some of the ugliest urban landscape in the world.

In the Fifties, this was emblematic of the dynamic modern France promised by de Gaulle. The RN7 sweeps by the remaining *pavillons*, their high fences a hopeless defence against the barrage of traffic in what was once a semi-rural suburb. Gradually, these once desirable houses – miniature chateaux and fake mountain chalets – were torn down to make way for the new housing blocks and the superwarehouses full of instant kitchens that sprouted on the outskirts of French towns, announcing not least a merchandising revolution.

It was all part of the Plan, as it was known, conceived by Jean Monnet in wartime exile in America. A scion of the distilling family from Cognac, representing the Monnet brand in the US fired him with faith in a potential new France. His engine was American style growth, his slogan 'modernisation or downfall'; freely toasted by the disparate groupings of unionists and bosses summoned to negotiate quotas at the Plan's official HQ – with the state using its powers of legislation and patronage to stack the deck and kick ankles.

Powered by a population shift to the towns after the war, the resulting Five Year Plans helped streamline France, laying the foundations for de Gaulle's decade of political stability. The first Plans concentrated on industry, later ones encompassing housing and welfare. For the technocrats at the Plan, technology equalled expansion equalled progress. In their Left Bank think tank, they studied Ford's mechanised production and sketched Le Corbusier's cities in the sky. Heroic draughtsmen of a new, polyvalent French society, they held tight to the rails of the ship of state as the Fourth Republic rocked from government to government. Their enemies were the bureaucrats, staid products of the élitist *Grandes Ecoles* installed in their *positions acquises*.

And so, even by the Sixties, the myth of ageless France was falling into disrepair. It was being zoned and paved to make way for new housing projects like La Défense to the west of Paris, a cubist symphony of eccentric skyscrapers with fountains rising and falling to muzak; a 1,700-acre car-free coloured concrete bazaar, representing the highest aspirations of the plastic art of urban planning.

The road to Orly resembles the highway out to JFK but, in a flourish of engineering style so beloved of the French, it appears to hurtle into the terminal building itself, only to plunge down an underpass and emerge on the other side – brushing past a stationary Concorde on display at the corner of the airfield – before tearing on to disturb the ancient repose of *la France profonde*.

It went on for hours, the roads curving with an elegant camber, unfamiliar and sensual to the English driver. For the French, the road, *la route*, was incontestably female. She ran into the distance, lined with tall leafy trees, their intervals marking a subdivision of the French subdivision of the circumference of the earth and also showing – as any English schoolboy could once have told you – the way for German tanks.

I recall French roads as one long middle overtaking lane, with its exciting possibility of a head-on high-speed collision; every half-hour, the welcoming wink of a red and blue *Les Routiers* sign, and a hotel-restaurant with a carpark full of dusty lorries.

The towns that we passed through were then still at war with the heavy lorries whose air brakes hissed and engines gunned as terrified mothers yanked their children out of the way. Their pavements were barely wide enough for an old man wearing a beret and carrying a baguette. Whilst the residents of these towns welcomed the passing tourist – or at least enjoyed the spectacle of unfamiliar, overladen vehicles, and returning the curious gazes of their occupants – they rose in civic fury at the accompanying disturbance as the traffic grew busier each year and the tourists queued with the lorries in congested, grimy medieval squares. The bypass was the most significant detail of change in the French countryside. Year by year, town by town, they were painted in dashes of grey across the fields, sweeping around spires and red tiled roofs and allowing these towns to return to their fitful slumbers, linked now to the autoroutes that were growing clogged and dangerous.

At Fontainebleau we sometimes stopped to view the palace, the one preferred by Napoleon. Compared to Versailles it is correct in scale for an enlightened despot; and with its different wings added over centuries, a reminder of continuity and evolving tradition, though needless to say it was the ostentatious Versailles that was widely copied by European royalty. What I liked most about the old palace were the gardens. Accustomed to the contrived disarray of English parks, they appeared to me vast and intricate, laid out according to a grand scheme, like the plan that subdivided the circumference of the globe.

Does it seem strange that the English should yearn for disorder, for the fury and sensibility of Nature, while the French crave harmony and structure? In the different styles of national park is dramatised the dilemma of the Romantic versus the Rational; the right half of the brain in conflict with the left. The one living the life of the senses awed by the power of the intellect; the other living a life of order and logic seduced by the power of the senses.

Rue de Dépôt

IT GREW HOT and uncomfortable in the car as we wound our way through the Bourgogne, past the monument marking the house where photography was invented, finally climbing over hills into the Rhône-Alps. Mâcon, Dijon, Bourg, towns in the south-east that seemed to me to be forever dozing behind steel shutters in the afternoon heat.

At last we came to Ambérieu, the town where, upon marrying her third husband, my grandmother had come to live. In the square, an old woman sold us ice-cream. She had new teeth that gleamed as she smiled but seemed not to fit her mouth, and made her words hard to distinguish. She had been selling ice-cream most of her life. She used to have the pitch just outside the station, but during the war had fled with her son, and when she returned, a rival had taken it over. From a position across the square, she sold the ice-cream that her son made at home, resigned to having lost the profitable flow of customers. I pitied her this injustice, since my grandmother insisted that hers was the better ice-cream.

Positioned at the foot of the Alps, the town benefited from its position under the west-facing slopes, ideal for the cultivation of vines, which require good drainage and plenty of sunshine. Only a few kilometres away, as the valley rose into the mountains, the slopes grew rocky and steep, good only for the raising of a few goats. Ambérieu, which like many French towns could trace its church back to Roman times, was at the head of the route into the mountains, and thence to Italy. It was here that travellers once changed horses for the ascent into Haute-Savoie, and here that, from the end of the last century, trains changed locomotives for the climb over the Alps.

The town thrived as a railway junction and, like most of the men living there, my grandmother's new husband worked for the SNCF. He was an engineer riding the footplates of the locomotives that steamed out of the large sheds, going south to Grenoble and Turin or north and east from Lyon to Geneva. But with the coming of diesel and electric trains, his skills at controlling the old steam engines were no longer needed.

The status of his job with its generous pension and the small vineyard that he owned on the nearby slopes made him a notable catch in the small town, though it was he who had for some time been wooing my grandmother. Their marriage nevertheless caused a stir among the eight children that the old man had sired, mostly grown up by then but some of them still counting on some portion of their father's estate.

His scattered holdings – several strips of land on the hills and one at the back of the town – were themselves the fragments of his father's property, split up under the Napoleonic laws of inheritance whereby everything was divided equally among heirs. Far from smoothing the transition of property from one generation to the next, this caused undignified scrambles among siblings to snatch as much as possible in goods before the sad day. As populations grew, so individual holdings multiplied and, protected by high tariff walls around France erected in 1892 by Jules Méline, the pattern of the landscape itself changed, subdivided into a tapestry of small fields farmed by a multiplicity of small producers.

My grandfather – we called him that in the curious way that children have of assimilation – used the patch of land at the back of the town to grow wheat that he gave to the *boulanger* to bake into large rings of dark, chewy bread, from which he cut chunks with a deft turn of the Opinel. On the slopes above the town he grew sinuous vines that hid fat purple grapes, his sons gathering to harvest them. The first topic of conversation on our arrival each summer was the quality of the coming vintage. Had there been enough rain at the right time? And later, would there be enough sun to fully ripen the grapes?

Housed in a shack not far from the vineyard was the communal '*granjon*', two huge stone wheels to press the grapes. The lower one was cut with rivulets, allowing the juice to be collected as the upper wheel ground down slowly on creaking wooden gears.

The wine fermented in wooden barrels in the cellar under the house, the key to which was never allowed out of the old man's sight. It was guarded like the instrument of a precious sacrament, a source of mysterious power that went beyond the flush of pleasure it brought the adults at the table to influence somehow the destinies of families. As I grew older, I was sent to fetch wine for the meals, drawing the frothy liquid with careful awe, my head light from the cool, moist smell of the wooden barrels twice my height. On shelves behind were cobwebbed bottles filled with wines as old as 20 years which my grandmother reserved for cooking those chickens among the ones she kept in the yard of which she was especially fond.

Kept on the higher shelves were bottles of clear alcohol distilled from *marc*, the stalks and peel left over from making wine. Allowed by law to brew untaxed up to ten litres each year, my grandfather, like most farmers, brewed more. He never drank it himself, except in coffee. My grandmother used it to pour on cuts, though sometimes she would wake me early with a bowl of black coffee, spiced with ground chicory and a shot of this raw alcohol, sold now as Vieux Marc, but which we knew as *Eau de Vie*, the Water of Life.

As a *bouilleur de cru* my grandfather counted on a certain respect, dispensing this water of life to the postman and other tradesmen who passed. Since Pierre Mendès France curbed the home-distilling privilege in 1960, the *bouilleurs de cru* have been slowly dying out. It was French monks who invented the distilling process in the 11th century, searching for a universal curative, an Elixir of Life mentioned in the Old Testament. Employing obscure alchemical formulae, the noble monks braved centuries of foul distempers to unlock the secret of the grape. The technique soon spread through Europe, farmers trying it out with whatever was at hand, from berries to cereals to potatoes. This surely ranks as one of the great French contributions to civilisation, along with the Enlightenment, the accidental invention of champagne in the 18th century, the bikini and the pneumatic tyre.

Having retired from the railway with a sizeable pension, my new grandfather sat at the table of his house in the rue du Dépôt and awaited the visits of his sons, some of whom made it their routine to pass by on their way from work for a glass of wine, taking away with them a bottle. They wore the same faded blue overalls as their father – that light, fast blue that is the uniform of the worker in France. They had red-veined faces that contorted with the phlegmatic vowels of the language. They spoke loudly and incomprehensibly. What they were talking about was often too thick with regional dialect for me to understand or else too adult for anyone to explain to me. They were always amused to see us, however, the family who came all the way from England. At any rate they pretended to be, making laughing, friendly grimaces that threatened to erupt in a hefty cough of spittle. No doubt they also resented and feared us, since we could drink and eat as we pleased during our stays and who could tell what we might embark on, having free run of the house and, more worryingly, the cellar.

Meals lasted for three hours, lunch from midday to three and dinner from six to nine. During the afternoons, my father would saunter out into the garden with the old man to poke and prod at the plants, swapping English and French names for the pumpkins and yellow beans in a laughing, drunken semblance of communication. Sometimes they would try to start up the small tractor that sat rusting in the shed, a legacy of Monnet's first Plan that sought to mechanise French farming. My grandfather would go juddering along the street on the back of this tractor, barely able to control the machine and using it for just a few days each year. It was bought, like the TV later on, as a status symbol, and hardly ever used.

More typically after lunch, the whole family would just fall asleep. And in the evenings they would switch on the TV. French TV inspired me with its eroticism, employing a parade of painted, smiling females to make announcements and even read the news, while British TV, preserving the no doubt important distinction between facts and titillation, adhered to a reassuring rota of ponderous masculinity. But the programming was less than enthralling, dubbed serials and semi-nude showgirls apart. Then we would bring out faded ochre photographs. The old man would recount his march to the front in 1916. He had made the journey on foot – and back again, bearing a silver medal. During the Second World War, he was obliged by the *Boches* – a word spat out with hatred – to run trains all the way into Germany. He tried to sabotage them but feared reprisals on others. He shuffled slowly in the heavy boots that he wore most of his life, raising up his flat cap to scratch his short-cut silver hair, a corn-paper Gitane smouldering on his lip. Later, he would grow sentimental and, swept by memory, would begin to cry.

In the town, manners had not much changed throughout his life. Entering a shop or bar, people greeted each other with a general '*M'ssieursdames*'. The market came once a week, like the one at Vaison, and the fair came every summer, filling the square with fireworks. I rode my bicycle between the bridge and the station and I was warned to be careful of the teenagers who rode their motorbikes recklessly to and fro, local heroes roaring against the boredom. Changing too fast for some, France was not changing fast enough for them.

Armenians had taken over some old carriages next to the railway lines, adorning them with flowers and washing and finally removing the wheels. I was told to avoid the flats near by, five-storey blocks painted a once-bright yellow, their doorways cluttered with dark little children. These were the *pieds noirs*, the 'black feet', Moroccans and Algerians. They were *sale*, dirty, and, to judge from the distaste with which the word was uttered, as repulsive as I – by now half inculcated with British instincts – found certain of the vinous, garlicky, hawking French. I was always warned not to mix the grape and the grain. Wine or brandy, when mixed with beer or whisky, would produce a lethal hangover. And it was clear that for the French themselves, beyond the grape was to be found a dangerous sensual elation.

The foreign language of love

MY FIRST SEXUAL contact with the French came unbidden, though in my adolescent heat I sought such a moment with every desperate glimpse of imagined and untouched femininity – any femininity, not particularly French.

She was a granddaughter of the old man and had come to visit him from a town somewhere in the north. I was 15 years old and she was perhaps 17 or 19. She had grey-brown hair and spoke no English, which didn't prevent us becoming friends. She looked at me with undisguised curiosity, unafraid of the silence between us. I hid my unease at this with anxious sentences describing my life in London. She was short, plump and not beautiful, but I fantasised incessantly about her.

One afternoon, I was lying on my bed in the quiet that always followed the long family lunches. These stifling, protracted afternoons seemed to me an impossible hiatus in the advancement of any civilisation. As a boy, I sweated against this lacuna in the middle of the day but finally learned to give in.

The door opened and she entered noisily, making no effort to respect the quiet of the afternoon or the peace of the house. She was bored. She signalled me to move across and lay alongside me on the bed, looking at me with an interrogative half-smile. Unable to interpret it, my senses bristled. I could smell the flowers for the tisane that lay drying on old newspapers on the floors of the rooms above. I wanted to stop talking, but I couldn't. She wore a long, high-waisted dress that lay in pleats between her knees, cut low at the neck. Her skin was spotted with pimples like the flesh of a peach. I tried to avoid staring as I reached across her to adjust the radio that was quietly fading in and out of Radio Luxembourg. She leaned forward abruptly, still smiling. It was certainly no accident: her breasts pressed against my arm and she looked up at me, without trying to pull away. I was startled by their softness. Confused by this unexpected impression, I froze. She must have been grateful, at least, that I stopped talking.

In the silence we heard footsteps outside the door. The old man opened it without knocking and, seeing us both on the bed, told her harshly to leave the room. She obeyed, irritated, without looking back at me. Her grandfather didn't say anything to me, but followed her out of the room.

I think she got as much pleasure from disturbing the old man's afternoon nap as she could ever have had from me. Later I learned that he regarded his daughters as his sexual fiefdom. He had slept with one of them, said my mother, though I was never sure if this wasn't a mistranslation on my part. Certainly, he took what in someone of his age seemed to me to be a morbid interest in his granddaughter that went beyond her being his favourite. The sex life of provincial France is full of such transgressions, both cruel and delightful.

Years later, French friends told me it was not uncommon among aristocratic families for close female friends to take on, with the parents' connivance, the task of a boy's sexual initiation. Though he was by then too old to do anything himself, I'm sure that my grandfather was jealous of his granddaughter, and could not rest for the thought of what we might have been getting up to – had I only been a little less nervous. In the dark of the house, we could have lain there for hours, and it was not the possible scandal that was uppermost in his mind.

Growing up in Puritan England but exposed to sensual France I was almost at ease with the French attitude to sex. Accepting nature and revelling in its fruitful chaos, the French view sex as a biological pleasure. They indulge in it with the satisfaction of people taking a spa cure. As with food, they enjoy it and cultivate the accompanying rituals. Encouraged by divorce laws that used to tolerate a husband's affairs but discriminated against a wife's, discreet infidelity became a courtly game of love. In fact, the French have made so much of the ritual that they often forget its consummation.

'It's more the packaging around it than the act,' a woman tells me. 'Girls I know might lead a man along for days and then when they finally went home together and the man undressed, they would get turned off completely if the guy was wearing the wrong kind of *caleçons*.'

Lust, in fact, is not a French vice. Sex is not a cauldron forever threatening to boil over, or even a kettle as in Britain, where, safely controlled, the steam is put to proper use. This is why advertising in France uses sex with far less reserve – it's harder to get people's attention. If anything, the problem with representations of sex in France is that they're too *élégant*. Not for the French the pallid ghastliness of a Reader's Wife bent over a chair with her knickers half off and the lights on full.

Minitelevisions

THE CHAIR I am sitting in is a version of the chair favoured by programmers at MIT and designed by Phillipe Starck, who also designed the all-black television room in the President's suite at the Elysée palace and the three-legged chairs in the Café Costes, rendezvous of the *branchés*, the unstintingly trendy Parisians of the Eighties. What is unusual about this chair, though, is not the fact that I kneel rather than sit on it conventionally, but that I bought it through the Minitel.

I saw it in a brochure, tapped a code on my phone, was interrogated briefly via a small TV screen next to the phone, tapped out my credit card number, and received the chair a few days later at my door. I was entirely satisfied. With a simple transaction I felt I had been initiated into the new age of *telematics*.

Telematics is a French word coined in the late Seventies to describe the marriage of telecommunications and informatics (an American word coined in the early Seventies to describe the marriage of computers and information). In Britain it gave birth to the Prestel service, which languishes like a toy nobody wants. Its offspring in France was the Minitel, installed in 20 per cent of French homes in under five years.

A small TV screen with an alphanumeric keypad, the Minitel sits beside the phone, a communications marvel in brown plastic. I collected mine from the local office of France Telecom, who give them away to the public. With it, I can consult the computerised telephone directory, which costs nothing, or, for a fee, access the endless array of services. Unlike Prestel or Teletext, the Minitel is interactive. I could spend a whole day in front of it. Here's what my day is like.

I start by consulting my horoscope. I tap 3615 ASTRO. A page appears on the screen telling me I am in touch with the service and asking for my date of birth. I can choose between traditional and Chinese astrology, or I could see my biorhythms.

I type 'Leo' and the page changes. There is a graphic of a lion and a short message.

'LEO WILL ENCOUNTER A STRANGER TODAY. DO YOU WANT TO KNOW MORE?'

Too busy. I exit this service and tap 3615 LEMOND. On the Minitel I don't type, I *tap*, a French neologism that captures the abbreviated flavour of digital communication.

A contents page appears for the service offered by the daily newspaper *Le Monde*. I can see what the weather will be like in France or in 140 other countries. I can see the headlines of the day. 'TRANSPORT STRIKES CAUSE CHAOS IN THE CITIES.' Luckily the Minitel means I don't have to leave home. But if I did I could tap 3615 RATP for the best itinerary for my journey within Paris. Or reserve a seat on the TGV. Next to the large Métro stations, similar terminals encased in yellow plastic stands even print out the itinerary on a handy ticket.

'IN THE ASSEMBLY, CENTRISTS REFUSE TO JOIN WITH COM-MUNISTS IN A VOTE OF NO-CONFIDENCE.'

This is good news for the stability of the new Socialist government. Still with LEMOND, I consult the Bourse. To make a transaction, however, I would have to phone my broker. The French stock exchange still awaits its telematic overhaul.

First I better look at my finances. I tap 3615 LION. Before I look at my account, the bank service asks me first if I want to borrow money. I would like to reply that I have already donated, but it is one of the horrors of computers that they don't understand sarcasm.

With the digital money I have borrowed – money, curiously, that I didn't ever actually see except as a row of figures but which it will take me 15 years to repay – I decide to see if there are any interesting acquisitions to be made in the art market. I tap 3615 ART. A page appears offering me advice, price indexes and small ads from people holding Minitel auctions. Art Nouveau, recently slow, is picking up. The progress of Art Moderne is noticeable. Anticipating the imminent recycling of the late-Modern period, I leave a message saying I would like to buy an early Starck chair, an inflatable see-through plastic one.

This is the goal of telematics, the interactive society: people communicating via computer terminals, atomised individuals associating through the telephone lines – the computer their intermediary and host. The French could not resist such a fascinating experiment with their society. It's a game they have played in real-time, with all their technocratic drive and passion for novelty.

Now it's real-time to have lunch. I tap 3615 BADOIT, the mineral water company that is offering a selection of Minitel recipes in association with master chef Pierre Troisgros. I choose something absurdly exotic, for the language alone. *Poached Lobster in a Fondue of Tomatoes with a Curl of Cucumber*. These menus are the erotica of eating. I invite myself to a *Hot and Cold Carnival of Fruits*.

Before I switch off my Minitel, imagining a microwave oven that would deliver my selection in an instant, I glance at the corner of the screen. The cost of my morning on the Minitel: 60 minutes at just under a franc a minute. I have bought a newspaper and placed an ad in a specialist magazine, been to the bank, and consulted a recipe book in the library without leaving my room. I have spent six pounds, which will be shared between France Telecom and the companies who devise and run the services.

In 1986, the fourth year of service, 30 million hours were spent on the Minitel, not counting directory calls; 285 million calls to 4,000 services. It was three times the figure for the year before. After deducting their share, France Telecom forwarded to the services some £80 million. All involved were very pleased indeed. Conjuring with technology and society, they had created an entire industry.

At the start of the Seventies, France had fewer lines per capita than Greece. The waiting list for a phone was 18 months. Modernisation had been costly, but one of its fruits was the Transpac system, a digital relay essential to computer communications. The decision to proceed with the Minitel project was taken by the Giscard government partly as a way to maintain employment. It was attacked as technocratic and high-handed, and praised as a leap into the information age. It was hoped to create '*communication tous azimuts*' – communications in all directions. Official reports resounded with the French zeal for remaking society. Information, previously descending vertically like wisdom from on high, would find a new locus of *necessity*, spreading freely, laterally. The bulk data of society would become a new reservoir, 'each community communicating with its like and with the centre'.

Of what, then, did the 30 million hours of interactivity in 1986 consist? Banking services, home shopping, reservations and theatre tickets took up much less than half of the time. Some of the rest was spent on games like those played on home computers and on horoscopes, quizzes and tests, the standard fare of magazines. By far the greater part of the time, however, was spent in the *messageries*, anonymous electronic 'mail-boxes'. The name suggests a cross between a massage parlour and a zoo. These were digital meeting places where you could communicate in three-line bursts. They were conceived as a kind of postal service, but rapidly turned into a playpark for the fruitful French sexual imagination.

Lured by advertising, people tapped 3615 CHAUD looking for typed conversation with a member of the opposite sex. In the informatic equivalent of dry ice at a disco, messages floated inciting sexual fantasies, signed with elusive pseudonyms. Strangely, it caught on. It was daring and safe, public and private at the same time. Parading in the system disguised as someone else, the French found an intoxicating liberty and an unexpected telematic frisson, conversing with someone who was also masquerading. It was a new kind of social encounter.

From the start, the tariff for the system was deliberately based on time rather than distance. The whole of France was to be one informatic village. Part of the system was reserved for businesses to connect with their branches or reach customers. The newspapers who cried that their functions would be usurped and their businesses ruined were given rights to run the services. Only *they* had the media experience and social responsibility, they argued. In '82 one of the journals in the pilot scheme offered a service called Gretel. This functioned in the same way as services allowing users to play chess among themselves. Instead of a chess move, they were able to transmit a three-line message.

Left to themselves, the French public lost no time in turning it to serve their second favourite pastime after eating. The intellectual packet-switch of information imagined by the technocrats had delivered a bundle of steamy pornography.

Ah well. The responsible family newspapers who ran the services and the banks who funded them at first tried to ignore this fact. It was at least *literate* pornography, proving that France remains a literary nation. And it meant that everybody could have a free digital directory. It was a new twist to the sexual hypocrisy of the French: a tax on loneliness and sexual misery, paying for the informaticisation of France.

Along with the TGV, the new high-speed train that is shrinking the physical distances between cities, the Minitel is helping to transform the social geography of the country. Terminals in every home have created the first interactive society, giving instant lists of like-minded adults and instant public polls. Already, viewers are asked to respond to advertisng and to issues raised by TV debates. The information bulk is fragmenting and starting to flow in different directions. It is not impossible to imagine the government of the Republic itself, with its fondness for extending democracy, proceeding via the Minitel, an instant digital ballot box.

For the moment the *messageries* are a cross between the bar at the corner, extending right across France for the same tariff, and a fantastic literary masked ball. It was a surprise to everyone how readily an innocuous little black-and-white screen acted on the imagination; everyone but Jean Baudrillard, the French philosopher who long ago concluded, to the exasperation of his colleagues, that the screen is the surface of modern reality. Until the Eighties, the content of the screen was beyond the control of the consumer. The effect of entering into communication via the screen, making contact with someone through the telematic ether, was considerable. 'The Minitel,' according to one study, 'allows you to extract yourself from reality, to free yourself from social conventions, to converse intimately with unknowns. In the relational game of the *messageries* you can lead a fantasy life without disturbing your own life.' The *messageries* created Minitel addicts and, as their phone bills rocketed to £200 a month, these addicts created Minitel millionaires. There evolved a new subculture of lonely tappers at the home terminal. The girl at the supermarket checkout and the man in the Métro were swapping intimate fantasies. A cross between a church, psychiatrist's couch, disco and public masturbation zone, the Minitel gave sudden vent to the sexual neurosis of French society.

3615 PERVER

I TAP 3615 PERVER on my Minitel. A page appears with a line drawing of a woman reclining in bra, panties and fishnet tights. The curves of her body are represented in little steps and she has black pixels for nipples. This is the page welcoming me to the service.

To start the masked ball rolling, there is a list of sexual domains that might interest me: *Dialogue Direct, Lettres Erotiques, Pervers Vous Repond, Lieux Pervers*. I choose direct dialogue. Anonymity removes any need to be coy. A second page appears, asking for my code – the disguise that I will wear to the ball.

I tap TATI, since I wonder what the lanky French comedian, forever entangled in the quirky paraphernalia of modern France, would make of the Minitel. Perhaps he will even strike a romantic chord.

There is a lengthy list of pseudonyms of those already there. Names encoded in a strange new language, an abbreviated slangy spoken French: Cquin, Jouuiiiir, Bit-a-Cul, Fesseur 75, Sex Fou.

I ask Sex Fou what he or she is crazy about.

De Ton Cul? comes the reply. About your arse? The question mark is disturbing.

Name your perversion, I demand boldly. There is no reply. Obviously Sex Fou wasn't going to waste his, her, its time with a nervous novice.

However, Cristian leaves a message for TATI: *H Marie 45ans BCBG Grand et mince, rPa ch F sympa et liberee*. Oral or street French, such as the popular reverse language of *verlang* or backchat, is transcribed into Minitelese. Paris, 'ris-Pa', becomes rPa, for example. A 45-year-old married man, tall, lean, a professional living in Paris is looking for a woman, cool and liberated. Good luck.

There is even an *Homme Sensuel*.

Ca sert a quoi?

A une femme sensuelle.

Curious. And not very perverse. But there are other correspondents: 'A Violer', for example, 'To Rape'.

Je vous dis meme pas bonjour alors?

But after a few more desultory exchanges, the fun wears off. It's a weekday night, but hundreds of thousands of people are still busy tapping to each other. I do the Minitel equivalent of going home; I tap 3615 KASPAROV and play chess with the champ for a while, or with a computer masquerading as the champ.

The animatrice

THE MESSAGERIES OFFER the French equivalent of telephone sex. They are primarily a commercial activity. To generate traffic, they must use publicity to get people to call. The result has been a heavy turnover of posters of naked women; passing the hoardings of France over the last few years has been like flicking the pages of a pornographic magazine. But the conversations, once connected, tended to flag. They needed someone to keep them going. This is the job of the animatrice, who animates the conversations, pretending to be a private tapper.

Isabelle is an animatrice. She was working in the press office of a large company when she was offered a job animating a *réseau* or network. She did it for fun at first but soon became engrossed in it. 'The Minitel is a new kind of social therapy,' she says. The network she animates is not strictly sexual, and part of her task is to police it, since hardened *dragueurs*, people looking for pick-ups, come cruising knowing that the correspondents in the sexual *messageries* are often bogus. Posing as private callers, the animatrices keep dozens of conversations going at the same time. It is a particular skill. Using entry codes, Isabelle shows me the activity going on in her system. Run by a popular cultural journal, it offers games (which technically are just endless variants of Battleships) plus listings, information and a *messagerie* called *Delire*, which invites people simply to express themselves.

She approaches the terminal with slight hesitation. She is never sure what she will find going on on it. If fantasies on this public notice-board become too heated, she has to calm them. Her trepidation is noticeable. This is more than a job. It is as though she is dealing with a potential flasher or an errant child.

At the moment everybody is swapping quotations. This has been going on for days, she tells me. Someone launches an idea and others pick up on it. 'Because of the magazine, our network is a kind of vanity publisher for people who want to be read.' She shows me the list of pseudonyms that people choose. There are more than a thousand, of which about a quarter are currently connected. 'A lot of them are doing it from their offices – it must cost their companies a fortune.' The pseudonyms also function as message boxes. I could leave a message for ToTiTo for example. Isabelle tells me that she recently came across messages from a man to his mistress. Curious, she followed the exchanges. The man, who, she realised from his comments, was actually a *député* in the Assembly, arranged meetings with his mistress through the Minitel, because she couldn't telephone him at home.

Isabelle's job is a kind of telematic equivalent of the concierge of old. She has the codes to all the electronic mail-boxes and can see who is coming and going from the network.

'The Minitel itself is a kind of *cocu*,' she says. A cuckold. Many people do it in secret, at the office, and wouldn't want their partners to know. What are they looking for? 'They seem to want communication, discussions, meetings.'

The first question they ask each other is always *H ou F?* – man or woman?

'They want to know what the person looks like.'

Décris-toi . . . is a favourite opener.

'Men fantasise about themselves, creating a macho or sensitive image. There is one paralysed woman who enjoys making her male correspondents fantasise.'

Isabelle can see from the phone numbers where they are calling from. 'Many are in small provincial towns. There are a lot of little moralisers. But you have to have an identity that meshes with the others. It's an egocentric way of letting go but behind the mask there are fears and mental acnes of all kinds. You find everything from hymns of love to bursts of visceral hate. These are the really deconnected people. There are all kinds of pathologies,' she says, 'paranoid, schizoid, or simply lonely.'

It's a psychological disease dump for society, a telematic confidant or confessional. Isabelle notices that a system of social support, which is disappearing in the cities, is re-forming in the Minitel, substituting for things like *SOS Suicide*. 'Everybody *tutoyer*s each other on the Minitel. It is very intimate. One woman came on and said she had just lost her nine-year-old child. It was very strange. People found her message and left messages of consolation and support.'

These are murky, muted cries. Listening to the signal traffic on the Minitel is like putting a stethoscope to the French soul.

A woman was strangled by someone she met through the Minitel. By searching through a list of names on the Minitel, her boyfriend found the trail that led to her murderer. There are happy endings too. People marry after meeting through the Minitel. In an atomised society, new affective networks are forming, as the planners hoped. Life goes on – on the Minitel.

A red balloon

IN A BAR, a red-haired boy is playing pinball. On the juke-box are records by Les Chats Sauvages and Elvis Presley, the American rock and roll sensation. The red-haired boy is angry and morose, more so than usual today because he has just found out why there will never be a French Elvis.

At the town hall there is an official list of the names you can give a French child: names like Claude and Anatole, Prosper and Eugène. Nowhere on the list, according to his cousin who works in the town hall, is the name Elvis. And so it's all in vain. Johnny Hallyday can dress in black leather like Gene Vincent and swivel his slim French hips, but there will never be a French Elvis.

'*Tain! Me-e-e-erde!*'

He bangs the corner of the pinball machine with the palm of his hand, causing the machine to register *Tilt!* with a nerve-jangling clang.

'*Bof!*'

The red-haired boy throws up his hands in protest, though he is really too familiar with his adversary to care. He spends most of his spare time and all of his spare cash on it.

'*Vraiment, ça me fait chier, ça. Tu vois?*' He looks at me earnestly. '*En France, c'est toujours comme ça.*'

His name is Philippe, but he tells me to call him Phil because, perhaps as a result of the same list at the town hall, in his class at school there are four other Philippes and, though it's beside the point, they are all doing better than him. He thinks it's fine that I can sing all the Beatles' songs and I know who the Animals and the Rolling Stones are, even if I am four years younger than him. He is pleased to know somebody that lives in London. He introduces me to his friends and they say 'Carnaby Street! *Vous connaissez les Beatles?'*

Short, chubby, freckled, Phil chews gum constantly and speaks a few words of English, mostly culled from the titles of rock and roll songs. His father drives a delivery van for the local supermarket, the sight of which causes Phil to freeze and dodge into side streets. Sometimes, when it rains, he takes me to a house with walls lined with creeping vines. He pulls snails off the cracked cement and sucks them out of their shells, swallowing them with a grin. For the sake of our friendship, I try one. I can feel the live snail convulse like phlegm in the back of my throat. Phil explains that they die straight away. He pats his stomach. Already a gourmet, he says they taste better in April.

For my part, I am glad to have someone to go into bars with. It's difficult being a boy in a small, foreign town. Without friends, you become introspective, which in turns makes you less approachable, a reinforcing circle of isolation like the endless tours of the town that I trace on my bicycle. In this isolation I dwell on curious details, like the streets named after forgotten statesmen or just historical dates, a litany of obscure glory.

Phil's best friend lives, for example, on the rue du 19 Janvier, in an egg-yellow block of flats beside the railway lines. He is older than Phil, tanned and with longer hair and he has a motorbike that he keeps locked in the downstairs hallway of the block. Phil confirms my grandparents' description of its denizens as *pieds noirs*, though he glances around before he says it and pronounces the words not with distaste but with surreptitious glee. He tells me that his friend was born in Algeria but had French grandparents, and he came to live in the town after the war. He and Phil converse intensely about the mechanics of the small Japanese bike. I sit on the stairs and read the comic strips in *Spirou*. Familiar in English, a duck exclaiming in French becomes once again preposterous. It is early evening, and there are spicy stews cooking upstairs. The hallway is wreathed in the doughy vapour of simmering *couscous*. Women returning with shopping step past me on the stairs, quickly identifying my face without looking me in the eye.

Later that evening Phil's friend makes the same tours of the town on his motorbike that I had been making on my bicycle. He goes faster, shortening the time and taking longer routes, stretching the perimeter to compensate for his accelerated boredom. Phil and I take turns to ride pillion, returning breathless and cold-faced to the town square, where girls gather to meet us. There is one girl in particular who twists the black throttle on the handlebars, lolling her head indecisively, evidently tempted by something. She rides away with Phil's friend. Cheering them as they roar off, Phil accepts this as inevitable, but he is also annoyed now. He takes me to the bar by the station, where we order lemonade with grenadine and he feeds more coins into the pinball machine. Flipping the change, I realise you can't tell heads from tails in France because the franc, since the Revolution, has no image of a king or queen on it. Accustomed to a monarch's reassuring profile, I am dubious about French coins in that their value is guaranteed by only a wispy female wreathed in a scanty dress, and dangerously unbalanced by this *chasse à la femme* in that they thus appear to have two reverse sides, as though doomed to schizophrenic antagonism.

Within minutes, Phil has registered Tilt. He does this almost deliberately, out of frustration, since, like all French boys, he is an expert at the machine. Calming a little, he easily gets a replay, which he turns over to me.

'*Moi, je m'en fous, moi,*' he says. And then, '*Tu sais, j'aimerais bien aller à Londres. Mais c'est loin comme l'Amérique.*' He asks me if motorbikes are expensive in London. I tell him I don't think they're as expensive as in France, although I have no idea.

'*Tain! C'est chiant.*'

The next day, on the platform waiting for the train to Lyon with my family, I see Phil's friend. He is wearing a porter's cap and pushing a barrow full of parcels. Smiling, at ease with himself, he comes up and says hello, shaking my hand. My grandmother greets him politely, questioning me afterwards about who he was. She makes no comment and the train pulls in.

When we returned the next year, my grandmother told me that Phil had been in an accident. He had stolen a motorbike and, foolishly trying to dodge the barriers of the level-crossing as they swung closed, had skidded and been sent flying, crashing through the windscreen of an oncoming car. '*C'était horrible. Tu vois ce que je t'ai dit? Les motos sont dangereuses!*'

Phil had been disfigured and lost part of his arm, she said obscurely. I tried not to imagine what she meant. The accident had happened three months before and he was still in the hospital in Bourg-en-Bresse. To my mother, she added that it had been the Algerian boy's bike. And that one, *celui-là*, had got a girl pregnant. Her father had gone after him with a gun, but he was so drunk and in such a rage that he shot his own dog instead. And now, nobody knew where the boy had gone.

The following year, I saw Phil again, riding with his father in the delivery van. There was a zigzag of thin, wrinkled skin around one eye and he proudly lifted his shirt to show me the long scars on his chest and shoulder. I was glad to see that his arm was intact but he held it up and dangled his limp hand, which swivelled sickeningly.

'*Euh. C'est fini pour moi, les motos,*' he said with the air of a 15-year-old war veteran.

He had nearly lost an eye and perhaps also the use of his hand but had been reconciled with his dad, with whom he was working to repay his friend for the wrecked bike. He told me that this friend had returned and married the girl. I asked him if it was the girl that used to come to the square.

'*Elle? Tu rigoles. Elle est toujours là. Mais pourquoi tu veux savoir?*'

The outsiders

LATER, I GOT to know Phil's Algerian friend, whose name was André. He was not Algerian, but a *pied noir*, an Algerian of European descent. Phil insisted, when André displayed a quick temper, that he was '*un peu Arabe*'. From his childhood nanny, André had learned to swear in Arabic – a language made for cursing – but he never acknowledged to me any Arab part of him, except to say that he had an uncle married to a Chaouia, a strident woman who did not wear a veil. She was not an Arab, he insisted, but a Berber.

André counted Spanish, Italian and Maltese among his forebears, though he stressed a line of descent from farmers of the Midi who emigrated after the outbreak of Phylloxera in 1878 that devastated French vines. Launching the wine industry in Algeria, this blight gave a marketing fillip a century later to US viniculturists who reminded the public that it was vines reimported from California that replenished the French stocks.

André's family had long since sold the farm they dug from the fetid marshes of the Mitidja. And he was ten years old when they had to give up the shop they owned in Oran to come to France, part of the exodus from Algeria of the million or so 'Europeans' who lived there at the violent close of the war of independence in 1962. His memories were vague of this bitter colonial war. The family lived near the poor white district of Bab-el-Houed, where André's father reckoned the paramilitary Deltas were doing a necessary job machine-gunning Muslims suspected of aiding the FLN. His father referred to Arabs as *figuiers* at best, implying that they spent their days under fig trees. At worst they were *sales ratons*. He condoned the murderous *ratonnades*, 'rat hunts' inspired by the French-Algerian terrorist group, the OAS. At school, André was bullied by boys who called themselves 'ultras', imitating the rebels in the French Army who tried to seize Algeria and overthrow the Republic, bringing France itself close to civil war.

In Algeria, André's family were *petits blancs*; in France they were *pieds noirs*. In fact, they had been Maghrebised, by culture and temperament – and by temptation. They drank mint tea and slept in the afternoons in shaded courtyards. Even the poorest had *fatmas* to do the housework and, like the white settlers of Rhodesia or South Africa, they regarded this as their due. They had built the bridges and roads and irrigation systems, settling lands across which had drifted only the shadows of an ancient nomadic population. Like the South Africans, they saw no injustice in an electoral system that ensured European minority rule. In the end, the *pieds noirs* were betrayed, André's father told him, by the France to which they felt they belonged, but which, until they disembarked at Marseille, they had never seen.

Since the family's arrival in France, André had grown to resent his father, who worked as a stock clerk in a Co-op depot. He was ashamed of the obsequious, *pastis*-sodden respect that the older man still had for *la France*. André saw that she was a *pute* dealing at every turn a genteel snub to the coarse *pied noir* with his taste for *couscous* and heavy red wine. With an irony whose weight was fortunately lost on him, the old French-Algerian was regarded with the same contempt that he had once reserved for the *sale* Arabs. He acquired the habit of counting his change in shops, which kept him from noticing the blank regard of the shopkeepers. It was the most icy of all affronts, as though they were serving someone who didn't really exist.

La France entertained her new arrivals dutifully but without warmth. She could not comprehend their brooding, vengeful passions, acquired perhaps from decades of contact, albeit unbidden, with the fatalistic Arab sensibility. The Arab believes himself at the mercy of an implacable God, harsh and unforgiving as the meridional sun. Resigned to this, he is protected from its worst effects. By overexposing himself to the musky, heavy-lidded and ultimately oppressive sensuality of the far Mediterranean, the European, like a sun-worshipper falling asleep on a beach for a whole lifetime, developed an ugly melanoma, a rash of alienation and irritable self-contempt.

One day, seeing that I always carried paperbacks with me, André gave me a copy of *The Outsider* by Albert Camus, telling me with pride that the author was a native of his home town, Oran. In the novel, Camus's anti-hero, renouncing morality, murders without emotion. 'I learned not to separate these creatures bursting with violent energy from the sky where their desires whirl,' he wrote of his fellow *pieds noirs*.

Ill-assimilated, André rode his motorbike restlessly around the outskirts of the town in a black leather jacket, defining for himself, as did his French friend Phil, a new identity derived from record sleeves and bubble-gum cards. They shared an interest in movies, rock and roll and comic-books, the one out of boredom with French culture, the other in a spirit of mutual rejection. In the Fifties, Prime Minister Pierre Mendès France had tried to encourage French children to drink milk. The programme was a failure. In other ways, France with its rigid society, its high tariff barriers, its sense of a tarnished and belatedly protected culture, did not know how to nourish her new generation.

Phil and André asked me once what I thought of General de Gaulle. He was a comical figure to me, I explained, pear-shaped and absurdly tall, so it was impossible to miss him saluting his pointed head at official ceremonies. They were shocked. De Gaulle was many things to people in France but never a figure of mirth. Phil's father was a Gaullist. André's father hated him. 'He betrayed us,' said André. He did not believe that himself, however, though he said I couldn't imagine how central he was to a country ravaged and dispirited by the war. I explained that he was mistrusted by the British. It seemed to be a wartime grudge. It also had something to do with the British suspicion of the presidential style and memories of Bonaparte. They feared the entry of a military man into politics, since he would be disposed, in the last resort, to favour order over the chaos of democracy.

Announcing that he was available if needed as the military revolt in Algeria threatened to spread to France itself, de Gaulle was given decree powers to dissolve the Fourth Republic and frame a new constitution. The Right thought he would side with them, but he declined to become another Franco. He made agitated pleas to the unsettled French people, rising out of his seat and thumping his desk for democracy and reform. The Fifth Republic was born, and between Fraternity and Liberty, Algeria chose Liberty.

Discussing French films

IMPATIENT, TESTY, CHOKING from adolescent claustrophobia at the old-fashioned, constrained pace of life in France, Phil was a lot like the teenager in François Truffaut's first film, *Les Quatre Cents Coups*. Made in '59, I saw it only a few years later. But for me, it remains Trauffaut's best film; better than *Jules et Jim*, which is just the sort of sentimental confection everyone adores from France; or *Day For Night*, a film about making a film, self-referential in the worst French intellectual way.

To *faire les 400 coups* means to have done it all, run amok, taken every ride in the fair. The director claims it was autobiographical, the story of a bored and semi-delinquent kid growing up in Paris in the Fifties. His parents argue incessantly in their small apartment and one day, playing truant from school, the boy glimpses his mother in the arms of another man. The film ends with his first sight of the ocean, a bracing expanse of freedom that comes as he runs away from the remand school to which his mother has sent him.

It was one of the films that announced the famous New Wave in French cinema. As the Fifth Republic was being born, so the cinematographic style of a group of young French film-makers was being acclaimed for its realism, intimacy and speed. Indeed, the golden age of French cinema was long past. The plots had grown heavy, the dialogue stagey, and stars like Gérard Philipe, Michèle Morgan and the great Jean Gabin met each other time and again in productions as predictable as a reproduction Louis XV chair. The French film business consisted of 237 people, each of them instantly identifiable to the head waiter at Fouquet's.

Hunched over his typewriter, a young film fan who preferred the most underrated American B-movie to the academic products of France, bashed vitriolically at the keys. 'What's the use of an anti-bourgeois cinema made by the bourgeois for the bourgeois?' François Truffaut had just turned 20, one of the youngest of a group of cineastes running a film fanzine called *Cahiers du Cinéma* in which this famed broadside appeared. Together they decided to ignore the production cartel, which was anyway ignoring them, and organise a co-operative to finance each other's efforts.

Working on shoestring budgets, making a virtue of their amateurism, they succeeded in producing ten films in three years: *Le Beau Serge* by Claude Chabrol ('57): *Le Bel Age* by Pierre Kast, *Moi, un Noir* by Jean Rouch, *Paris Nous Appartient* by Jacques Rivette, *Hiroshima Mon Amour* by Alain Resnais, *Les Cousins* by Claude Chabrol and Truffaut's *Les Quatre Cents Coups* ('58); *A Bout de Souffle* by Jean-Luc Godard, *Le Signe du Lion* by Eric Rohmer and *L'Eau à la Bouche* by Jacques Doniol-Valcroze ('59). Similar only in that their makers were all under 30, these were the films tagged *nouvelle vague* by a journalist at *L'Express* as Truffaut's effort was selected for the Cannes film festival.

Wily, as any French aristocracy must be to survive, the film establishment rapidly embraced these upstart film-makers who had ignored the long apprenticeships of French cinema and actually revelled in their lack of craft. Chabrol joked that he didn't even know where the lens was on the camera, and framed his scenes through a washer he carried with him. The most radical of the group, Godard, took his camera into the Champs-Elysées, following Jean-Paul Belmondo as he circles Jean Seberg, the anxious hoodlum trying to preserve his cool in the pretty face of a not-so-prim translator who is not so sure she wants to continue the affair. While the young British couple in *A Kind of Loving* stood beside the kitchen sink trying to decide if they should, these two already had! To the documentary urgency of the improvised camera angles, the freshness of the acting duo adds emotional realism. Ignorant of editing technique, Godard crammed his scenes onto the precious film stock. In this 'fault', announced excited French critics, was the beginning of a style, a new grammar of film resembling the spoken word in literature.

With its youthful audacity, its breezy freedom, the New Wave threw open a window on the coming decade. In front of the cameras the directors placed young and little-known actors: Belmondo, Jean-Claude Brialy, Jean-Pierre Léaud and Gerard Blain. Played by Anna Karina, Juliet Berto and Bernadette Laffont were female characters whose make-up ran with their mouths.

Intellectually restless, the French have never given up the search for a new definition of feminity. In the Fifties, they found that definition in Brigitte Bardot, star of *And God Created Woman*, who blithely hung her wet underwear out to dry, hinting at an innocent, if thoroughly corrupt, sort of liberation, while her co-star fought back his blushes.

Meet Baby Dalle

THE FILM BEGINS with a medium close-up of a young couple making love. They are naked on the bed, the girl beneath with her knees drawn up. As the credits finish and the camera approaches, she begins to moan.

Minutes go by, and the camera – like the viewer – is unable to turn away; it draws steadily closer to the bedside until the man rears up and the face of the girl becomes visible, full-lipped and glistening.

There are many ways to make it big in French movies – some of them requiring years of patient work. And then there is the other way – naked under tungsten light, glazed eyes signalling that there is enough of you to go round all the darkened cinemas in the world. That's the way Beatrice Dalle did it. For her first screen appearance – as a convincing ingénue in the highly successful *Betty Blue* – the 21-year-old newcomer was obliged, among the other discomforts of screen celebrity, to simulate sex with her co-star, Jean-Hugues Anglade. It can give a girl a reputation.

'Since *Betty Blue* I've had plenty of offers of sub-*Betty Blue*s,' says Beatrice staring at her feet. 'I must have read a hundred scripts and its always the same role: girls with psychological problems and a vicious temper and guys in love with them.' She shrugs and her voice grows defiant. 'Not a single one where the guy leaves my clothes on! It's terrible!'

Beatrice Dalle complains about this a lot – to her friends, to interviewers on TV, to her agent Dominique Besnehart. This is the same agent who called unannounced and told her to be at the studio the next day for a test. She told him to ring back when he had acquired better manners, and hung up. And of course he did ring back, introducing himself as a casting director for the new film by Jean-Jacques Beineix. Beatrice didn't even know what a casting director was. Though she went to the cinema often, she had never heard of Beineix either, despite the success of *Diva* and *The Moon in the Gutter*.

'I knew the names of actors if I liked them but average people like me don't know the names of directors. Only people who are really interested in the cinema know who directors are.'

And anyway, the studio was too far away, so she refused . . .

What would be happening now if it had ended there? Beatrice would not be having her photograph taken today. And there would be one less figure of celluloid sexual fantasy. I had never met a Monroe or Bardot in the flesh before. If Beatrice is any indication, they are shorter, less fulsome – and engagingly candid; more like a little sister. I am not surprised when she tells me flatly, 'I don't get along with women.'

She is wearing a dark velvet fur-trimmed mini-coat that hangs off her bare shoulders, revealing a butterfly tattoo ('I'm getting another one done soon') and she has her hands on her waist, raising the hem of her already short skirt. Pressed forward against the painted frescos of the luxury hotel suite, her back to the camera, her legs slightly parted, she licks her lower lip. In her purple tights and high-heels, the five-foot actress is doing her best on behalf of the top fashion magazine to look like a cheap and possibly under-age prostitute.

As she gazes at her reflection in the lighting mirror, Beatrice is thinking about looking her best, concentrating on her expression for the camera. She says nothing to the photographer. He sweats as he squeezes the shutter, throwing rolls of film to his assistant, maintaining an endless barrage of praise in mid-Atlantic French. '*Voilà!* That's great. Don't move. Don't move an inch.'

She pouts. 'Yeah. Don't move at all. *Ne bouge pas.*' She sticks her bottom out a little. '*Ne bouge absolument pas.*'

A friend comes into the room and she doesn't look at him. She is concentrating. She is thinking about how she looks. Beatrice thinks she has a bit of a 'dirty' look – and if people say otherwise then they're only trying to flatter her. She knows that guys imagine she'd be a pushover; even if, up to now, there haven't been many for whom it has been at all easy! But she has heard things you wouldn't believe!

Everyone is thrilled with the Polaroids, which lie on a table in rows like the cards of a game of fashion snap. Beatrice reclining on the bed; Beatrice dangling from the bed; Beatrice draped over a chair; Beatrice regarding the viewer in a mirror regarding her. Always the same 'dirty' look – lips lasciviously parted, revealing her best feature, the gap between her front teeth.

It is a hot day, and the windows to the balcony have been open, giving office workers opposite a spectacle in which, this being Paris, they seem barely interested. The activity in the room has been suffocating: frequent changes of clothes, reapplications of make-up and redoing of hair. A large tinfoil mirror reflecting the light has served to raise the temperature further. Then there is the strain of getting it right. Everybody is anxious that everybody else is happy: the client, the stylist, the photographer, the star. There is a warm tension in the room, as before a storm. Under her powder, Beatrice remains dry. I ask her if she is bored. 'I'm concentrating,' she says.

Like many children of the Seventies, Beatrice always knew she would be a star. Before *Betty Blue* she never had a job. She went out to nightclubs where men bought her drinks, slept on sofas at friends' places and could always find 15 francs for a lunch at Burger King. That was in Paris, between the ages of 16 and 18, and then she met her husband and her life become more stable. But still she was content to do nothing. She couldn't face the idea of working for 40 years for a pension. She knew something was going to happen to her. 'Me and my friends, we didn't care about anything. We all thought we were future superstars!'

And as these things go, the future superstar was walking down the Champs-Elysées one day when she was stopped by a man she recognised as an ex-model. He had an agency near by and asked her to come and see him. Too short to be a model, Beatrice was exactly what the magazine *Photo Revue* wanted for a story about Lolitas. 'They had a tarty Lolita, a chic Lolita, I don't know what. Obviously I was the tarty Lolita and because they liked the photo they put it on the cover.' Since then, Beatrice has done plenty of photos. Being photographed is easy but making films is more difficult.

The photographer pronounces himself happy, asks if Beatrice is too, and everybody breaks for food. Cheerfully Beatrice helps the photographer's assistant prepare the table and serve the food. The salmon mousse has started to melt but there are radishes and *fraises des bois*.

Beatrice sits next to her friend Sophie, who has just found a backer for her first collection of clothes designs. They knew they were going to make it. And here they are surrounded by luxury rented by the hour and sipping success from plastic cups, talking about Jean-Paul's latest stuff and how weird it is to work with Helmut, who lives in Monaco now.

Sophie is the same height as Beatrice, with round shoulders, greasy hair and a bright smile. Together they look like the sort of girlfriends you might meet on a seaside holiday, one pretty, one plain. In fact, having decided at the age of 15 to leave school and their native Le Mans, where nothing ever happened, the two girls set out for the Punk capital of the world, London, only to be sent back by immigration officers at Dover because they had no money and no idea where they would stay.

Like many children of the Seventies, Beatrice grew up fast. At 13, she was already going alone to local nightclubs. Her mother didn't mind. 'Go ahead if you want to enjoy yourself,' she would say, distracted by her favourite actor, Blake Carrington, on the TV. And so at 16 Beatrice went to stay with a friend in Paris. 'I don't want to pretend that I've seen it all, but at 23 I feel like a lot of women of 30.' At the end of last year, her marriage to a young painter broke up. 'C'est la vie,' she says, looking sad and distant.

Beatrice tells Sophie about her holiday in Rome with her new boyfriend. They were followed everywhere by paparazzi. She met him at the Cannes film festival in May. Beatrice was there for the première of her second film, *La Sorcière*. The organisers asked her to present the prize for the best director at the closing gala. Then she heard that she would be presenting it with the British actor Rupert Everett. 'He came to my hotel to get me on the night. I ran down from my room and almost jumped into his arms. Usually men are too timid to try to get off with me. I have to chat them up. It was me who made the running with Rupert.'

The couple converse in French when they are together – which is not as often as she would wish because Beatrice lives in Paris, where she has a modest apartment with a bathroom refitted in the Seventies that she hates.

'He speaks French really well,' she trills. 'I love the English accent. He's even learnt French slang in a year and a half. He's really intelligent.'

'Is it love?' asks her friend Sophie.

Beatrice makes a face.

She brightens, proposing to show Sophie a top that the stylist has brought with her from London. Disappearing into the bathroom, she returns wearing a dark-blue velvet bodice that pinches at her waist. The bodice is so tight that the veins pump blue on her small breasts, now inescapably displayed. She covers her décolletage modestly with her hand as she talks, making it much easier to return the habitually direct contact of her yellow-brown eyes.

Later, Beatrice tries to sneak out wearing the bodice under her denim jacket. She prefers to wear her own clothes for photo sessions, she tells the stylist ingenuously, mixing them with ones that are provided for her.

Does she play any sport, asks the stylist.

'No sport. I don't like it at all. Except boxing. But that's just to watch.'

I ask her what kind of music she likes.

'I listen to the Doors.'

'Isn't that a little depressing?'

'I know but it's better than this kind of pop that you hear all over the beaches at Cannes.' She gestures at the portable radio in the corner.

So they sent a car and Beatrice did the test. And while she waited for the decision she read *37.2 Le Matin* by Philippe Djian, the cult French novel about an ill-fated affair between a failed writer and a disturbed waif. And, like a trouper, she found that she could identify with the character of Betty, even down to the physical description. 'It was really me. I didn't have to try to interpret the role at all.' The only difference was that Beatrice was extremely shy. 'Even with a guy I was intimate with I could never parade around a room naked like Betty.'

This gave rise to some loud disputes between the starlet and her director. Beatrice had to understand that this girl was very liberated; she had no problem with nakedness. The first-time actress had agreed to some nudity for dramatic reasons but balked when it was suggested at the last minute that she should be nude for some scenes to make them more erotic.

'Making guys dream is fine but not by taking your clothes off. Why did Monroe or Bardot make them dream so much? Because you wanted so much to see them naked and you never did and so you fantasised about them. If I spent my whole life making films like *Betty Blue* who would want to undress me afterwards?

'This stuff about nudity is really something from the Sixties – for 40-year-old guys who think that a liberated woman is one without any clothes on. It's really old-hippy and really dumb! That's all over. Today you don't have to sleep with everybody and strip naked on the beach to be liberated.'

In fact, just about the only place where you still have to be naked to get anywhere these days is in French movies. What can a girl do? For her second film, she selected a script that was a bit unusual and – for dramatic reasons – took her clothes off again.

'I'm used to grand hotels,' says Beatrice, as we sweep away in the stretch Mercedes. 'I like this life. Who wouldn't?'

Some tramps jeer drunkenly as we turn a corner. Beatrice jeers back and then shrinks timidly in her seat. 'I've always had luck. Ever since I was born I've been lucky. I have no fear that things will change.' She clutches at Sophie. 'Anyway, I still have my old friends. That hasn't changed. With me it's always passion, so either it ends or it doesn't.'

As we drive back to her apartment in the anonymous streets behind the Sacré-Coeur, Beatrice explains what it means to be a sex symbol in France.

'There was an article about the new French philosophies and they put me in it. I was supposed to represent the new sexuality.' She shrugs. 'Of course I like being a sex symbol. Are you kidding? What more could you dream of than to make films that are good, that are dramatic like *Betty Blue* – it's saved because of that – and be a sex symbol? There aren't many women who would be bothered by that . . . I was flattered that they thought I expressed it. They ask me what I think all the time – about drugs, politics, morality. I've no advice to give anyone but I'll happily give an answer. Just because you didn't go to college doesn't mean you're stupid.'

She sits up defiantly in the back of the limo.

'I'm not against anything!'

Libération

'THE SILENCE OF the people is a lesson for kings,' said Mirabeau coldly to the Assembly.

In this silence, Louis XVI heard only the beating of his own faint heart, while in Paris, the citizens loosened paving stones for further ammunition, and artisans from the narrow streets of the Faubourg St-Antoine, next to what were now the ruins of the Bastille jail, made ready to erect new barricades.

The militia hurriedly gathered under Lafayette were given cockades of red and blue to wear, the colours of Paris, to which, after a little reflection, a band of white was added, the colour of the King, a phantom colour that is merely the absence of colour.

Referring to the National Assembly by name for the first time, the King announced the withdrawal of his troops surrounding the city. A prudent and, moreover, just decision in the view of those who would soon be known as the Jacobins, it was not to be his last feckless act in the eyes of the royalists.

Three days after the fall of the Bastille, having considered flight and made his will, the King came to the Hôtel de Ville, the town hall in Paris, to answer the calls for the resignation of his Minister of Finance. French people consumed a kilo of bread a day and after a poor harvest prices were rising steeply. In the countryside, hunger was turning peasants into brigands. The villages had grown into towns and in bustling towns like the Faubourg St-Antoine on the edge of Paris, pamphlets quoting the *philosophes* offered dignity to an emergent urban population of artisans, *commerçants* and guild-workers. Fearful of the Church – which the Reformation had failed to evict from the business of everyday life and restore to the chapel of the soul – and jealous of an aristocracy that disregarded them, these new citizens, the makers of the Revolution, proclaimed their hasty approval of the looting of mills and manor houses and the dunking or worse of hoarders and speculators.

The King's route to the Hôtel de Ville was lined with citizens bearing knives and muskets and crying '*Vive la Nation!*' His Majesty was led, according to a shocked English observer, like a tame bear through the streets. Upon entering the town hall, he was presented with a red, white and blue cockade, the colours of the Revolution. Nobody was quite sure how the King would react.

After a moment, he took the coloured feathers and fastened them to his hat.

'Sire,' enthused the Comte d'Estaing, 'with that cockade and the Third Estate you will conquer Europe!' But to speeches from members of the newly created Third Estate, which now represented the prospering merchants and artisans alongside the estates of the Church and the aristocracy, he made only faltering replies.

And so, the King gave his soul to the Republic, but it was a morose king, and an uncertain republic. Outside, the cries of '*Vive la Nation*' gave way to cries of '*Vive le Roi*', not a reconciliation so much as a conflict of loyalties that has confused the French mind ever since.

For it is a curious fact that revolutions are usually made in the name of the king – a special brand of courage or dementia being required to make the world anew in one's own name, more likely to give rise to a cult or religion.

Nationhood too is a kind of faith, its vessel a spiritual vacuum in which, at the wrong moment, any idea, any tyranny, can lodge. And revolution is like a sneeze – a pleasurable, vacant spasm. Long before there were revolutions, the soul was thought to be momentarily unguarded during a sneeze, allowing evil spirits to enter, which is why to this day complete strangers, and also complete non-believers, will bless you when you sneeze. There is no such formula to safeguard the makers of revolution, however.

Transported by the success of their initiative, the failed lawyers and intemperate journalists who made the French Revolution set about the task of redefining the French nation. Never was such a heroic and fascinating venture undertaken in Britain, where over the centuries society has been shaped and hammered like a shield. And perhaps this was all to the good, for in France, the process of liberty soon resulted in a savage, bloody fight.

The implosion of politics

'SOMETHING COULD HAPPEN tonight. I can feel it.'

Christophe has been on the phone all day. A former member of the JCR, a Trotskyite group committed to the overthrow of society, he now laughs at his old self and wears braces designed by Jean-Paul Gaultier and inscribed with meaningless Soviet lettering. He tells me a meeting has just been called at the new faculty at Jussieu, near the Sorbonne. Feeling an old exhilaration, he grabs his satchel and runs from the office of the magazine where he works.

It is the 22nd of March 1988, a day bristling with historical implications. TV crews and reporters have already arrived for the meeting in the hall, which is thronging with students who chatter excitedly and clamber over their friends to find spaces on the benches. There are some older students with long hair and beards. Their faces are lined but their expressions are dreamy and even rejuvenated. They are recalling other meetings and the intervening years. The majority of the students are young enough to have only folk memories of May '68, the pivotal month in post-war France. These students grew up in the world that the older ones wrought. They queued for burgers in the Champs-Elysées. They listened to punk rock and didn't fret too much about losing their virginity.

But there is an unmistakable tension in their chatter to one another. They talk loudly like anxious expectant initiates in a new rite. With the re-election of the left-wing President Mitterrand still uncertain, they are conscious suddenly that history is not given but can be overturned. As if to remind them, the meeting is attended by Daniel Cohn-Bendit, one of the founders of the *Mouvement du 22 mars*, now a teacher and green politician in Germany, and by Pierre Juquin, a breakaway Communist candidate in the coming presidential election, his banner part red and part green for ecology.

Ironically, it was an ardent young Juquin who in the early Sixties helped purge the Communist Party of student militants, the Trotskyites, Maoists, Althusserians and Italian-line Khrushchevians – the French love to turn a leader into a movement – thereby arranging the factions for the civil war of '68. Significantly, he is now the only person in the hall wearing a suit. Cohn-Bendit is casually dressed in a baggy grey sweater.

'What are these two former foes doing on the same platform? Who is the hostage of whom?' Christophe asks. He is keen on the chess game of politics. He wants to see if, as he suspects, Cohn-Bendit will lend his support to Juquin, who has been trying to rally youth, immigrant and ecology groups in a new 'alternative' left-wing bloc. 'The old *Parti communiste* is in flux,' Christophe tells me. Having left the Revolutionary Young Communists through disillusionment with the political apparatus, he is pleased to be here as a spectator. 'Tonight we could see the birth of a new party!' A once-in-a-generation event in the UK, such births occur more readily in France. There is no space left in the 1,000-capacity auditorium and still more people are arriving. An hour after it was due to start, the organisers are untangling cables under the makeshift bench at the front. 'The Left still can't get a microphone to work,' sighs Christophe.

The election is important because of the executive powers of the French President. In the new constitution prepared by de Gaulle and his future Prime Minister Michel Debré in 1958, the President was given power to control the parliamentary agenda. De Gaulle was the first popularly elected President since Louis Napoleon in 1848 and, like the emperor's nephew, took on the mantle of national sovereignty. This satisfied the royalists but angered the republicans. The President nominates a Prime Minister who then forms a cabinet that drafts bills on which the elected deputies vote. He can determine the character of the cabinet and the speed with which reforms are passed. The timing of the two ballots – every seven years for the President and five for the deputies – meant that for the last two years of his term, the left-wing President has had to nominate and 'cohabit' with a right-wing Prime Minister – an unprecedented dysfunction but, to the relief of all in the unfinished republic that is France, not a catastrophic one.

The President also embodies the French state. More than the election of deputies, a presidential election, with its national personalities, stimulates the interest of the electorate. It is as if the whole of France was electing a new king – a figure who will give shape and voice to their hopes and fears, their foreign policy and political passions.

Juquin knows that he cannot win this election. He can only hope to amass a block of votes large enough to horsetrade later on. From the constant shuffle of the fractious French Left, he hopes to deal himself a hand recalling the glory days of '68. With a tight campaign schedule, he is the first to speak.

'I have never stopped reflecting on those days,' he confides. This intimacy brings an immediate rush of applause. He speaks firmly, arms folded in a professional gesture of reflection and not crossed in obstinacy. Whether from nostalgic emotion or the smoke in the hall, his eyes are moist. He talks of his political shifts as evidence of his maturing.

Christophe shrugs. 'He is a Social Democrat reformist who took a while to get rid of the old slogans, that's all.'

Juquin says he doesn't want to participate in another *petit* political party. 'The choices of industrialisation are rarely discussed. Marx and Engels thought those forces were given, but we *have* a choice.' Calling for a 'Movement of Red and Green', Juquin reaches the end of his short speech. 'What worries the bourgeoisie is not the *petit parti bien rangé* but a movement. I am the movement!' He raises his arms but there is a vague rustling in the audience that threatens to turn into a hiss. 'But I am not alone,' he adds quickly. 'You are here with me if you want to be. *You* are the future.'

The invitation to self-congratulatory applause prompts barely a ripple from the sceptical students.

Cohn-Bendit speaks next.

'I have reformed a lot more than he has,' he jokes, gesticulating at Juquin who is seated now beside him, staring at the back of the gallery.

'I sense something in this moment. The problem for me is that . . .'

Muttering, his words dribble away.

Looking around slowly, he grits his teeth and, dismissing with a wave the 'alternative Green *machin-truc* that we're talking about here', he says that what's really needed is the dissolution of the Left!

For this he receives a round of eager applause from the students, delighted that the old political southpaw can still hook from so far on the left that his ideological sparring partner couldn't see it coming. He doesn't want a new party block fighting for its morsel of cheese, he emphasises. What he would like to see, come to that, is the dissolution of *all* political parties! Next to him Juquin, who has devoted his life to political parties, keeps his eyes fixed on the back of the hall.

'This is the great debate of the future,' says Cohn-Bendit. 'The ecology debate is really about an alternative politics that we want to construct.' He speaks in hoarse, jumpy phrases that belie the repetition of conviction and appear to be fresh, spontaneous arguments. He calls finally for the 'autodissolution of politics'. Suited to the idealistic yearnings of the students, this idea inspires noisy hoots of encouragement.

Cohn-Bendit rocks back grinning on the heels of his chair, satisfied with himself.

Love revolution chaos action

On the 8th of January 1968, a new swimming-pool was being opened at the University of Nanterre. Hardly had the Minister for Youth and Sport finished his inauguration speech than a youth – chubby, red-haired, freckled and blushing – rose impudently to heckle him.

'I've read your white paper on youth. Six hundred pages of ineptitudes! You don't even *mention* the sexual problems of young people.'

'With a face like that,' the minister unwisely cracked, 'I'm not surprised you've got sexual problems.'

In fact, it was the governors of the university who were having problems with sex. They wanted to stop the circulation after midnight between the male and female dorms, to damn the tide of the new sexual freedom or at least to draw across it a discreet prophylactic curtain.

The students responded to what they termed the 'fascist' remark of the Minister for Youth and Sport – whose title of office itself gives an idea of how youth was then officially regarded – with demonstrations and slogans daubed across the walls of Nanterre: Down with the bourgeois university! Down with Daddy's world!

Two years before, to show his undimmed revolutionary vigour, a 73-year-old Chairman Mao swam the Yangtze, trailed by a shoal of red-flag waving youth. These were the Red Guards, shock troops of the coming youthquake.

In the US, desegregators in the civil rights movement were joined by the draft card burners, protesting their country's attack on North Vietnam in the Summer of Love.

In France the schools were full of Beatle caps and Little Red Books. Jacques Dutronc sang, *'Il y a neuf cent millions de chinois/ et moi, et moi, et moi.'* By tearing down temples and sending teachers to work in the fields, the Red Guards showed that history itself could be vanquished – a self-perpetuating system of values toppled as easily as a statue. Theirs was the victory of the future over the past. And so the most radical of French fashion designers, Pierre Cardin, cut a collarless jacket, 'as a distraction, to change my outlook. I've always worked for popular taste and it's worn by the maximum number of people.' Director Jean-Luc Godard made *La Chinoise*, about a Maoist cell plotting their individual upheavals in cafés and, of course, in bed.

In the halls of residence at Nanterre a tract written in 1936 by Wilhelm Reich was circulated. 'What is sexual chaos?' asked the German mystic. 'It is to contract a lifelong sexual liaison without having sexual knowledge of one's partner beforehand. It is to mentally paw every picture of a half-naked woman. It is to sleep with a proletarian girl because she is not worth anything more, while one would not ask the same of a decent girl.' Morals were all the more chaotic in a France at once Catholic and libertine, where, as little as 20 years before, brothels had still been officially licensed.

Jean-Claude Killy scored a triple gold at the winter Olympics in Grenoble – the beginnings of a ski-wear empire – and the students at Nanterre were still ignoring the curfew on their dorms as de Gaulle, President for ten tranquil years, gave his New Year address. 'Thanks to efforts at all levels of industry, I feel sure '68 will mark an important step towards a new social order,' he promised. Despite the clipped moustache, the knees held rigidly together under the desk at the Elysée, the old man still had force and animation. 'Let me be quite clear,' he stressed, leaning forward. 'Towards the direct participation of workers!' It was the same room, lined with gold carvings, from which, a decade before, faced with a possible military coup, he had made agitated appeals for support in the Jupiterian voice of Free France.

On 20 March, as the American and Vietnamese envoys were being introduced to each other in a house just outside Paris, windows were smashed at the American Express office. Two days later, protesting against the arrest over this affair of two students, demonstrators surged into the administrative buildings at Nanterre. With two against and three abstentions, 142 of them decided to occupy the building. In the modern conference room that evening were Young Communists, Trotskyists, Maoists, members of the '*groupuscules*', the twilight groups of the student Left, rejected by the Communist Party and the student union. Among them was the same red-haired heckler who had been so impudent to the minister, a 23-year-old sociology student of German origin named Daniel Cohn-Bendit. That night he gave up his small apartment in a tower block in the 15th arrondissement and became 'active'.

Familiar to the media already from the swimming-pool outburst, it was to Cohn-Bendit that the press came for an explanation of the aims of what was called, with the confusing French penchant for tagging political events by date, the Movement of the 22nd of March. A little breathless with nerves, short-haired, serious, his pupils narrowed in an intense gaze that would soon be aggravating all France through full-page photos in *Paris Match*, Cohn-Bendit stood outside the administrative building in his duffle-coat and addressed the reporters.

'The students refuse to accept their role in society: to become the future bosses exploiting the workers,' he told them, hesitating slightly. 'This movement is born in the university, but it doesn't want to be confined there, it wants to form a bridge with the workers or the peasants.' He stared into the TV lights for a second. 'That's more or less the nature of the movement.'

It was an urban guerilla offensive lodged in the unfaced bricks of a newtown university.

Throughout April their sit-in continued at Nanterre. Public support came from, among others, Herbert Marcuse, the 70-year-old German Marxist whose *One-Dimensional Man*, published four years before, announced that the Communist Parties were 'bankrupt' because the revolutionary potential of the worker had been bought off by the consumer society, and predicted that youth, led by an intellectual vanguard of students, would constitute the new revolutionary force.

Not long arrived in France, the consumer society, its cash registers chiming to the orchestrations of Monnet's technocratic élite, its public secure in the comfort and delight of modern living, paid little attention to the students at Nanterre.

The key concept and buzzword among the *groupuscules*, meanwhile, was 'action'. There were 'action committees' and even an irregular newspaper,

Action. To be active was to have gone beyond the creaking, left-wing machinery of the student union, the UNEF, centred at the Sorbonne and stillborn at Nanterre. To be active meant leaving home for good, renouncing the university and with it the family and the state, becoming wide-eyed and argumentative from the electricity of living of each moment a revolutionary critique.

When Rudi Dutschke, leader of student radicals in West Berlin who had occupied their own 'critical university', was wounded in a shooting as he rode his bicycle to college – a week after the assassination in the US of Martin Luther King and a few months after the slaying of Che Guevara – the students felt spurred to action. The previous September 15,000 students had enrolled at French universities, easily filling those such as Nanterre, constructed four years earlier in the crumbling heart of an industrial suburb of Paris. The Faculty of Letters was devoted to history, literature and the relatively new human science of sociology. Faced with this overcrowding – a little sociological bubble signifying that the baby-boomers would soon be coming to boiling-point – the government revealed in April that it was considering measures to curb university entry. At this, the students at Nanterre noisily convened, the same ones who had been defying the curfew and who had broken the news about Rudi, occupied the buildings and daubed slogans on the walls. They called themselves the *Enragés*, a name chosen to stir vague alarms in contented Gaullist France.

The original *Enragés* were the militants of the French Revolution, who ousted Danton to dominate the *Cordeliers* Club in 1793. Led by Jean Varlet, a postal worker, and Jacques Roux, a former priest, the *Enragés* organised the *sans-culottes* (literally 'without trousers'), the Parisian rabble in the more radical of the 48 *sections* of the city. Roux was one of those whose task it had been earlier that year to escort Louis XVI to his death. The King had tried to give him a letter for the Queen. 'I'm not your errand boy,' he snapped.

As the rhythm of revolutionary 'days of action' established itself and Paris was periodically swept by the delirium of protest, so the *sans-culottes* grew more assertive. They imposed a *taxation populaire*, invading shops and forcing merchants to sell at what they considered a fair price. Attempting to block their conservative *Girondin* opponents, the *Jacobins* tried to exploit the popular fury stirred by the *Enragés*, who called for the death penalty for hoarders and speculators whom they blamed for galloping price rises. The

Girondins, many of whom had a few speculations going themselves, saw the *Enragés* as crazed and dangeous extremists. And so, to deal officially with those for whom the *Enragés* threatened mob justice, both parties favoured the idea of a revolutionary tribunal, unwittingly erecting the scaffold of the Terror under whose blade many of them would soon find themselves.

But as they listened to the appeal of Jacques Roux in the Convention, they must have been seized by another sort of terror. 'Why have you not climbed from the third floor to the ninth in the houses of this revolutionary city?' pleaded the former priest. 'You would have been moved by the tears and sighs of a population without food or clothing, brought to this misery by speculation and hoarding, because the laws have been cruel to the poor, made by the rich for the rich. You must not be afraid of the hatred of the rich. You must not be afraid to sacrifice political principle for the salvation of the people, which is the supreme law!'

Like Godard and Coca-Cola

ALONGSIDE COHN-BENDIT in the demonstrations throughout April '68 was Alain Geismar, a civil engineer and science teacher representing the lecturers who were sympathetic to the student cause. Aged 29, he belonged to an older generation of left-wing activists. When the OAS had taken their campaign of terror to metropolitan France in 1962, disfiguring a four-year-old girl with a bomb intended for André Malraux, he was among those who, despite an official ban, thronged the streets around the Bastille in protest. As the crowd grew to 10,000, nervous police charged without warning. Fleeing down the stairs of the Charonne Métro station, demonstrators found the doors locked. They were helpless as police hurled down iron railings and marble tables from the nearby cafés, leaving eight dead, including three women, and establishing, in the minds of Geismar's contemporaries, an indelible reputation for violent repression.

The 1st of May came and went. Prime Minister Georges Pompidou said not to worry and flew off to see the Shah of Iran. Two days later, Friday, the Dean decided to close Nanterre, expelling certain students. Finding the doors locked, they descended on Paris early in the afternoon to rally support at the Sorbonne. It was overcast that day, sharp and cold. While police massed in the streets of the 5th and 6th arrondissements, Sorbonne students left their classes to join the others. As dusk fell, the police received orders to expel the *Enragés*.

This caused the students milling in the old courtyard to start, uncertain if they should run or fight. Cohn-Bendit seized the mike. 'Politically, we must know exactly what we are going to do because the situation is new.' He appeared excited but cool-headed. His earlier hesitation had vanished. 'We have been told to leave the Sorbonne but we are here,' he affirmed over the PA. And then the logic of the moment came to him. '*De fait*, we have occupied the Sorbonne!'

There were a few half-hearted cries of '*Ouaaaais!*' but nobody paid much attention, uncertain of the implications, first of their commitment, and now, for their safety.

The rumour spread rapidly through the city. The Sorbonne was now occupied! The police charged with their truncheons drawn. Driven out into the streets, the students were joined by more young demonstrators. Skirmishes flared on the margins of the crowds. Tempers exploded, tear-gas grenades flew and skulls started to crack. In the Place Edmond-Rostand some cars were overturned to make the first barricades. Suspected student militants were dragged away in Black Marias.

The next morning, tourists enjoying the romance of springtime in Paris stumbled over the broken paving and pondered the upturned vehicles. The Minister of the Interior labelled the demonstrators 'villains'. In the Communist daily *L'Humanité* Georges Marchais, the stern, outspoken keeper of the French proletarian conscience, derided the '*faux* revolutionaries presuming to give lessons to the labour movement'. Speaking for the Party, he noted the German-Jewish origins of Cohn-Bendit.

Five French Nobel Prizewinners including François Mauriac publicly asked the President to appease the students by reopening the Sorbonne. But on Monday the university remained closed, provoking demonstrations which again ended in riots. In the *Quartier Latin* that lies between the Seine and the labyrinth of old colleges around the Sorbonne, street battles raged into the night. To support the 66 mobile police divisions, 29 *Compagnies républicaines de sécurité* (CRS) were called in. There were 400 arrests and almost 1,000 injured. The intoxication of upheaval took hold, and a cycle of revolutionary violence began. The CRS, with their helmets, overalls, shield and *bidules* or truncheons came to symbolise oppressive authority. But their task was as much to keep the sorely provoked and less disciplined police apart from rampaging students.

Copycat demonstrations were held in provincial universities. The scenes in the capital were replayed in Grenoble, Lyon, Bordeaux and at Strasbourg where the *Internationale Situationiste* addressed the consumer society with subverted comic strips and soap powder ads, bringing Dada to dialectics. They criticised the 'society of the *spectacle*' – meaning both spectacle and show or performance and, in this context, distraction. If they persuaded nobody in the supermarkets to try Brand X-treme, the Situationist thought bubbles burst over the heads of left-wing committees with a nihilist bang. 'The student is a product of modern society,' they proclaimed, 'just like Godard or Coca-Cola.' Whereas it seemed to many in France that a student was someone in a brown suede jacket with a Little Red Book, their face covered by a handkerchief, head protected by a motorcycle helmet, hurling a paving stone at a bleeding policeman.

The Minister of Education decided that the Sorbonne should remain closed. This fresh provocation reached the students on Thursday, just in time to set in train a second 'Red Friday'.

The students gathered in their thick coats and at dusk the first barricades went up. Street signs and fences were heaped on the upturned cars and draped with red flags to incite the coming police charges. The agitated voices of on-the-spot reporters from Radio Luxembourg added to the impression that the 30,000 university and high school students had passed from riot to insurrection. Yet such was the reverence surrounding de Gaulle that it was not until dawn, as the street battles died down, that the President was woken to hear that Paris had been 'close to civil war'. The Army Minister had to dissuade the General from calling in troops, warning of the risk of young conscripts making common cause with the students.

Over 300 cars had been burnt that night by the students, who were coming to be seen as the spoilt kids of the consumer society, not content with two decades of peace, growth and stability; eager instead to smell the acrid stench of tear gas.

Prime Minister Pompidou opted to defuse the situation by giving in to the immediate demand of the demonstrators to reopen the Sorbonne. Revolutionary violence gave way to revolutionary exhilaration. The students surged over the Sorbonne, flying the red flag from the dome. Now it was the turn of the two major unions; the Communist-controlled *Confédération générale de travail* and the moderate *Confédération française democratique du travail* which, influenced by youthquake themes of environmental concern and *autogestion* or self-management, began to take a radical direction. So as not to be pre-empted by their own members, they announced a general strike the next day.

The spring buds fell on empty streets while the students set about covering the walls of the Sorbonne with slogans in imitation of Mao's Red Guards. 'Professors, You Are As Old As Your Culture.' 'Abolish Alienation.' Taking post-Marxist analysis into the streets, they proclaimed that: 'Underneath The Pavement Lies The Beach!' By decree of the Sorbonne Occupation Committee on 16 May at 19.00hrs, these slogans were to be 'daubed over paintings and posters in the Métro; announced in cinemas during the film; when emptying your glass in the bistro; before making love; after making love; in the lift'.

Another orderly march was staged by workers and students, apparently united, calling for the resignation of de Gaulle. With their sombre, dignified clothes and heavy steps, the union chiefs walked uneasily behind Cohn-Bendit, who described them at a separate rally that evening as 'Stalinist leftovers' – their general strike an attempt to overtake the Movement after a week of silence. Cohn-Bendit, now known and feared as Dany the Red, had grown alluring with his confidence. 'I think we're facing the eternal problem in France,' he opined. 'The Communist Party will always absorb any movement that overtakes it on the left. That's right, I said *on its left*!'

In response, the CGT shut the doors on them as students massed outside the Renault factory at Billancourt. Old shop stewards smoking cigarettes cheered half-derisively as they passed. What did these spoilt rich kids know of the struggle?

Organised by the students, the Sorbonne became a prototype for the new world, a Utopia in the centre of Paris where only forbidding was forbidden. There was a crèche, canteen, hospital, dormitory and even a security force, leather-clad delinquents who later had to be evicted. Lectures were replaced by debates. A group of *Enragés* stormed the nearby Odéon. They marched onto the stage of the theatre famed for productions of Brecht and Genet, and declared it occupied. The Odéon became a public forum, an echo of the Revolutionary clubs of St-Honoré, but with no membership, no manifesto and, like the ideal society, no rules. Anarchists and drunks, cab-drivers and Castro-ists, the discourse was open to all. Tramps came to lodge in the corridors. At the film festival in Cannes, the party was suspended. Directors

Godard, Loluche, Malle and Truffaut called an Estates-General of the Seventh Art. 'Why film?' they asked. With no trains and no petrol, the French had nothing left to do but ask what they were doing. In the countryside, meanwhile, they began hoarding food.

If many professionals were touched by their euphoria, workers were wary of the students, receiving with caution their delegations and their delirious ideas: to leave prosperity's ghetto, to escape the ennui of the production line, to be free of the whims of the technocrats, to be self-motivated and self-determined. The CGT warned against mad Leftists and, like a dog with an old bone, put up specific wage demands.

Somebody even raised a black flag of Anarchy over the cathedral of Notre-Dame! It was becoming too much. Cohn-Bendit had imprudently left for Germany. He would not be allowed back. Hurt by the calls for his resignation, the General addressed his people. Clearly moved by events, he called for a vote of confidence to 'open, where necessary, structures closed to the new blood of France'.

The following day was to be the third and most turbulent of the Red Fridays. Twenty thousand people gathered to protest the banning of Cohn-Bendit. 'We're all German Jews!' they chanted. And a more disturbing whisper: 'To the Hôtel de Ville!' Several police stations were set on fire. Some rioters tried to force open the doors of the Bourse, others attempted to take hostage the Minister of Justice. Not just students but workers, professional people, hoodlums and young girls; whether they had come to tear down society or just to meet the opposite sex, they were soon drawn into the orgy of riot. Ominously, the police began to concentrate their efforts against the students.

At the Ministry of Employment, meanwhile, a young undersecretary named Jacques Chirac was keeping lines open between the bosses and the unions. Frustrated at the magniloquent but uncertain gestures of the ageing President, Pompidou quietly convened union leaders to discussions.

While this went on at the Ministry, a vast rally took place at the Stade Charlety. Here, the student revolt passed into its Baroque phase. Speakers paraded at a carnival of the Left: CFDT unionists behind their works banners (Sud-Aviation, Renault, Citroën, Radio-Tele-Française); socialists of the SFIO and PSU; radical Mendès-ists; members of the Jean Moulin club; militants of the *Mouvement du 22 Mars*; Maoists marching in formation under portraits of the Chairman; anarchists brandishing the skull and crossbones; Trotskyists waving red-and-black flags; Revolutionary Young Communists; Castro-ists; Guevarists; hippies carrying flowers; Hell's Angels carrying chains and volunteering for policework; trendy Catholic priests; Red Cross activists. The event had the flavour of a French Woodstock, with words serving instead of music in philosophical France to rouse the crowd of 60,000. 'Today the revolution is possible,' declared one speaker to a wild ovation. 'We have to organise very rapidly!' The carnival passed to the hallucinatory. Cohn-Bendit reappeared, or what appeared to be Cohn-Bendit, his hair dyed black, declaring, *'En mai, fais ce qu'il te plait!'*

Elsewhere, too, dreams merged with the real. 'There is no longer a French state,' declared François Mitterrand at a press conference. The leader of the French Left in the Assembly, Mitterrand had forced de Gaulle to fight a second ballot in the presidential elections of '65, a chink in the General's armour. His aplomb a mite premature, he keenly presented a three-point plan to 'get things going and organise the succession'.

As the unions prepared to accept the government's offer of a 35 per cent rise in the SMIG, the minimum wage, plus a 10 per cent rise in salaries, the General himself suddenly vanished. He left with his wife in a helicopter, without a word. Was he, like Louis XVI attempting to flee under the protection of his Swiss guards, about to end up, by his own vicissitudes, a hostage to the revolutionary students? Had he retreated like that unfortunate monarch, rejected by his people, suffering the agonies of a wounded lover?

His capricious mistress, *la France profonde*, chose this moment, apparently, to respond. A Gaullist deputy organised a massive counter-demonstration of support for de Gaulle. A million strong, with an ageing André Malraux propped at their centre, they marched on the Arc de Triomphe. It seemed as if the silent majority had found its voice.

In fact, de Gaulle had flown to Germany to secure the allegiance of General Massu in case a counter-revolt came from the Right as it had threatened ten years before. He returned that day in a fighting mood to declare over the radio, in tones recalling his wartime broadcasts from *la France libre*, that he had reversed his decision to hold a referendum, saying that it would only be used 'to deprive the French people of their voice, as they are being prevented from living their lives, prevented from studying, from teaching and from working'. Proposing a ministerial reshuffle, he added that if the violent confrontations persisted, he would 'take measures other than the consultation of the country'.

That night, the 30th, petrol was delivered to garages in the Paris region for the first time in two weeks. Services slowly resumed their timetables. With jubilation and relief, or with discouragement and despair, the French began their Whitsun holiday weekend.

The end of the spectacle

WHATEVER THEIR FEELINGS at the failure of the student revolt, French people were unaware how deeply that month of May had marked each of their lives. The press reported a 'return to normal' after the union deal and the massive Gaullist demonstration. While many factories were still closed and all that had been eased was the discomfort of the Parisians, the government had won the propaganda war. From their critiques of the 'society of the spectacle', the students should have known that this was the immediate theatre of battle, not the cycle of protest and arrest on the street or even the chickens they brought from the countryside to distribute at the occupied factories – to demonstrate, as Cohn-Bendit told a meeting at the Sorbonne that Whitsun weekend, 'that our fundamental project is to explode the old separations between the towns and the countryside'.

As 10,000 students gathered outside, not knowing what they should do next, he must have sensed that the revolt had failed. He wanted to extend the system of Action Committees to factories so that the Movement of the 22nd of March wouldn't be 'ossified like all revolutionary movements in France'. He wanted to create a 'democratic movement based on workers' councils'. In the meantime, he proposed 'to continue the discussion, even in small groups, to break with the passivity of the spectacle on the platform'.

The government now began to mop up. *Gardes mobiles* and the CRS reoccupied the Renault factories at Flins a week later and then the Peugeot factory at Sochaux. With moderate opinion mobilised against the students, there was little outcry when, at Flins, a Maoist film student drowned after being butted with a rifle, and two workers were killed at Sochaux. The following day, 11 June, the students organised their last protests, ruthlessly broken up by police, who made 1,500 arrests. Immediately afterwards, the government outlawed most of the radical groups and banned all demonstrations.

It was the French revolutionary tradition that gave the students their hope (that seemed to them so close but now seems only naïve) of transforming society. Equally, it was the revolutionary tradition that allowed France to absorb the convulsions of May '68. Having a context in French history, the protestations of the generation of '68 could be absorbed. It was to be far longer before their grievances at a stolid, repressed, agonisingly slow French society would be settled.

What happened to those small groups that Cohn-Bendit wanted the students to go outside and form, breaking with passivity and turning away from the spectacle on the platform?

With more money and a shorter week, at least the workers were temporarily nullified. But where do urban guerillas go to retire when the circumstances deprive them of a martyr's hail of bullets? Nowadays we assume that they were wasting their time. We have the privilege of cynicism; they had the gift of naïvety.

If the students knew that the working class had been bought off, one wonders why they expected workers to side with them? They should have learned from Mao and gone for a ruthless all-out purge to establish themselves as the new ruling teenage aristocracy. Instead, disconsolate at their failure to snatch from the moment and from their reading of Marx a swinging new Jerusalem, the demand-fed baby-boomers stared gloomily at their Che Guevara posters, losing focus, growing self-critical, introspective and paranoid.

In the concerted action of the Government and the Army, they saw a conspiracy of repression. And they were not wrong, except that it was not a conspiracy so much as a consensus. They had been wrong to think that the French worker, or anybody else for that matter, would want to be in complete control, in that heady state of day-to-day free democratic dialectic with their own lives.

Having been 'active' was a badge of courage. But this adrenalin-heightened state of constant self-criticism (which peasant am I oppressing by buying this soap? In being charmed by this woman, am I guilty of sexism?) was difficult to sustain. The pupils grew small and fixed, the eyes wide, the complexion pale as political sensitivity forced the plight of others upon you: a rush of suffering engulfed you, a deep and terrifying moan of the tortured and the hungry and the worn-out wailing from the burns of Napalm or sealed alive in South African mines.

But if one could not remake the world, then better at least not to despoil it. Do not add to the unrecyclable mound of greed's discarded plastic shopping bags. Think global, act local.

A few regrouped in violent cells, dedicated to armed revolution. They called themselves *Action Directe* and put bombs under the cars of bankers. They thought that by pulling out some linchpins the whole structure would collapse. They failed to understand the complexity of the structure, of which, by their actions, they themselves became a part. Some of them went on trial in this anniversary year, accused of assassinating a judge. Demanding political status, they went on hunger strike. 'France is a free country,' shrugged the minister responsible. 'Everyone has the right to choose their own slimming programme.'

A life study class

I LAY ON the bed of the hotel in the rue des Saints-Pères and stared at the narrow gorge of zinc roofing visible from the small window. I had left school the year before and, nursing what I thought was an irreparable heart, had come to Paris, haven of the sensitive and the lovesick, with the aim of losing myself in a room somewhere. There were no vacancies in *Libération* that morning. It was a hot spring day and I wondered what to do. Towards midday, the chambermaid entered.

The night before, we had spoken to each other as she waited on the reception desk. 'You don't look English at all,' she said, 'you look more Italian.' She was petite in that Parisian way, with straight black hair, brown eyes and in her gaze was a frank self-assurance absent from the regard of English girls I knew. She was confident of an illusory charm. We had talked the night before about our reasons for being in Paris. She was studying for her *baccalauréat* in the evenings. I told her I had taken a year off my studies, though the year was nearly over and I had no intention of going back. I was grateful for the conversation, as I knew no one in Paris and in my deepening introspection curt exchanges with shopkeepers and the landladies who placed ads in the newspapers echoed loudly.

I walked along the Boulevard St-Germain looking at the antiquarian books and imagined myself becoming a writer. I had confused the reality I reconstructed from written words with the act of writing. Any modern French critic could have explained my dilemma. I was half lost in literature, that daydream of experience. But my slumber had been disturbed and I grew restless after meeting the chambermaid. I read pages of meaningless words and wondered if she would have dinner with me, imagining how the exchange would go. *'Oui, avec plaisir!'*

I could find no way of asking her. I grinned as casually as I could. Seeing the newspaper on the bed, she spoke first. 'Have you had any luck?'

I told her how my search was going. She sympathised. It wasn't easy to find a room in Paris. She pulled the pillowcase away and replaced it. I told her not to bother with the sheets. She folded the old ones down neatly.

'There might be a room at the house where I live. I'll ask if you like?'

It was a large old three-storey house on the edge of the Parc Montsouris that belonged to the bourgeois family of Patrice, who lived in fine anti-bourgeois disarray on the top floor. He called a meeting of the house committee in the large kitchen to discuss my possible tenancy. The meeting was a simple affair. They asked why I was in Paris and nodded at my imprecise shrug. They were surprised to learn that I was 17. They were all in their twenties. They were all students or ex-students. I told them I thought there was no point in going to university just for the sake of it and, since there wasn't anything specific that I wanted to learn, I had no intention of going. They asked me what my politics were and I said I didn't know. Nobody asked if I smoked or ate red meat. They looked at one another and Patrice said I could have the room if I wanted.

Apart from Patrice, there were three other residents of the house. There was the quiet Véronique, who had a boyfriend from Hamburg with long, thin blond hair and who, to her ill-concealed anguish, came and went in an old Beetle, carrying an improbable black briefcase. She was from Strasbourg, and unusually tall and fair for a French girl. There was Alain, who sat reading at the kitchen table behind the oval-shaped glasses that in France had somehow acquired intellectual sex appeal. And there was Ann, who asked me after the meeting, as she opened the door to the room on the second floor, 'Are you really 17?' I tried not to be coy about it. I was staring at her knees, two small miracles.

Ann was 23. She was studying for her *bac* now because she had given up before to work for the international Red Cross. It was just after the famine in

Biafra. She had been very idealistic in those days, she told me. She was the first person I ever heard use the phrase, 'the politics of hunger'. She asked me if I had heard of Bernard Kouchner, a doctor who wrote in *Action*, the journal of '68. He had made her realise that the problems of disease and famine in the Third World were not practical but political. It was '*pour lutter contre cette politique*' that she intended to study law. I realised she was a serious girl. She wore a black and grey Persian shawl which was political enough to me in that it reflected the silver in her dark hair.

As I had suspected, the act of studying was dangerously inconclusive. Patrice and Alain had been students in '68. Alain had been at Nanterre, Patrice at the Sorbonne. They told me the police were worse than the CRS, but the Trotskyists were worst of all! You couldn't hold a meeting without being harangued interminably by them. Six years later, it seemed that the events of '68 had fixed all their political libidos like the first glimpse of a woman unclothed.

Patrice wore an oblong Lip watch, which he had bought the year before at the height of the strike that, he said, was the most important thing that had happened in France since '68. On learning that the new Swiss owners planned heavy redundancies, 1,200 workers at the Lip watch firm in Besançon had occupied the factory unprompted by unions. Action committees proposed selling the watches they produced and soon, wearing a Lip watch meant on the Left that you knew what time it was. At the Socialist Party conference, Jean-Pierre Chevènement, the present Minister of Defence, ordered 2,000 of the 'liberated' watches. The way Patrice told it, by seizing the means of production – rather than just strangling it – the Lip workers had seized the national destiny. 'It's Possible! We Make, We Sell,' read a banner outside the factory gates. To which someone later added, 'And Get Paid!' They ignored union delegates who were 'too busy arguing among themselves' and, capitalising on the euphoria they stirred, set about marketing their watches. A Lip car even followed the Tour de France. A month later, an industrial tribunal ruled that the firm should be restored to its owners, and – a frequent end to events in modern France – everybody went off on holiday.

Ann had gone with Patrice and Alain that summer to Larzac. 'It was important to make a statement about the French landscape,' she said. On the Larzac plateau of southern Aveyron, not far from the town of Béziers, the government wanted to buy up land to extend a military firing range. The sheep farmers there were not to be easily herded off ancestral lands, however. Their cause was taken up by Occitan regionalists, who daubed slogans over the Midi in the old Franco-Iberian language, and by hippies who came to lie down in front of the contractors' bulldozers. They would be going again this summer, they expected, but since Patrice wasn't going there would be a spare place and maybe I wanted to come?

'I no longer believe in revolution,' Patrice explained airily. This lay at the end of a long trail of his reasons for not going to Larzac. If I believed in anything myself at the time, it was that anything that required the sustenance of faith was liable to crisis.

This made Alain laugh. A Trotskyist in '68, Alain now thought that there was no political answer to the spiritual crisis of modern society. The remedy for alienation was not to be found in the short-lived comradeship of revolution. He had gone only half-heartedly to Larzac, having lived on a *communauté* in 1970, a *margi-bouzer* looking for *autarky*, the sun-bright fusion of autonomy and anarchy. 'We dropped out of the city. There was no property. We shared everything, from sexual partners to kitchen utensils. It deteriorated into a fight.'

In France, he said, there was nothing like the tradition of pioneer communities that sustained communes in America. They were also resented for reasons more complex than the fact that they didn't attend mass on Sundays. They were throwing away the supposed social advantages that the locals struggled to give to their children – a *bac*, a salaried job in the town that did not mean getting up before dawn and returning after dark in muddy boots.

Alain was a Giscardian now, which I had never heard of before, though it served what I suspected was his dialectical aim of rousing everyone to anger.

He told a sceptical Ann that Giscard intended to make reforms favourable to women and was even going to create a ministry for women. She scoffed at this, calling Giscard a *faux aristo* and saying she knew the type only too well. She came from Dijon, a once prosperous commercial town where the socially mobile often acquired aristocratic pretensions along with new suffixes such as d'Estaing, which she accused the presidential candidate of having done. She said that a ministry for women would only be a *prosthèse* of male imperialism. She added pessimistically that women in France would never be emancipated because they didn't want to be. I chuckled at this, which annoyed her, since she was not trying to be witty. Later she told me she felt the dead, unseen hand of French society like an old man's on her thighs.

'What has really changed in France since '68?' asked Patrice, pouring more wine from the bottle as we sat around the table smoking *Disque Bleu*. I waited for the answer.

'You have no idea how bad it was,' he said, 'how *sclérotique* French society was. Much more so than English society. There was a wall of conformism. In the good French bourgeois milieu you couldn't even belong to the Beatles' fan club. That would have been a waste of money. There was no fun, only duty.'

Once the symbol of all that was immutable in France, de Gaulle had resigned in '69, after a referendum rejected his plans for regionalisation and the reform of the senate. He died a year later. There was no Leftist candidate for the succession, and Pompidou became President with a 30 per cent abstention rate.

The blonde girl broke her gloomy silence to chide Patrice. 'You know that nothing has changed,' she snapped. She said that in Germany they had despaired of 'what Rudi called the long march through the institutions'.

Patrice said he took heart from the fact that Mitterrand was now head of the Socialist Party which had made a pact with the Communists two years before. 'Revolution is futile,' he said airily, 'but at least there has been some evolution.'

'And reform?' asked Alain. 'Look at Chile.' The mention of Allende's popularly elected socialist government, which that winter had been brutally reversed by General Pinochet, brought the conversation to a predictable turn. 'You know what Marchais said. "It's always the Right that refuses the alternation of power" '.

'*Bof!* Not Marchais,' groaned Patrice.

Ann got up to pour herself more coffee. 'Is it like this in England?' she asked me.

'Yes,' I said, since I supposed it was. I was conscious of a lack of political sophistication, worse than not knowing which wine to order.

'*Tu veux venir avec moi?*'

'Where are we going?' I asked as we got into her little red Renault. '*Tu verras.*'

We drove around the newly opened Boulevard Périphérique, swooping around Paris watching the lights flicker on the advertising hoardings.

Soon, we were slowed to a halt in the traffic. She pushed at the horn, giving a long wail.

The autogestion of truth

SERGE JULY WAS studying philosophy when the *Mouvement du 22 mars* reared its little red Maoist head. The dark-haired Parisian son of a former Radical Party candidate, July was a vice-president of the student union, in charge of information. In 1970, as the government set about prosecuting vendors of the Young Communist journal *La Cause du Peuple*, information seemed all the more dangerous. Serge July took charge of a project for a 'revolutionary *agence de presse*', a network of news sheets and correspondents aligned to the Maoist movement.

To July, the need for a 'revolutionary' news service was in no doubt. The aptly described Gaullist media, when not overtly partisan (jarringly so compared with the 'objectivity' of the British press) filtered information in the service of the government, whether through patronage or by the nature of the people who worked for it. And flawed and biased Nature – that mystical touchstone of the British intellectual – had been revealed by French Structuralists to be merely the accumulation of prejudices.

French radio and TV stations were carefully controlled, with senior appointments in the hands of the state. De Gaulle didn't like TV, calling the evening news a 'moment of enchanting pessimism', but he grasped its power. Ministers were never seen being questioned and no opposition member was given airtime until the presidential race of '65, when French *telespectateurs* saw François Mitterrand being interviewed.

There were no periodicals like *Rolling Stone* in the US and *International Times* in Britain to supply information to the growing counter-culture – which in France remained obstinately political in character, and fanatically lefter-than-thou. Humorous journals like the old *Hari-Kiri* and new comic-books like *Geranonymo* provided light relief. Barricade bulletins like *Action* came and went, their turbulent schedule tied to the momentum of events. But in 1970, with the help of a young journalist from *L'Express* named Jean-François Bizot, the founders of *Action* launched *Actuel*, based on the provocative British *Oz*, that for the next five years would be an only semi-regular radical digest. With its coloured inks and irreverent, penetrating texts, it belonged to a cartoon era of colourful, hallucinogenic revolt. Harassed by police and menaced by changing times, the first incarnation of *Actuel* eventually folded with that era.

July meanwhile approached the widow of a Resistance hero whose daily paper *Libération* had appeared until 1964. She gave permission for the title to be used and Jean-Paul Sartre agreed to be a director of this new journal, whose precept was that 'information comes from the people and goes back to the people'. The first issue appeared in February '73. With four pages instead of the promised 12 the new *Libération* announced itself as a newspaper like others but with the news from 'workers, peasants, shopkeepers and under-managers'. It would feature comics, cartoons and *photoromans*. There would be debates on racism, sexuality, 'the oppression of women by men'. In the first issue was practical advice on how to read date codes on frozen products and a scoop about speculators planning to redevelop Bon Marché in Paris – the world's first department store – with a loss of 300 jobs.

True to the plan to develop alternative lines of information, this scoop came from the workers at the store themselves. To ensure editorial independence, there was to be no advertising. *'Safety breaches by car manufacturers are not reported because they are the biggest advertisers. It's time to assemble, 28 years after the original Liberation, against the systematic manipulation of our lives.'* The paper asked readers to form 'committees of liberation' throughout France, weaving a 'spider's web' of 'free information'. As subscribers, they would be the owners of the new paper, bringing information to it. The journalists would work collectively with them.

'The source of information is people but it's hidden in the people.' The paper was to contain the direct accounts of ordinary people, a style of verbatim reportage close to the *écrit-parlé* cherished by Sartre. In the first issue Michel Foucault began a column recounting workers' oral histories. But in an interview with José from Renault-Billancourt, Foucault does most of the talking. Going further, there were free small-ads to encourage the exchange of information, and the typesetter too was given a commentary, while the journalists, who all received the same wage as the typesetter, took turns on composing.

The newspaper was to be a working model of the new society. Alongside articles about toothpastes that ruin the teeth and sausages that lose weight after packing, there was an interview with a Catholic priest in favour of legalising abortion.

The newspaper supported such causes as Larzac and the Lip strike. But this was to be the last optimistic battle of the French worker, for the oil crisis and competition from the East meant that coming strikes in the coal and steel industries of the north would be long-fought and bitter. It was reassuring to read of these events in a newspaper that shared their point of view but the idealism of the project was not sufficient. By the end of the first year, *Libération* was selling only 12,000 copies a day.

And yet, in the curious way that journals unite diverse opinions, distilling a social bloc from the amorphous crowds, the paper survived and came to represent its generation, the '68-ers. It chronicled their hopes and crises: the revolution in Portugal in '74, the war in Angola, gay lib, regional autonomy, drug abuse, punk, and later terrorism and the *radio libre*. The readership grew as quirky, marginal causes such as pollution attacked the beloved French countryside, 'natural' food became a supermarket label, and environmental concern became a political cosmetic.

Abandoning in the second year the job rotation schemes and the reader editorial committees, though maintaining equal salaries which, says editor July, cemented the spirit of the paper, *Libération* was financially stable by the end of '75. Its Saturday supplement of free small-ads was the clearing-house bazaar of the French counter-culture. Sales continued to grow, but by the end of the decade, the paper had come to an impasse. Energetic and eclectic, to expand it needed the authority that a sparky editorial content often lacked. While they enjoyed the lateral, affective work structures, the staff were frustrated by the informal chain of responsibility. Finally, things came to a head and the paper closed for several weeks. At a meeting of the 140 worker-owners in 1981, July proposed a new hierarchical management structure, with himself at the top.

It was put to the vote and carried. In many ways, it was the presidential-isation of the paper. Would-be democrats, the French still cleave to a sound aristocracy. Reappearing soon after, partly refinanced by the owner of Club Med, the new *Libération* has steadily gained respect and power, at the same time as its formerly radical public has taken up reformist posts. The Sixties were finally over. But who ate whom? All it is possible to say is that the centre of French society has moved closer to the '68-ers, who have moved into the centre of French society.

Revolt into nostalgia

THERE ARE FEW paving stones still to be seen in Paris. They have all been asphalted over. But in an auction room twenty years after May '68, to the amusement of the bidders and the spectators, a paving stone has turned up. It has a ticket attached to it marked Lot 49 – though perhaps it should read 'integration', or whatever is the opposite of alienation.

In a smooth voice, the grey-haired woman in charge of the sale reads the title of the next work. *'Bourgeois – vous n'avez rien compris.'* She smiles almost maternally at the chortles of ironic laughter. She has gathered 200 posters, tracts and documents for the sale, the angry warnings of a once imminent revolution now preserved behind plexiglass, their passing into artefact tolled by the auctioneer's hammer. The auction is taking place at the Paris salerooms of Drouot, under the avid scrutiny of TV cameras and journalists. Twenty years later, May '68 has itself become part of the spectacle.

Beside me is one of the artists. He pulls at his chin as a poster of a CRS brandishing a truncheon over a shield marked 'SS' goes for 3,800frs – or two-thirds the current minimum monthly wage.

Somebody asks him if he feels nostalgic.

'A bit. But in my head it's still clear.'

Looking around the room, he snorts. 'It's very strange . . . I don't see many ties. I suppose that's fashion.'

His hands are fat and rough and his hair greasy, though he wears delicate oval glasses. He is 47 years old and twenty years ago today, as the song goes, he was on strike from his job as a lab technician.

I ask if he is still on the far Left.

'*Bien sûr.*'

'Any party?'

'No.' He taps his skull. 'It's in the head.'

'Where is the beach now?'

'It's still there.'

He explains that he will vote for the Communist candidate Pierre Juquin in the first round of the presidential election, and for Mitterrand in the second.

'*Normal.*'

'Against Le Pen?'

'*Contre Le Pen.*'

A member in 1968 of the Action Committee of Ris Orangis, in the suburbs of Paris, he used to go and collect the posters from the *Ecole des Beaux-Arts* and also design and print his own in a local workshop.

He grins as one of his posters goes for 4,000frs. It shows sheep responding to the newspaper headline 'Back to Normal'. 'I know him, he's a bourgeois,' he says of the buyer, as if he were an old adversary. 'It amuses me a lot to profit from the bourgeoisie. With the money I can go and make Molotov cocktails!'

I think it more likely that he will buy his wife a microwave.

In front of a new generation of students at the Sorbonne, there is another speaker. Of Algerian descent, tall and thin and tonight a little nervous, he begins a short, impassioned speech, referring to the women's rights movement, and the anti-racist movement of which he is one of the founders. 'These people have no voice. To give them one requires more than a meeting in a hall.'

Turning to Cohn-Bendit, he says that it's rather feeble of him to hedge his bets, to call for a boycott of the political system. 'You have a vote, the message has to pass and you should use your vote to pass it clearly. Abstention never served anybody.'

Cohn-Bendit screws up his face as though trying to recall the proof of this.

This only drives the young speaker on. 'You have to vote,' he implores, 'because Le Pen is rising!'

There is a roar of approval for the speaker, whose name is David Assouline, one of the founders of an organisation called SOS Racisme whose anti-racist concerts and rallies have massed what in Britain would be thought of as simply hundreds of thousands of young people, but in France is considered a new political powerbase.

Raising his palms to forestall the audience, Cohn-Bendit swings forward again on his chair and, chin almost touching the table in supplication, he pleads his defence.

'It's not good enough to give rights to unicyclists, battling here and there like the Greens in Germany. The problem is greater. The unemployed are supported by the workers of the Third World. We've known too many false hopes, false movements. I'm too much of a hard-nose from experience!' To cheers now, he calls for a social movement and not a political deal. 'Demonstrate for issues, like the right to vote for immigrants, not candidates. As soon as a movement forms an organisational structure, it becomes the hostage of that structure!'

In the hall there is a murmuring swell of agreement. My companion Christophe nods. He says to me, 'In politics, the winner is usually the person who can sit it out the longest. That's what used to happen in the JCR. Whoever was left arguing after all the others had gone home, carried the motion.'

There is one person left to speak, a young woman with long black braids who, like David Assouline, is a founder of SOS Racisme. Still at college, Kaisa Tirous is working as campaign director for Juquin.

Trembling with anger, she says that it's easy for Cohn-Bendit to say don't vote when there are racist crimes each week in France and a fascist party at 10 per cent in the polls. She is the daughter of a Renault worker who went on strike in '68 and was told by police that if he wanted to stay in France, he had better get back to the factory.

'Any candidate who used to break windows' – she nods at Juquin who glances away modestly – 'is worth keeping an eye on. I would vote for him because he speaks about the problems of women, of immigrants. But as the daughter of an immigrant, I have no right to vote!'

There is a silence as she speaks. Frail, almost distraught, she touches the audience with her fiercely uttered reasoning, neither tactical nor theoretical but impassioned. Listening to her words, Cohn-Bendit lowers his face and covers it with his hands, looking down at his clean desert boots. As Kaisa finishes and gives the final word to Juquin, he begins to fold and unfold a yellow Métro ticket, without looking up.

The following day on TV, Pierre Juquin's old comrade puts the PC's case. He has a bar-side manner and the round vowels of a southern, working-class accent that has not been polished for the media. Like Juquin, André La Joinie believes that unemployment is not a 'given'. But in his view there's no need to choose what to do with the forces of production. He calls for a new brand of Socialism, one that takes charge of the forces of production, which doesn't seem very new at all.

Asked if presidential candidates should consider new speed limits, he first reflects on the contradiction between advertising that emphasises the speed of autos and crash statistics that are not publicised. 'Why not limit the speed of automobiles the world over!' he proposes. He says he is in favour of giving the right to vote to immigrants because they pay local taxes. It is a position that has cost the Communist Party votes to Le Pen, who places the jobs of French workers before the democratic rights of others.

Though I have various cryptocommunist friends, I have never seen a Communist on TV before. It is not a little surprising that this movement born in France, nurtured by Jewish intellectuals in Palestine, brought to fruition in Russia and China, in the embrace of which still live a third of the world's population, should have in Britain no representative innocuous enough to be seen on TV. With his gruff, red-wine sincerity, La Joinie is like a character from a soap opera that nobody watches any more, who will turn up next advertising country-style loaves.

There is in Britain an intolerance of extremes that doesn't quite contradict the tolerance for which the British are renowned. Introverted northern people who warily place their deck-chairs in the sun, the British view climatic, emotional or political extremes with caution. They have developed potent antibodies that isolate and repel anything that threatens to disrupt rather than find a place in the status quo. The constitution and the judicial system are based on this famous and incontrovertible status quo, the legitimacy of which derives from the *status quo ante*.

And yet, their governments forever the hostages of extremes, their society caught between revolution and reaction, it is this social stability that the French yearn for, the clear-sailing of modern social democracy.

The Communist candidates together will poll less than 10 per cent of the vote in the presidential elections, the *Front National* leader 14 per cent. It is the vote of the fed up, the disaffected and the frightened.

That same day at a reunion meeting at the Faculty of Letters at Nanterre, Alan Geismar says, 'I reckon it's better to be reformist every day and revolutionary when it's worth it.'

To be reformist 20 years ago was to display a pathetic lack of courage; now it seems to be a token of common sense. Bernard Kouchner, a founder of the charity Médicines du Monde and now Health Minister, says, 'Revolutions have to be studied case by case. I don't have any use for global solutions.'

What happened to the desires of '68 for a society without war, without class, without police, without bosses? It passed into history, into hefty tomes of detailed recollection and onto anniversary TV panel discussions. Some of its principle articulators are now in positions of influence.

In Britain, we look back on that period now with only scorn, so complete has been the cultural reassertion of the new Right. The nihilistic cult-priests of the succeeding Punk generation interred the values of the '68-ers. Replacing them with nothing other than alienation and self-laceration, they prepared the way for a born-again Tory resurrection. There were never any Punks in France, however, and if some of the values of '68 have been relinquished here, the memories are still warmly held.

On late-evening TV at the end of the week, Daniel Cohn-Bendit recalls a moment of 'ecstasy' – utopian and hedonistic. And he smiles. 'At least it got people talking,' he says. 'About immigration, about psychiatry.' But there are still oppressive silences. 'The debate about Greenpeace is very difficult in France,' he remarks and, as if to prove him right, there is a murmur of disquiet from the studio audience.

A gnomic, red-haired former firebrand in brown leather trousers, I wonder what kind of music the former student radical listens to these days: classical, new age, rap?

The debate goes on. A young student who demonstrated against Chirac's education reforms two years ago says she was shocked that the police responded with such violence to their peaceful protests. The older Leftists gathered for the discussion laugh like men in a bar. Someone else says the Left has changed in France, but the Right not at all.

They are wrong. It has been seduced by the Left. Chirac invites visiting pop star Madonna to dinner and, concerned for the quality of life, sends into the streets of Paris an army of fluorescent green roadsweepers. Because of May '68, the calendar that stopped in France before the war has been moved forward.

The final statement belonged to the studio cleaner. As the programme credits rolled and the discussion continued into the night, he switched on his Hoover and went to work.

One night in Paris

THE ENTRANCE WAS under a nondescript modern apartment block between the supermarkets and restaurants of the 13th arrondissement, the Chinese quarter of Paris. We pressed the entry code and went through the glass doors. In a long straight corridor was a man in a black bow-tie. He asked if we were members. Our host, who had brought us here with an air of excited subterfuge, said yes and we paid the entrance fee. We came in through a door at the end of the passage.

The interior was unsurprising. With smoked glass and piped lighting, it could have been any French discotheque of the Seventies. But the music was not at the usual ear-splitting volume. At the bar we were introduced to the owner. He touched one of the girls' legs and asked, 'Are those tights or stockings?' The girl flinched. She didn't know that this was only the beginning. The owner was short with hooded eyes from years of living through the night. He wore a shirt without a tie or jacket. He looked fifty but was probably younger.

We had come for dinner, I thought; the entrance fee had seemed excessive even for Paris. There were four of us, two men and two girls. 'This seems so normal,' said one of the girls. I didn't know what she meant.

The dining room was decorated with palm trees sprayed gold and lit from beneath. The tables were lacquered black. On one side of the room was a large buffet and on each table some bottles of wine. The lighting was very low. There were other people already eating. We sat at a table and after a while a man came and sat down beside one of the girls.

The atmosphere in the club, with people joining strangers at the tables, seemed to have been imported from a Club Med, those exotic holidays without cash or inhibitions. Touching the girl's knee, the stranger smiled at her and asked how she felt, as though it was a perfectly ordinary gesture. Not knowing how to respond, she smiled emptily and continued eating.

The coffee came, and our host drank it very quickly saying, 'Shall we have a look around?'

Leaving the restaurant, we came to a passage where, instead of a cloakroom, there was a small lingerie shop. In the window were pairs of red crotchless lace panties.

After this we came to a large room full of mirrors. On the black velvet low-backed sofas, people sat languidly, embracing. If one couple began a kiss, others gathered around to stare openly. I realised that I was in the ante-chamber to an orgy. With a long and secretive tradition in Paris, the *maisons closes*, orgy houses, have gone underground since the war, but evidently have not ceased operating.

In the next room, a woman was performing the vague motions of a striptease. She was about 40 years old; already naked, she continued to writhe, oblivious to the stares of those who passed. As she came to the end of her improvised dance, a group of men who had been watching approached her. She disappeared behind them. All we could see now were the hairy legs of the men under their white shirts.

In the club there were an equal number of men and women, the result of a strict admission ratio. They were aged between 20 and 50. It was an elegant nightclub crowd of the kind that you might expect to find elsewhere in Paris; some wealthy types, and some personalities from the fashion and movie businesses. I was told that sometimes you would even see ministers and their wives. Apparently you could either participate or watch. The girls hid their faces after a few moments, and tried to remain aloof as the *habitués* of the club approached and, without saying anything, caressed their thighs and breasts. One of them had been here before, and like our host was enjoying the libidinous atmosphere. The other girl, also a first-timer, was like me aghast but unavoidably fascinated.

In the last room was a full-size pool table, lit by a powerful lamp. On the table was a woman wearing only her bra. Her heel was dug into the corner pocket. A man approached her, climbing with one knee onto the table. The corners of the room were hidden in shadows.

'I feel like I'm caught in a labyrinth,' said one of the girls. Her face was pale. In the toilet, she said, she had been attacked by a lesbian. She wanted to leave but thought there was no chance of finding a taxi alone outside an orgy house.

We went back to the restaurant and sat at one of the tables. It was impossible to have a normal conversation. There was no point in talking about what we would do on Sunday as people in their underwear came and went from different rooms. We met someone we knew, who at first was surprised to find us there and eager to show us around. Soon, though, he was talking haplessly about the best ski slopes in Val d'Isère, from which he had just returned.

We were still there at three o'clock, waiting for our companions to return. A fresh buffet was laid: tartines of *pain poilâne* with pâtés and cheeses. The debauchery had evidently given everyone an appetite. They began to drift back into the restaurant, the men standing and eating in their shirt-tails, with ties undone and no underpants. Some of the women were naked. It was time to leave.

Not everyone can afford to spend a night at this club. But at the end of Avenue Foch, the most exclusive street in Paris, there is an alternative. Traffic queues up on weekend nights as couples looking for partners for domestic orgies arrive and drive slowly around. They switch the light on inside their cars as a sign and if another couple are interested they follow. These cars trail around the Porte Dauphine before heading off to their suburban Bacchanals.

'We like it,' said a couple interviewed on TV.

City of shadows

THE PÉRIPHÉRIQUE IS always blocked on a Saturday night. Oddly, it's the time of the week when the worst traffic jams occur; everybody going nowhere, trying to get in or out of the city. Stuck in a stationary car, unable to reach the cinema or show in time, they finally surrender to the Périphérique itself. It is a new kind of motorised urban *fête*. People crawl along, with music blaring, laughing and gesticulating at the occupants of other cars.

These are the *banlieusards*, the suburbanites who swarm in and out of the service city – a different city to the one promised in romantic weekend breaks with art nouveau iron railings covered in verdigris, bustling museums and shops full of models of the Eiffel Tower. The Parisian now inhabits a concrete, computerised city, zoned and policed.

There is another city, the capital of refined, expensive indulgence, home of the best cuisine in the world and the most beautiful women; shelter to some of the greatest art treasures and most infamous tyrants. It is no small irony that the Revolutionary capital offers an opulent sanctuary to the worst despots. The Shah of Iran owned apartments in Paris, as does General Noriega. Usually *nouveau riche* in the worst way, these rulers can find in Paris staff who aren't paralysed by the fear of ending up in pieces in the fridge, like those of Emperor Bokassa, who only wanted to be liked, and gave diamonds to President Giscard d'Estaing because that's what ugly potentates do. Michèle Duvalier bought her diamonds from Bucheron by the tray. Having fled from Haiti – where the five biggest killer diseases were all preventable – the wretched woman still shops at Valentino, who used to fly gowns over by the plane-load, and wonders why society now looks askance.

This is the Paris of lavish but transient wealth, the city that furnishes planes and bombs and stylish uniforms to the one-arm republics led by Sandhurst-educated buffoons. Their emissaries reside in the west of the city, in the elegant, calm 16th arrondissement. A vast luxury hotel for passing diplomats, the *Seizième* is also a home to widows who promenade their coiffeured poodles around the *café-dragues* of Trocadéro, eyeing young gigolos with a voracious glint of abnormally sapient vigour, the result of regular visits to a Swiss clinic to be injected with a commercial serum made from foetus of mountain goat.

Returning occasionally to Paris – a refuge from the dismal, depressed Britain of the early Eighties – I spent the weekends in another city of seamless wasted nights. I found in Paris a lurid, alluring decadence alien to my native London, which is a city founded on sound commerce that goes to bed at a reasonable hour so as to be able to get up and work. Paris was a city that tolerated the frivolity of pleasure, encouraged the vertiginous embrace of self-abandon.

The parties in nightclubs like Les Bains-Douches recalled the hedonism of pre-war *bals*, which were often held near-nude in search of an adored negro sensuality. In the modern Paris of the night playboys and models, artists and junkies swirled in a round of moneyed, narcissistic seduction. Le Palace opened in 1977, a few months before New York's Studio 54, throbbing heart of the disco decade. And elsewhere, in Le Tango and L'Emeraude, where they served only white rum and sugar-cane juice at 6a.m., Latin and African musics seduced anew the French sensibility.

Waking from this libidinous, licentious Paris of the night with an inevitable hangover, I realised it was already late morning. Throwing open the shutters I was assaulted by the glamorous, grimy city. I dressed and went out.

The elegant boulevards are clogged with angry, noisy traffic and the grand buildings have been sullied by decades of pollution. It hangs like accumulated snot from their intricate carvings, notwithstanding a forgotten law revived by Malraux in '58, obliging the cleaning of façades every ten years, and his restoration of the original sandstone hues of the Louvre, the Opéra and

Notre-Dame. Malraux dreamed, like all French cultural politicians, of rekindling the beacon of the Paris of the *lumières*. He would have been enchanted by the lucid white of halogen lamps that now illuminate the city like pearls against the grey skin of a wealthy widow. These new light bulbs are everywhere and, lit by them, the *ville lumière* of the 19th century has regained some of its lustre.

The City of Light, its cultural radiance visible around the world; Gay Paris, city of pleasure; these are different cities from the choking, crumbling, blackened and peeling Paris of rotating governments. The city is regarded with mixed affection by the nation as a whole; a showpiece of French civilisation and a dangerous urban blight at the centre of the true, rural France. But Paris thrives despite the rest of the country, to which most of its better-off citizens desire to escape each weekend, fleeing the commotion and the lack of green spaces.

But the cultural radiance has been tarnished. In the cafés of Montparnasse, there are only drunks and failures now to rub Bohemian shoulders with the tourists who come regardless.

Hemingway arrived in the Twenties to write, attracted by the literary glow of Balzac and Flaubert and by the exchange rate. A dollar was worth 25 francs and a three-course meal cost only five francs. A girl sold herself for even less, and brothels charging over 40 francs entry were not subject to police inspection. These were thriving businesses which changed hands for large sums. But this seedy traffic is not recounted by the likes of Henry Miller in their quest for manhood. And nobody looks for traces of the fabulous Harry Crosby, the American playboy publisher who sailed naked down the Seine at the head of a Byzantine orgy and left his wife's fortune in a taxi, expiating a variety of sins by dying at 30. Man Ray read about the Surrealists and shipped out of Long Island for Montparnasse, where he married Kiki, artist's model, nightclub floozy and woman of enchanting insecurities.

What of the Paris of the painters? Van Gogh only lived here for two years and most of the great Impressionist works are now in foreign museums. In Pigalle, the cultural heritage has become a tourist trap. Fortunately, there are still some Swedish hostesses who stage artistic evenings away from the commercial galleries – and some Japanese artists who, with that selfless Japanese sense of imitation, keep the painterly idyll alive.

They pose their easels by the banks of the Seine, stragglers in the queue for an old whore. If I were a painter, the light I would try to capture would be that of the RER tunnels, somewhere beyond the sombre in the spectrum of response, a creamy, grey paleolithic light with the dull sheen of coal dust that seems to emanate from the bowels of the earth.

Like an ingrowing cancer, Paris engulfs itself. Disembarking here in the 18th century, Laurence Sterne thought it a city of dwarfs. Constrained by the Périphérique, unable to spread outwards or upwards, Paris is driven downwards, down into the twilight tunnels of the RER, the new supersubway opened in 1977 that links the suburbs with the centre, its focal point the seven-acre subterranean fusion of the old stations of Châtelet and Les Halles. What were once two distinct *quartiers* are now part of the same multi-level pedestrian zone. In the RER, people work, shop, eat, sleep and even watch TV. A new underground human society is evolving. Tramps and runaways sleep in the warm corners, ignored by the commuters who pause only to shop for provisions or cheap watches and jewellery or to buy a pair of jeans from a vending machine. TV monitors dispense a soothing stream of colours, jingles, pop video segments and incomplete infoflashes, a new channel called Le Tube. People gather in front of these monitors as their trains arrive and depart without them. The monitors are housed in vandal-proof plastic cocoons. But it is as if these monitors, weird new urban totems, were protected by a powerful taboo. None of the teenagers who swagger through the tunnels at weekends, 'bombing' and 'tagging' any appropriate surface with their obscure spray-painted signatures, seem to want to efface the boredom of the flickering hydra.

As I step over the sleeping beggars, avoid the tall, green-garbed African cleaners lethargically pushing their brooms, dodge the pockets of commuters transfixed by the TV screens and try to judge, so as to avoid them, the cars carrying pin-eyed jazz geniuses and guitar-wielding acid casualties with amplifiers strapped to their legs, I feel that the famous Métro, the best urban transport system in the world, has become an assault course for the urban future. It takes me equally to a destination not marked on the tourist map, a Fourth World of teeming poverty under the paving stones of the First World.

The beggars on the Métro grow in numbers and vary their ploys. A young man with combed black hair and grimy hands recites a poem he has written. He sells xeroxed copies of his poem, but most simply bark their story of misery and misfortune and invoke your responsibility to help them avoid descending to crime. A woman of 50 swallows her pride and walks the carriages with a pathetic, hand-lettered sign, asking for help to feed her hungry children. It's getting like Bombay or New York.

'She's a professional,' a woman scoffs. 'Is it like this in Britain?'

I tell her that in Britain, we've banished these people to the north or to ghettos where the municipal transport doesn't run any more.

The beggars can be devious in their psychology. They know what little sympathy the sight of suffering elicits from busy, cosmopolitan people. And like the British, the French prefer simply to avert their eyes. Shame is a greater discomfort than poverty. Many of the beggars sit hunched, their heads bowed, not wanting to embarrass potential benefactors. One wily beggar is accompanied not by a sob story or a pathetic child but by a thin, hungry dog. The dog is the recipient of much generosity from the many Parisian matrons who care more for poodles than people.

From a nearby poster, candidate Jacques Chirac gazes down, radiating *ardeur, courage* – qualities which are spelled out beneath him. He too understands the psychology of appeal. He knows that people are more concerned about themselves and their dogs than about their fellow beings. As mayor of Paris, he sent motorised *ramasses-crottes* out into the streets, motorbike-mounted hoovers that tour the pavements sucking into their innards the abundant turds.

A simple law, penalising the owners of offending dogs, has no effect, since the first impulse of the Parisian is to ignore others. They are bound up by elaborate rituals of politeness but are incapable of basic courtesy in shops or their cars. They are unable to park without causing inconvenience and throw away most of the resulting penalty notices. I begin to understand the purpose of the Napoleonic Code; that tangled, heavy legislative masterwork that seeks to balance the snarling, petty, cross-eyed self-interest that is affectionately described as the natural anarchy of the French.

The Parisians

In Paris, it's true, even the ugly women are beautiful. Parisians are convinced that they live in the city with the most beautiful women in the world. Like the inhabitants of any major city, they are self-possessed and intensely proud.

The Parisian is the supreme connoisseur. He knows which is the best wine, sporting gun, yacht, pen, etc. He will be happy to flaunt this knowledge for hours. In fact, he would prefer just to talk about it, sitting around in the perfect pale-green shirt somewhere in the South of France. This is because, being an aristocrat *manqué* or merely aspiring, he can only afford selectively to indulge his exquisite taste. And also because, despite his fondness for action holidays (though rarely outside the fawning francophone world), he prefers to let others get their kicks for him.

Aristocratic, bourgeois or impoverished, the Parisians live enclosed lives. Preferring to socialise in restaurants, they rarely invite you to their homes – which are often so small that the kitchens are confined to a cupboard, while the entrance hall, making a bourgeois pretence of adequate means, strives to be as large as the salon.

An estate agent describes to me the characteristics of the inhabitants of some of the other *quartiers*. In the 15th live very unpleasant people, bitter and frustrated because they would like to live in the 7th, the best and oldest part of the city, but they haven't enough money. In the 9th live fading aristocrats, either very rich or very poor but aristocratic to the last; generous, dignified and modest. People who live in the 5th are very egotistical, very special. Even if they think they could live elsewhere, they can't.

In the Métro, no one speaks – normal for a major city, especially one like Paris with a population density twice that of London and the equal of Manhattan. As people live so close together, privacy is at a premium, and silence is golden.

Assaulted by noise pollution from Le Tube and from the busking musicians who fill the subway cars, Parisians arrive at work numb and jumpy. These are the lucky ones. Their colleagues are still stuck in traffic jams.

Having started the day with a hopelessly inadequate breakfast – usually just a bitter dose of concentrated caffeine – they are so agitated that they spend most of the morning jabbering frantically, without actually getting anything done.

That is if they manage to get to work at all. Working in Paris, the first thing I had to do was learn to be late. I used to arrive at ten o'clock and there would be no one there until twelve. Then they'd be so hungry because they hadn't eaten a proper breakfast that the first thing they'd want to do would be to have lunch.

The Parisian concept of a power lunch consists of a plate of raw meat, a steak tartare. Propelled by this protein fix and jolted by yet more caffeine, the Parisian is now ready to work through until 7p.m.

They will then spend the evening getting drunk, which is not the social hazard it might be in other countries. While most people drink to lose their inhibitions, Parisians – whose nerves are by now quite frayed after a long day of dealing with other Parisians – drink to become civil.

What foreigners find it hard to get used to is the level of inherent aggression – in shops, in cars and even from pedestrians who step out on the corners, challenging the motorists.

This is the justly famous rudeness of the Parisians. Arriving in the culture capital of the world, the visitor to Paris faces a major hazard – condescension. To each other as well as strangers, Parisians display a formidable mix of snobbery, impatience and caffeine-frazzled nerves.

And yet, impressed by the daily garbage collections, by the fresh water sluicing clean the gutters, the visitor may gaze upwards to admire a newly washed monument, and at once risk stepping into a newly laid dog turd.

Dogs have too much civic status in Paris and, encouraged by the general sighs of affection, their owners have the impression that they can let their coiffeured pups dine in restaurants and shit where they please, and that smiling, vote-seeking mayor Chirac will clean up after them.

Choking by now on exhaust fumes, the oxygen-starved visitor to Paris seeking fresh air and parkland finally reaches the sinister woods at each end of the city. These precious green spaces offer but a few stray shrubs by day and a pornographic charade by night.

Like noise pollution, another urban hazard to which Parisians, in their old-fashioned urbanity, remain oblivious is secondary smoking. Barely conscious of the dangers of smoking to themselves, they happily fill cafés and restaurants with a brown fug of cigarette fumes that passes for a charming atmosphere.

And yet Paris isn't such a bad place to live. It has the best Métro system in the world, charming apartments, fine restaurants and grand boutiques; it offers a leisured, cultured life of encounters on café terraces. The only thing wrong with Paris is that it's full of Parisians.

L'odeur terrible de la joie populaire

WHAT IS LEFT of old Paris? The Revolution took place in a medieval city; narrow, timber-frame houses overhanging streets of mud. It stretched along the Seine from the fashionable Marais to St-Honoré. It was flanked by the *faux bourgs* beyond the city gates – rebuilt but still in place at St-Denis and St-Martin – and by villages like those of Montmartre and St-Germain. Displaced by the Revolution and by Bonaparte's campaigns, homeless peasants threw up their shacks in the spaces in between, the beginnings of a harsh new urban poverty.

A tough weed, the city grew as the economy swirled and power lurched between monarchists and republicans, checked by Louis Napoleon's coup of 1851. He saw himself as a sentinel of order in a France at the head of nations. Needing a proper seat for this gilded role and impressed by the classical revival that produced the Georgian cities of Britain, he commissioned a prefect, Baron Haussmann to draw up plans for a new Paris – a city salubrious, modern, prestigious, and in which public order might easily be maintained.

The Baron proceeded with military aplomb, redrawing the map of the city as though it were a battleground. Annexing villages like Montmartre and Neuilly, he traced new city limits at the fortifications constructed in 1845 – now the Périphérique – enclosing 20 newly created arrondissements. He sliced two long axes, from what is now the Arc de Triomphe to Nation and from the Gare de l'Est to the new Opéra, which was to be the cultural centrepiece of the Second Empire.

The new industrial material, iron, was confined to the suburbs and only stone was used for the 16 years of construction in the city that followed, during which 100,000 homes were demolished and twice that number built, and the medieval chaos of Paris was pierced by new boulevards fanning out light and order. A limited choice of models for the buildings was imposed on developers, but ornamentation was left to the architects whose names are inscribed on the fronts. Luxurious or modest, each type had its strict proportions, but always a front entrance two storeys high, a balcony on the third storey, maid's quarters under the zinc roof and conduits at the back bringing proper sanitation and the new gas supply to illuminate the *ville lumière*, a beacon to the highest values of civilisation. The boulevards themselves were furnished like a salon, with benches and poster columns and *pissoirs*. And beyond the boulevards . . .

Uprooted from the city, a miserable population took refuge under bridges and along the canals. In the Faubourgs, a crowded and degrading promiscuity ruled in streets too cramped for light and order to penetrate. Out of this moral and material misery came the Cabaret.

In what was once the village of Montmartre, the old country *fête* still took place around a windmill, symbol of gaiety, of sowing and harvest, but it was a fake windmill or *moulin*, painted red, under which locals converged for dances in imitation of the splendid *bals* of the beau monde.

With their pleasant rural aspect, the slopes of Montmartre had been a fashionable address of artists and musicians. Delacroix moved there in 1822 on the recommendation of his new neighbours Chopin and George Sand. He noted his first impression: a woman's calf casually displayed as she descended from a carriage.

Within two decades of urban growth, the idyll was spoilt. Writing in the Paris Guide of 1867, Baudelaire described the area: '*Chauds parfums ici, là l'odeur terrible de la joie populaire.*' In the gardens and courtyards, workshops and small factories sprang up, turning the slopes to the north of Paris into a semi-industrial abyss, a vertiginous warren of harsh lives and rude pleasures. Steep was the climb out of misery but, as Victor Hugo confirmed, easy and not without a vicarious frisson the descent into degradation. Montmartre became a place of easy morals, where the prostitutes abhored by Napoleon and chased by him from the precincts of the Tuileries came to lodge, thriving behind the hypocrisy of the grand boulevards.

In the rue Frochot lived Degas and Renoir and later Manet, benefiting from the light on the hill where, in another street, the infidelities of Maupassant's *Bel-Ami* were taking place.

Behind lace curtains, amid red velour and palm fronds, delighting at Balzac's *Comédie Humaine*, the insouciant Empire grew wealthy on the new industries in which work began at the age of seven and continued for 12 hours or more a day. Launched by the new republican government into a shambolic and soon reversed assault on the Austrian empire, Parisian workers, hungry, weary and now frightened by rumours of a siege, rejected the rule of the Third Republic and, in 1871, beat drums on the hill to proclaim the Commune. Led by Louise Michel – a thoughtful young woman with the stern countenance of a nurse who prayed to God but read Voltaire and confessed she had come to like the smell of gunpowder – they swung the cannons of Montmartre round on the city. The hill glowed white as the Hôtel de Ville burned, and with it the city archives. The Elysée-Montmartre became an infirmary as soldiers arrived to crush what was the first proletarian revolution.

In the dog days of the century, her morale gone and her dream of enlightenment flooded dark by poverty and hypocrisy, Paris reclined and gave in, becoming the licentious capital of pleasure. A *demi-monde* lurked behind the sculpted façades of the beau monde, its frontier the Boulevard Montmartre descending into the penumbra of Rochechouart, beyond which no gaslight shone outside the infamous houses or lit the human traffic in the alleyways. On the boulevard, showgirls kicked their petticoats high displaying the tops of powdered white thighs, while Aristide Bruant declaimed caustic verse that satirised the fashionable crowds who came from the Champs-Elysées to rub shoulder with this *demi-monde*.

His friend Toulouse-Lautrec delighted in Bruant's disdain for the beau-monde that was his own, but which had shunned him as a cripple. In the supposed ugliness of the people of Montmartre, a rabble, sick and ravaged, diseased and violent according to the legacy of the Commune, he found asylum, and was treated with sympathy by the bar-girls to whose tainted beauty he held a sentimental mirror. His paintings decorated the walls of Bruant's cabaret, Le Chat Noir, paintings of dancers like La Goulue, a daughter of Montmartre like Zola's Nana whose sex was the downfall of all around her.

Behind his descriptions of social injustice, Zola had little sympathy for the denizens of Montmartre. In *La Débâcle*, his novel of 1891, he contrasts in two characters all that is noble in France: the soul of France, balanced and courageous, attached to the soil; with the faults represented by a Communard – the folly, the vain egotism.

After the Commune came this Montmartre of lurid headlines and lyrical complaints; printed ballads employing the *gouaille*, the Parisian cockney, an accent and a quick, sarcastic humour. After the boulevard had failed against the republic, there was only irony left to wield against might. The cynicism and arrogance of Montmartre became legendary – as did the violence, the violence of the undernourished, the rickety and the ruined. Made vicious by everyday cruelty, they took refuge in absinthe and popular song.

In search of old Paname

'IN THE STREET,' says Robert Doisneau, winding on his film, 'the show is permanent and free.'

The celebrated photographer, a contemporary of Cartier-Bresson, is now in his seventies. His blue eyes are clear and piercing. They radiate his contentment with a life spent photographing people in the streets of Paris.

I hurry along with him for a day working on a magazine assignment, photographing contemporary Parisian characters. A small, quick man, he fumbles like a mouse with his camera, looking around with a sly sparkle whenever he has taken a pleasing photo.

Since the war, he has been a witness to the accidental moments of life in the city. There is a black and white photo, taken in the Fifties, of a young couple outside a café, the boy buried in a large overcoat, one hand gripping the limp shoulder of a girl, the other nonchalantly in his pocket, lost in a passionate, hopeless, oblivious kiss. Doisneau took the photo, another in the roll, as he sat at the café. Entitled 'The Kiss', it is one of the most popular posters sold in Paris.

There is a satisfying economic logic to this. The photo that encourages the romance of Paris pays the pension of the photographer in love with Paris. Did his eyes glint as he took it? It was a long time ago and it has become for him a professional recollection. There were other photos, of drunken wedding parties spilling out of cafés, of women in the public wash-houses, of accordion players on street corners, of the empty streets themselves.

'Over the decades,' he laments, 'the street has been emptied of its gaiety. It has been antisepticised. The peddlars, the old inhabitants of the street have disappeared in the great clean-up. It's nothing to cheer about. The *ville musée* is like an artificial flower, a tart badly made up.'

Doisneau began his career at the Renault factory in Billancourt, taking photos of the production line and workers' picnics by magnesium flash. 'Now the photographers think they're princesses. Then, we were a circus act. Nobody thought we were doing anything important.'

Being a photographer, he says, is a bit like wearing a fireman's hat. It gives you courage. He went out into the street with his clumsy apparatus photographing '*décors sans importance, personnes inconnues*'. These were turned into postcards that tell the romantic and popular history of Paris.

At the sombre end of the rue St-Maur, between the Arab grocers and Islamic butchers, there is a café with a zinc counter. Inside the door, an old man, indecently tipsy at eleven in the morning, has one eye on arriving patrons and the other on an ever replenished – not to say eternal – glass of *pastis*. Cigarette butts are strewn at his feet since a law forbids the placing of ashtrays on the counter.

It was in this café that the Bonnot gang gathered to plan their robberies, though there are no longer any bullet holes in the wall – evidence of their glee at discovering the strategies available to any *voyou* with an automatic pistol. The tables and chairs have been updated too; that is, they were renewed in 1954. At the same time, the yellow wall lamps were replaced by strips of pink and blue neon.

What else remains of those days? The *avis aux mineurs pour la prevention d'ivresse publique* is still pinned to the wall, dry and brown at the corners, next to the *Licence IV* authorising the sale of alcohol. And there is the smell from the back of the Turkish *chiotte* – that uncomfortable abyss over which visitors hesitate to squat – still blocked up.

'*Bah, dis-donc!*'

Doisnéau grins and offers a Gauloise to Hervé, whom we have come to meet. Hervé gladly accepts. Nobody smokes Gauloise any more. The state tobacco company manufactures fake Virginia cigarettes to tempt the smoking public away from US brands – though these too are made under licence by the state.

The two of them draw contentedly on the rich black tobacco and soon we are wreathed in the confederate smoke of lovers of old Paris.

Hervé is 25 years old, spotty, with crooked teeth. He wears a beret hiding bleached, cropped hair. On the seat next to him is a strange wooden contraption, a Barbary organ. Three years ago Hervé decided to follow in the footsteps of his father and master the bulky instrument which, like the accordion, is impossible to tune because its tone depends on the physique of the operator. Hervé knows that this barrel organ has no real future in an age of digital music. There is only one man, living in Lyon, who can still repair them. Hervé built his own and, to update his repertoire with songs by modern French pop groups like Les Rita Mitsouko, laboriously perforates the long musical cards to feed through it.

His father has retired but still performs occasionally at old people's homes. His grandmother used to sing at café tables. Like his father, Hervé tours the *cours* of Paris, cranking out on the organ old tunes to which he has added his own contemporary lyrics; slices-of-life, tragic and tender in the style of Boris Vian or Jacques Prévert. Hearing the tumbling chimes, Parisians grow warmly nostalgic. The older citizens throw coins wrapped in paper, remembering Paris before the war.

It's always the same, says Hervé, the most generous are the people in the poorer, eastern parts of the city. 'It's difficult now to get into a lot of the *cours* because of the new digital codes on the locks.'

The sound of Hervé's barrel organ recalls the *Parigo* of Italian immigrants at the turn of the century, the *Paname* of the *apaches*. It was a crowded Paris of noise and rats; of carts laden with produce trundling over cobbles; of narrow, flaking gorges echoing with the sarcastic humour of the *gouaille*; the Paris of Henri Calet or Francis Carco, whose *Jesus la Caille* epitomised the *apaches*, those hoodlums who scorned the general mobilisation in 1914, preferring anarchy to either peace or war, family memories still strong of the Commune forty years before.

To the organ or the accordion that stop-goes with the rhythm of declaimed speech, couples danced the Java, a lewd popular waltz executed with both hands planted on your partner's haunches. After the First World War, jazz killed the Java and *apaches* drew their trusty knives to find themselves facing a Browning pistol. Stenographers jitterbugged with the frenzy of the new

Dictaphones. During a speech in 1920, President Deschanel liked the sound of a phrase so much that he repeated it – and didn't stop. The *bal masqué* gave way to the nude revue and the *Belle Epoque* gave way to the *Années Folles*.

Doisneau found the romance of Paris in the unexpected corners. After the war he went looking in the suburbs with his friend Blaise Cendrars; the same Cendrars who titillated readers in 1935 with his *Panorama of the Underworld*, poetic bulletins describing how to buy cocaine from hat-check girls or become a racketeer. Together they made a book of photos and prose called *Banlieue*, a homage to the suburbs where they had grown up. The poet and journalist hadn't written anything in years, but the book was not a success. 'It was a book about our childhood,' recalls Doisneau. 'It came out just after the war and I suppose it was too dark for the critics' taste.'

The suburbs are the *milieu* of our next subject, the crime writer Didier Daennickx. We meet at the beginning of the rue Watt, the most sinister of all Paris, extending dangerously over the railway lines; a favourite setting of precipitous events in the books of Leo Malet, grandfather of French crime writers. Daennickx wears a raincoat and a dark hat. He has a thin moustache and a look of steady concentration. For the photo he has brought with him a gun. He brandishes it with a smile. Nobody questions its provenance.

Daennickx listens closely to Doisneau, who is for him a legend. He solicits recollections of Malet and the great Cendrars, who lost an arm in the first war and typed his books with his left hand. He knows of their book on the suburbs. Doisneau admits that he is not fond of the new suburbs. He finds the décor *sévère*, stony. There is too much concrete.

Daennickx does not disagree. Here is his description of a block in Aubervilliers from his book *Lumière Noire*.

The entry was hidden back from a long road bordered on one side by an interminable factory wall and on the other by a series of anonymous warehouses. It was one of those buildings thrown up in three months, a game of prefabricated cubes that lost its freshness with the first rainfall. A neighbour called regularly to offer a range of beauty products sold exclusively through circles of acquaintance. Like a department store, each floor of the building had a particular saleswoman: perfume, frozen food, kitchenware, video cassettes . . .

A contemporary Cendrars, instead of the *quai*-side cafés, Daennickx frequents the airport at Roissy for his panorama of the latterday underworld. 'After two days you get completely paranoid, There's no life, just work and police.' A former printer, he wrote the book, his seventh, with financial assistance from the *département* of Seine St-Denis, which includes the district of Aubervilliers. He was born there 39 years ago and, apart from sojourns in the Far East, has lived there ever since. In his books, which sell around 40,000 copies, he describes a Paris of factories and bistros, of immigrants and cops, that begins at the foot of the tower block he inhabits.

'The Paris underworld is all around. You can find it in the cafés full of lorry drivers near the warehouses to the north. You make a sign and they take you out to the car-park to show you a stock of leather jackets or gold lighters. The prostitutes too have changed. They stand at the exits of the Périphérique. Fifty metres away, they park a caravanette. *Finis les taxi-girls, voilà les camping-girls!* '

'Where has old Paris gone?'

'It has almost vanished. But there are still a few traces, like the lines of communication; the *petite ceinture* for example, the old railway line that circles the city. I often walk along it. You can learn as much as in the Bibliothèque Nationale.

'The difference between old Paris and now is that, as late as the Twenties and Thirties, people still lived near their work, at the gates of the small factories. That's how they knew one another. You can still find that among the furniture-makers of the Faubourg St-Antoine and the metal-engravers of the 20th. Elsewhere it has changed. Half of Paris was already professional. What Chirac is doing is getting rid of the working people. In the old days, all the classes socialised alongside, provoking the pleasures and the revolts.'

Where the rue de Ménilmontant climbs to survey a grey, peeling Paris, between the video rental stores and the *chevaline* butchers, is a worn stone doorstep where, at the turn of the century, a newborn baby girl was abandoned. It was a common enough start to life in the teeming working-class slums to the east of the city. She was adopted by the Piaf family, who gave her the name Edith. She had a harsh, pure voice that pleased *habitués* of the local cafés, and as her popularity grew, she made her way west to Montmartre to star in the cabarets of the Cigalle, the Moulin-Rouge and, most famous of all, the Elysée-Montmartre. Maurice Chevalier too was a native of Ménilmontant. He made it all the way to Hollywood, croaking 'zank 'eaven for leetle girls' with kinky Boulevard charm, acquired in the cabarets of Montmartre. It was on these stages that the spontaneous gaiety of the street crystallised into the multicoloured extravaganzas of Paris by Night.

There is a Paris steeped in dangerous, intoxicating liberty, where a tap on the shoulder could mean an invitation to a gallant escapade or the menace of a tense, knife-wielding *apache*.

To the visitors who blink from panoramic buses on the rue de Rivoli and Boulevard de Clichy, Paris is the possibility of a life abandoned to romance and sensuality. To students slouched against back-packs in the stations, a temple of art and culture. Paris belongs to folly and escape, to the imagination, to no one. A city of cherished corners hidden in memory. A city of strangers, of adulterous encounters. A city to visit alone.

There is the Paris of Hôtel du Nord, still there beside the canal, and somewhere in the imagination, the *Quai des Brumes*.

There is the Paris of hedonistic nights, the streets freshly sprayed with water to reflect winking amber traffic lights, and a sweet nausea in the stomach from too much champagne.

And a Paris of the café-table poetry of Prévert, a city whose statues embrace on Sunday afternoons when the cinemas are full and the birds sing in the trees and only a blind child points at the astonishing scene.

At the age of 13, with a childhood friend, Jill Caplan passed her Sunday afternoons on a bench beside the Seine, peering at the reflection of Notre-Dame in the water and reciting together whole pages of Prévert – the sort of thing you do when you are 13, sentimental and precocious.

Now she is 23, a pop singer. She gives breathless interviews at the chewing-gum speed of French pop music.

We sit on the same bench and the water reflects her black hair and black T-shirt cut low to display bony white shoulders, the pallor of a city girl.

'I was born in Belleville. My mother was Blanche Leonie Hayez, a salesgirl at the Galeries Lafayette, and my father was Jacques Rene Guillen, a screenprinter. I took a stage name later, like the actress Arletty. The first record I bought was by the Beach Boys, in a sale in the local supermarket, but the lullabies of my childhood were from the idols of my parents: Barbara, Brel, Brassens, Ferre. I rarely listen to them now. You can't listen to them just like that, the way you can Midnight Oil. I have to be in a particular mood. I say to myself, *"Tiens, il faut que j'écoute une belle chanson française qui va me parler DIRECTEMENT dans MA langue, à MA culture".'*

'Tell me what happened to the spirit of old Paris.'

'For me, Paris is a certain music of accordions, an indefinable *gouaille*, an accent, a smell. In the morning very early; lunchtime on a sunny terrace; or very late when the Parisian night takes over. I don't mean the *branchés* of nightclubs like Le Palace, but the prowlers, the cleaners, the men that change the posters. You don't know where they come from or where they go.

'And then there are the cafés where you get teased by the *mecs* at the bar. "Well, my little lady, what'll it be? *Un petit noir? Une mousse?*" I feel heroic when that happens, I feel that I belong to a legend.

'Not long ago, I spent a *nuit blanche* talking with a friend at home. At six in the morning, we went down to buy croissants. To reach my apartment, you have to climb the top stairs to the *chambre de bonne*. There, seeing the sun rise over the zinc roofs, the chimneys smoking, feeling the warm croissants in my hand, I felt that old Paris hadn't disappeared.

'Paris is a city of love. It breathes love. You get the impression that in every corner lovers are hiding, under the Mansart roofs and behind the tall doors lovers are embracing. It's a cliché, but what a *beau* cliché!

Paris is a phrase of Clemenceau, "The best moment in love is when you climb the staircase!"

Inadvertent truths

How do the French see themselves now? Films, drama and television serials depict a disputable reality, linear but unreliable. There is another France, the France depicted on food packages and in TV ads; what Jean Baudrillard would call the 'hyperreality' of France. Advertising, without any pretence at truth, shows how people would like to be. Unrealistic, imaginary, it is the shared dream of France.

In the supermarket, there are stacks of *saucisson* on special offer, and above them an image of a farmer in light blue Lafont overalls sits at a wooden table, addressing the shopper with peasant sincerity. In front of him is a half-drunk glass of wine, a loaf of dark bread and a *saucisson* from which he has cut fat, glistening slices.

This is the Hovisland of France, realm of country goodness that has passed into myth, where at least it won't be disturbed by the new TGV lines cutting through the vineyards; the high-speed train is changing the temporal geography of the country, shrinking distances in the way that food technology freezes time.

Even as they enjoy the benefits of high-speed rail travel – traffic has doubled between Paris and Lyon since the introduction of the TGV – the French are nostalgic for the same France that millions of tourists come looking for each year.

Has it vanished, then, the rolling rural France of the colour supplements? Not quite. It is still alive in the wistful affections of the French – a powerful, poignant image of themselves. On egg cartons a middle-aged country couple smile with inspiring confidence outside their farm. The man caresses a chicken which he holds tenderly in his arm. That enlightened ruler Henri IV said every Frenchman should be able to eat chicken once a week. Despite EEC directives, calves and chickens are fed on steroids and there is a thriving black market in the illegal but profitable growth hormones, with unknown effects on Henri IV's Frenchman.

Little of this is related on television, of course. Adverts depict the French housewife as busy but glamorous, achieving a delicious gourmet dinner with a microwave and without shame. The dinner is usually suggested to be scandalous (she wants to tempt a man) but turns out cosy (it's her husband). She is dark-haired, though statistics reveal that the average Frenchwoman is blonde.

The suggestion of sex is less self-conscious in France and the circumstances are often amusing. The morning-after is a favourite scenario. Mami comes around and, ignoring the unfamiliar man in her granddaughter's apartment, recommends a family brand of bleach. She gives him a look not of suspicion but of admiration! A girl wakes up in a designer-dark apartment and prepares a new breakfast for a man, or is it breakfast for a new man? At any rate, it's something 'warm and crunchy like me' that he hasn't tried before.

There is not much to be gained from suggesting to the Frenchwoman that she might please the kids. While the tone of advertising has changed in Britain to show women balancing families with independence, beauty with achievement, in France women have another recipe for success. A business-woman comes to her office. She strides urgently to her desk, reaches into the drawer and takes out – a pot of jam! Turning to the viewer, she dips her spoon in and smiles conspiratorially.

The fantasies used to tempt the French male consist not of sex so much as adventure. Sex is more likely to be used to sell some utterly sexless domestic staple than to sell a car or hi-fi or other sexy male purchase. The French male when he is not, like the British male, the object of ridicule for buying the wrong computer, is most likely to be found hang-gliding, abseiling, on the telephone announcing an oil strike, or better still at the wheel of a dust-covered but still *puissant* little hatchback driving dizzily along the great wall of China.

There is one important exception to this male stereotype. A black man goes shopping in a large department store. He exits, grinning, with an oversize carrier bag. He is wearing a grass skirt and there is a large bone through his fuzzy hair. In French advertising there are no positive images of racial minorities. They are still figures of fun or invisible fear. There is no Arab behind the wheel of the latest Renault.

Carrying advertising only since the early Seventies, French TV has discovered in a big way the 20th century's most maligned creative form. The French themselves are determined to elevate advertising into an art – surprising as they didn't invent it. TV commercials feature the ad company's credit in the corner of the screen. There are magazines devoted to telling the amateur how current ads were made. Ads form a context in which the programmes are viewed. For a long time, people have been complaining that the ads are better than the programmes. It took Baudrillard to explain the significance of this – calling the screen the surface of reality – by which time it didn't matter any more because the succeeding generation is unable to distinguish.

Is French TV really so bad? Everybody in France tells me so. But what is the Degree Zero of television, where is the vanishing point of mediocrity? Does a *speakerine* equal the Mona Lisa? Is TF1 equal to Antenne 2?

At the annual party for the employees of TF1, hostesses in the blue uniforms of French parking meter attendants dispense coloured drinks and plastic watches. In the makeshift cloakroom at the back of the stadium to the north of Paris are rack upon rack of furs. The evening has all the glamour of a dinner at Hippopotamus, the American-style theme-park steak house that has taken off in the big cities with its piped pop videos, pictorial menus and rows of large, luminous cocktails to greet arriving diners.

The entertainment at the party is a *télévariété* spectacle, with showgirls, comedians and pop singers. The assembled employees of the station applaud happily, content to be a part of Entertainment France, though they must get enough of this stuff every day.

At the cocktail party afterwards, I meet a young man, bronzed and smiling, who tells me that his ambition is to be the presenter of a variety show. He covets the early evening slot, with its large public and the covers of *Paris Match* that will track his showbiz marriage, divorce, slide into alcoholism and painful recovery to marry a glamorous heiress whose last boyfriend is suspected to have died from SIDA.

On his morning show, he gesticulates frantically at the camera with a self-adoring smirk. Looking at the viewers he is really looking at himself, interrupting his guests and snatching things – usually books – to wave at the camera like a child desperate for attention. He asks me what I think of French TV and, to ruin his evening, I tell him my favourite channel is M6, one of the new stations created by the Socialist government, though probably nothing like their expectations. With its bright simple idents and unmemorable bought-in soaps, it has the forlorn look of a video game that nobody wants to play any more.

But is French TV really so bad? The fact that the most popular TV host is Bernard Pivot, who attracts an astonishing 14 per cent of the Friday night audience with a programme about books and authors, suggests that perhaps it is. Peering over bifocals in a friendly avuncular way, he epitomises for the French well-read conviviality, though he says nothing of consequence and has the wit of the schoolmaster which in any other country he would have been. He is therefore trusted for his impartiality and good judgement, but mostly because he is there. As such, he has become a marketing figure for armchairs and middle-age leisure interests.

France remains a literary nation with an estimated 900 literary awards each year – almost three each day – and I think I have found out why. Not a half-hour goes by on French TV without someone holding up a book. The cameraman, momentarily distracted from his primal directive to focus some-where between the legs of the nearest female, tries haphazardly to capture the title. There is little need to spend, as the Ministry of Culture does, three million francs promoting books (with images of an elegant woman, *livre ce soir!*). Even a Saturday night rock show, which you would expect to be doing its utmost to promote illiteracy and American junk culture, displays the latest books on the subject. Viewers have no hope but to turn to the books that Bernard Pivot recommends for a little excitement.

The only personality on French TV more popular than Pivot is Christina Ockrent, popularly known as Queen Christina, though I have no idea why since she is, inevitably, a newsreader. The ease with which these people assume a family role is not something that French intellectual culture has managed to counter. France has proved as weak as any other country when it comes to resisting the homogenisation, the narrowing and the confusion of television. It is the true Latin cultures that have most easily coped with TV. Brazilian TV and Italian TV, despite their inferior quality – that is their lack of highbrow pretensions – accurately reflect the tempestuous surface of Latin life, disturbing nothing fundamental. It is ultimately less distracting to have a cretinous television than a quality one.

The creation of two new TV channels by Mitterrand in the early Eighties has led to the inevitable explosion of mediocrity. The French have added their own speciality, however. The highest ratings on French TV were made last year by a show called *Sexy Follies*. A fairly ludicrous video-smut version of a game show, it involves blindfold male contestants fondling the breasts of a row of topless, giggling participants, the spurious aim to identify those of their girlfriends. As with all the best game shows, the prizes are irrelevant.

The contents vary from show to show, as the producers devise new situations for women to undress. In the tradition of the French nude Follies, no doubt, it departs from the showbiz of the boulevards in that it involves amateurs as well as professionals. Inspired by the New York cable-porn channels of the Seventies, *Sexy Follies* allows the adulterous French to covet other viewers' video wives.

But – hey! – it's Saturday night, you're drunk, the town centre is full of rampaging delinquents. You might be anywhere in northern Europe. But you're in France. No need to go to the video-grocer. Canal Plus, the pay-movie channel, programmes hot-pink four-square pornography nationwide from midnight. Simply switch on the decoder. Haven't got a decoder? So what? Ratings for these movies outstrip (forgive me) the number of decoders. More than two million French people spend their Saturday nights watching these jiggling flesh shows through a blur of jagged lines. It beats driving around and around the ring roads.

Where burger is king

DE GAULLE GROANED at the impossibility of governing a country that produces 365 different cheeses. During the Revolution, things were a lot simpler. Even a hundred years ago, according to the catalogues of large stores, there were only five or so cheeses available in urban areas. These were the boiled, hard cheeses that travelled well – gruyère, cheddar, parmesan – plus some local soft cheeses. Camembert was a village in Normandy that nobody had heard of. Cheese itself was regarded as unsavoury, liable to give rise to nauseating, deathly odours.

Such were the logistical and consumer awareness problems faced by Charles Gervais at the start of the Second Empire, when he took delivery of fresh rounds of light cheese on a wooden pallette, which he called Petit-Suisse. His solution was a horse-and-cart delivery network that also served to advertise the product whose light, fresh taste seduced the increasingly delicate French palate. It was an early coup of food marketing. The advent of refrigeration and the subsequent rationalisation of production did the rest. Accustomed to the odd smell of cheese by now, the urban population was ready to try the avalanche of curious shapes, textures and odours that arrived with the new cold storage systems.

If cheese was sniffed at, yoghurt was an aberration, the obscure diet of Bulgarian shepherds, fermented milk that, after a report from the Pasteur

Institute, acquired a vaguely medicinal reputation. A Spanish entrepreneur sold through the pharmacies of Catalonia a yoghurt which he called Danone after his son Daniel. Arriving in Paris in 1930, he changed the image of yoghurt from a cranky health food sold by prescription to a daily staple.

By this time, France was already learning to enjoy the delights of The Laughing Cow. In 1924, these quarters of a long-lasting cheese mix, individually wrapped and stamped *La Vâche Qui Rit*, became all the rage – one of the first food products to be sold in France without the benefit of gastronomic rosettes or the cachet of regional speciality. A snack food in fact.

The first French hamburger joint opened in 1972. The American import was an immediate success. With their well-known fastidiousness of palate, some Parisians used to make a special journey to the McDonald's in the Champs-Elysées, thrilled to note as they chewed the slippery burgers that the buns and the relish were flown in specially from the US.

Since then, things have improved. There is no longer any need to traverse Paris for a hamburger, as one might drive 400km to Lyon for a meal. The beauty of fast food, after all, is that it comes to you.

For a long time the fast-food business was viewed in the same dim light as might be the redevelopment of Windsor Castle as a fun park. Worse than the Japanese taking over the Paris high-fashion business and buying vineyards in Bordeaux and hotels along the promenade at Nice, this was a betrayal of the national trust, a cynical denial of France's heritage. Those involved on a personal level – other than the immigrants who staff the kitchens – committed a bizarre form of French social hara-kiri. And the consumption of fast food itself seemed to entail a cruel castration of one's national gastronomic libido.

But all of that has changed. As well as preferring instant, sanitised, homogenous modern foods, the national palate has developed a taste for the international, an appetite for novelty. A new restaurant in Paris serves 1,000 diners a night from five different kitchens: Italian, Creole, Scandinavian, Thai and Californian – each, it must be said, uniformly bland.

Fast-food emporia are now opening in France at a faster rate than anywhere else in Europe. Some of this is simply to do with catching up. The trade body concerned with *restauration rapide* envisages an eventual market share of around 10 per cent. In the nation famed as the home of gastronomy, Quick and Freetime have thrown off their shame to emerge as growth industries. Of course, you would be unlikely to find the directors of either of these companies dining in their own restaurants. The fast food revolution will have to spread uncontrollably before it can unseat the most powerful and enduring aristocracy in France, the aristocracy of food.

The rustle that screams

I AM HAVING dinner with Christian Lacroix and 2,000 other people. There are rich, velvety textures everywhere; on the tables, on the walls, hugging at the curves of the women. Diamonds cascade over cleavages. Lacroix is the new king of the curve, which was in danger of becoming a silhouette, almost disappeared into a dark box with Kenzo, but, thanks to Azzedine, is now a curve again. The men are indifferent. They are businessmen with their wives. People like Donald Trump and his wife. New money that isn't afraid to breathe: *made it!* And old money that doesn't want to lose it. The cast list of a modern Vanity Fair.

Perhaps you have heard of Christian Lacroix, the new king of the *haute couture* curve? If you haven't, the fault is not yours but Lacroix's. He is in the theatre somewhere. He was on the stage a moment ago, receiving a standing ovation and a giant birthday cake, larger than himself, to celebrate the first anniversay of the new couture house. We rose enthusiastically, and watched some excerpts from a ballet danced by Barishnikov for which Lacroix has designed the costumes. Leaving, we had a delightful surprise. The halls of the Opéra Comique – a smaller, plusher Albert Hall – had been filled with tables and chairs while we were inside. There were napkins monogrammed in gold with the initials CL, and ice buckets with two bottles of champagne on each table, even the one by the toilets. Sit down and pour a glass for yourself and the person next to you. Drink a toast to Lacroix.

What did you think?

Earlier in the day, at the couture house itself in the rue du Faubourg-St-Honoré, we saw Lacroix's third collection of fabulous frocks and gorgeous gowns. This year, a midnight-blue velvet dress furred across the bust, with a train of taffeta.

It wasn't as good as his first.

It was Lacroix who brought Barcelona to Paris, flamboyant Flamenco frills, pinched at the waist and worn with a lace shawl and a rose in the mouth. The flower-print fabrics were full of emotion. It was a fashion moment that burst with exquisite colour.

Lacroix learnt his craft in the venerable house of Patou where, after more than a decade, he came to be regarded as a promising designer. Balding, chubby, his dark, saturnine eyes appraise the shape of a woman's body with Latin impertinence, and apply to it a formidable technique in garment engineering.

He brought a dash of the *feria* of his native Nîmes to Paris. The bullfight and festival is a reminder of the Occitan culture that once spread from the mouth of the Rhône to the gulf of Valencia. He brought this Iberian style to *haute couture* not too long (but just long enough to be sure) after liberalised Spain had been 'discovered' by French artists and other fashion sentinels; a delirious realm of passion and liberty, with a glorious décor of crumbling tradition – as once was France itself.

Those Lacroix fabrics: dark, plush, torrid, the ripe fruits of a meridional temperament. With discretion and daring, he has put together shades of olive, chocolate, mahogany, bronze, Chartreuse. Given the sober extravagance of couture, Lacroix is full of *passion*: the French buzzword of the Eighties.

In the Cocteau-esque red and gold foyer of the *maison*, clients are received with diligent attention. There are videos playing of the shows featuring Lacroix's *mannequin de vie*, a girl in her twenties with stunning grey hair – the youngest looking 50-year-old you have ever seen. Coffee arrives unsummoned. This is where Madonna and Paloma Picasso come for fittings, in the circular mirror-lined changing rooms wreathed with gold-sprayed twigs that open like magical cocoons to reveal the Lacroix effect.

Conjuring this effect, amplifying the rustle of *haute couture* – that sweet, exclusive whisper of layers of hand-embroidered silk – has been a costly business. Bankrolled by Bernard Arnault, who moved from property development into furniture, retail and finally couture with a stake in Céline and Dior, Lacroix's *maison* in the rue du Faubourg-St-Honoré comprises 80 employees, half of them busy in the workroom from which each collection costs £250,000 in fabric alone. For its first year of operation, the house of Lacroix posted a net loss of £2.5m, five times their turnover! In any other enterprise, this would be announced with a funereal note of failure. In the business of fashion, it is called a success. If there are rumours of bankruptcy, the marketing director laughs them off. Those are just the envious whispers of competitors. As far as everyone at Lacroix is concerned, the launch of the new couture house has been a brilliant success.

As the European rich queue for more free champagne, let's look at how this success works.

There are 22 couture houses in Paris, venerable pillars of an empire of style. Together they form a guild that excludes all pretenders and share a clientele for their individually designed and hand-sewn clothes estimated not to exceed 3,000 fabulous women worldwide, who spend an estimated £30m per year (or £10,000 each). The combined turnover of the French couture houses, however, is 50 times this sum, most of it coming from abroad, generated by the lucrative trail of accessories and the perfumes that waft behind the fabulous women. Due notably to the media-conscious Pierre Cardin in the Sixties, the names of the couture houses have become luminous signs of elegance, glamour, chic, style, what-have-you. Every age invents a new code word for the ease and grace of wealth, but the names of the couture houses of Paris are fixed in a radiant, seemingly eternal setting.

Adding another name to the magic circle was never going to be like opening a new hypermarket. The house of Lacroix has a list of about 100 clients, the majority of them American and British; Frenchwomen are less prone to entrust themselves to the meridional milliner. From his first collection (for the winter of '87/88) he sold 120 items, from the second (for summer '88) he sold only 70. There are fewer than 200 women in the whole world wearing against their skin the black and white label Lacroix. None of them paid less than £5,000 for this rarefied frisson. There is nothing to be had in the Lacroix catalogue for less. However expensive that may seem, the price is still only half the actual cost of making the dress! Taking into account the work of measuring and fitting, the cutting and sewing by hand, a quality of fabric and finish whose caress is like that of a discreet admirer, it's a small sum to pay to be enveloped in exclusivity, in adoration, in envy.

Adding on the costs of the presentation of the three collections – the models, music, lights, invitations and slap-up dinner for 2,000 people – running the whole Lacroix enterprise for two years has swallowed all of the £5m that was allocated for the launch of the marque. More money will be required next year to keep going. This is not a financial crisis however. This is the cost of building a brand. Rather than actually selling garments, Arnault is more interested in the name of Lacroix, which, comprised of easily pronounceable French syllables and redolent of expensive girls' schools, is the whole purpose of the enterprise. He is apparently contented with a fat return in adoring, adjective-filled column inches and free pages of photographs in the fashion magazines, worth, it is calculated by the marketing chief of Lacroix, at least £6m.

This Byzantine, histrionic effort to clothe less than 200 women has all along been nothing but a ruse; the collections themselves a fantastic window display for a boutique that sells not clothes but the intangible ozone of fashion itself, the essence of luxury, grace and wealth condensed into the name Lacroix.

The name Lacroix has already been licensed to an Italian ready-to-wear manufacturer, an Austrian producer of spectacles and an Italian shoemaker, all of whose products will be under the discreet control of the parent house. Lacroix wants to design the handbags, belts and jewellery himself. The perfume will make its debut soon. At upwards of £20 a bottle for something costing a few pence to concoct, it is the sort of business you don't give away to licensees. The perfume will be the first Lacroix product that many women own.

It is a very modern kind of business, whose product is an image manufactured with less than a hundred employees and a massive chorus of gushing praise. The final result is the façade. The only enemy of such an enterprise, other than the silence of the media – and the fashion media never ceases to chatter – is the pirate, the illegal trafficker in this costly commercial identity. And even the pirate is repeating the name as he steals it.

The Sentier

NOT FAR FROM the theatre where Lacroix is being crowned king of the couturiers, there is a dim-lit passage where, in a dingy doorway, young Pakistanis sleep in cardboard boxes. They wake early and stand at the end of the Passage de Caire, waiting for work. Rapidly, with confusion, bustle and blocked traffic, the Sentier comes to life. The Pakistanis are hired as porters for £5 a day, to wheel heavy cartons of clothing between workshops and showrooms, or just keep an eye on the Mercedes 500 while the owner negotiates another delivery of cotton drill from Bangkok.

It is here that the pirates thrive. They are not pirates at all, however; they are in the fashion business, which is the business of propagating, multiplying, copying fashion. French kids want to copy their Italian counterparts who copy a mythical American teenager. Beyond a certain age, French men want to copy a mythical English gentleman. French women want to copy the sort of woman who can afford to shop at Lacroix. It is the business of fashion to fulfil these aspirations and in France the business of fashion is enormous.

The couture houses with their sophisticated marketing are merely the international flagships of a huge fleet of enterprises, and trailing behind, a flotilla of small entrepreneurs concentrated in the few square miles to the north of Les Halles known as the Sentier, the centre of the French rag trade. In apartments transformed into cramped sweatshops with peeling wallpaper from the steam iron in use 18 hours a day, Vietnamese refugees brought by taxi from Ostend take turns to sleep on the floor between the chattering sewing machines. In the streets below, in huge, halogen-lit showrooms stacked with garments by the thousand, the sign is pasted like a refrain on the window, *Ne vend pas au détail*, 'trade only'. Here, fashion isn't ravishing or delightful or even just fun, it's money.

The Sentier is the denim heart of the French fashion industry. The combined turnover of the thousands of businesses lodged here is reckoned to be larger than that of Renault – if it could be measured. Any attempt to measure it, with a view to legitimising it, would cause much of it to simply evaporate. Ask one of the men in leather blousons in the cafés of rue St-Denis what their turnover is and before draining their *double express* and vanishing, they will demur, 'If I told you, it would only make my competitors jealous!' They are adhering, after a fashion, to the Jewish tradition of discretion. Ask them the time, though, and they will think nothing of flashing a jewelled Rolex.

For it is here that flash fashion fortunes are made. The Sentier produces most of the ready-to-wear clothes that bear the label 'Made in France'. In shops in Abidjan, in Baltimore, in Villurbain-sur-Loire, they carry the same chic Parisian cachet issuing from these narrow streets clogged with vans double parked that spill rolls of cloth and receive bundles of finished clothing.

The Sentier is located in the middle of Paris – between the Black Sea, Calcutta and Hong Kong. Eastern European Jews were the first garment makers to arrive in the area, employing Yugoslavian and Turkish workers. Sephardic Jews followed after their expulsion from French Algeria. Now the Pakistanis and the Chinese have arrived. Fleeing repression and poverty, the Sentier gives them a chance to be exploited anew, and perhaps to reach a position themselves to exploit others. It works like this.

You arrive with no money. Somehow, you get hold of a garment. A single garment. It might be somebody else's copy of a Lacroix or a track suit covered in logos or an item of lingerie or children's wear. You take it around the retailers and get orders. You have it made, on credit, in the Sentier, and you are in business.

In the Sentier, everybody wants to do business. Soon, they will be finding you premises. Eventually, you will move from the Sentier and someone else will take your place.

Ever changing, fashion never really changes. The ready-to-wear revolution in the late Fifties, which launched the brands of Cacharel, Bailly, Rosier and Emmanuelle Khan, and was soon joined by couturiers like Cardin, has never expired the way most revolutions do. In the Sentier, they can turn a collection around over the weekend. Around and around, over and over.

Flowers of evil

LARRY WAS A junkie. Paris in the Seventies was full of junkies. The heroin arrived via Marseille at the same time as the Africans, though there was no connection. The drug worked its seductive ravagement on a generation of young Parisians, as it did in Rome around the same time and later New York. Syringes washed up in shoals on the beaches south of Rome. Aldo Moro was dead and with him the Italian Autonom movement. Between the Red Brigades and the *cosa nostra* there was not much to choose. Heroin is a gulf for the wealthy, an abyss of self-obliteration for the poor, but democratic as death. In New York, limousines pulled up outside shooting galleries and their occupants queued with the rest.

But in Paris, it was different. In Paris, the hangover from the Sixties' street party was long and numbing. It involved the ingestion of regular quantities of heroin, as Corsican and Sicilian families vied for the profit from processing the poppy mash brought from the eastern Mediterranean, and failed and traumatised would-be youth revolutionaries passed from activity to passivity, taking the extreme succour of the world's oldest painkiller to cope with their failure to transform French society.

But Larry was not escaping anything. He was enjoying himself, a cultural trafficker. Have you heard this? Have you read that? He was always excited about something. I never thought of him as a junkie the way you do with some people. He had what I would describe as an *epicurean* habit. It went along discreetly with his taste in free jazz and what he called – I had never heard the term before – punk rock. He was the first person I ever met who appreciated the music of both Albert Ayler and the Stooges. The black New York avant-garde jazz saxophonist and the white hoodlum rock band from Detroit were on the same continuum for Larry, extreme and uncompromising in their expression of disagreement with polite form, with commercial dictates, spitting back with violent, lyrical noise at the society that had spat them out. He listened to the Art Ensemble, black muslims from Chicago who preached racism against racism. He told me approvingly that the MC5 used to be the house band of the White Panthers.

Larry knew about jazz too. Connoisseurs of jazz since before the war, the French have long given the music and its artists a status once denied to them in the US. Paris hosted black jazzmen like Sidney Bechet and Mike McKendrick, as familiar in the Twenties as the Italian waiters and Russian cab drivers. Arriving from Kansas City, the composer Virgil Thompson reckoned, 'Paris is so cosmopolitan anyone can find an image of themselves in it.' Among those who came looking were Josephine Baker, a coffee-coloured chorus girl who became the queen of the *bal nègre*. Picasso copied masks from the Belgian Congo and tribal motifs were all the rage. Darius Milhaud composed his *Création du Monde*, inspired by African legends and the rhythms of jazz, a year before Gershwin's *Rhapsody in Blue*. After the war, Existentialists bebopped at the Club St-Germain to the cool, broken phrases of Bud Powell. A young French illustrator named Francis Paudras befriended this musical giant-in-exile. His experiences became the basis of a film, *Round Midnight*, and from a converted farmhouse in Poitiers he now runs one of the biggest jazz photo archives. Larry discovered pop and rock music the way Paudras's generation had discovered jazz. It was a modern, coded metropolitan sound. It had nothing to do with accordions and popular verse. They appreciated it profoundly, but would never do anything so crass as to try to imitate it.

The other thing about Larry was that he had a green beard. It's not every day you meet someone with a beard dyed green. I wasn't too concerned that Larry was a junkie, and I don't think he was one when I first met him. He was a Frenchman with a green beard and unusual but very precise tastes in music. I was fascinated by this aesthetic of extremes. Larry was a connoisseur of extremes.

He also liked comics. He collected American underground comics of the late Sixties, *Zap* and whatever. He liked the deranged humour of *Mad* and also the popular superhero comics like *Batman* and *The Silver Surfer*, doomed to surf a coloured-ink world of senseless, unjust evil, the character that GIs tripped out to in Vietnam. While most people dismissed this stuff – and I was even ashamed of liking it myself – Larry treasured it. Ever since I was a kid, most people, not omitting my own parents, thought it juvenile, banal, a waste of time and money. Their notion of value did not then extend to pop culture ephemera. Although as a teenager you can't easily introduce a friend with a green beard to your parents, I thought they would nevertheless like Larry, who sometimes spent a whole evening carefully cooking and straining vegetables to make a ratatouille, which he would finally leave to simmer, adjusting the pressure cooker like an engineer, and not eat until the next day.

Larry cultivated an aesthetic of trash. He had what I later realised was a very French taste for the repulsive, the underside: the spongy white belly of the cow, the gristly flesh of the pig's snout. Both of these are delicacies in France. Even so, Larry's rigorous delving among the discards, the rejects, in the bargain bins of American culture were not easily appreciated by his fellow countrymen, who were highly suspicious, if not openly hostile to anyone with a green beard. Larry also had bushy red hair, which the French regard as barbarian, and wore black crushed velvet pants with yellow stars, which they found easier to tolerate. He had thin legs and a chubby face, apt to break into a grin behind the by now famous green beard.

It was in the flea market to the north of Paris that I met Larry, enthusing over some dumb artefact, a record by Iggy and the Stooges. I visited him at his flat in the rue Quincampoix, in a sloping old building above what was once Molière's theatre, a fact which he remarked on with pride, showing breadth of appreciation at least.

As capable as any Frenchman of awarding a medal to a sausage or to a lump of force-fed goose liver, Larry had also developed a scale of infamous, black values. He liked ugly rock groups; grating, atonal jazz; cheap, stupid B-movies. In this, he was continuing a French tradition of assiduous and loving assimilation of American junk culture. What the Americans export, the rest of the world consumes, but only the French truly appreciate. Hitchcock was thought to be merely a good entertainer until Truffaut wrote a book in the Fifties hailing him as a genius. Not even in America was John

Ford regarded as anything other than a movie director until the French hailed him as a forger of national myth. In France, Walt Disney and Charlie Chaplin were recognised as men of universal stature, as important as Lincoln or Edison.

Larry brought carrier bags full of records, comics and books back from trips to the States, fingering their fresh stiff spines with pleasure, and he scoured the flea market to the north of Paris for other remnants. He was well known there to the record dealers and other urban pirates who staked out this pioneer cultural territory, French gypsies who wore long leather coats and earrings, who returned from Indochina with a crate of silk kimonos or from Texas with a pallet of cowboy boots.

Their successors now run the thriving boutiques of Les Halles. The Urban Cowboy look has become a staple and the French will go to obsessive extremes to imitate the American outlaw. A few years after I met Larry, I spent a day with the official Paris chapter of the Hell's Angels motorcycle club. The original members went to Oakland to earn their wings, giving the club proper status. They all have identical gleaming Harleys and official dispensation from the police not to wear helmets, but you don't laugh at them with impunity. They were escorting a rock band to a TV shoot. I rode in the limo, and back at the clubhouse, a garage in the north of Paris, they let go a little. France was a whore, they spat. There were too many immigrants, they laughed. They had an American pool table, a stash of drugs and a gaggle of ugly women to admire them. If there was a fault in their tribute to the original renegade bike gang, it was merely that, being French, they were far too tidy.

Since I already knew about the New York Dolls, Larry introduced me to Lautréamont, the French author whose anti-hero Maldoror had eulogised the 'beauty of a drunkard's trembling hand'. Centuries before Bukowski, Larry pointed out.

His favourite French novel was Huysmans' *A Rebours*, the morbid anti-hero Des Esseintes epitomising the moral decay of the *fin de siècle*, rendered febrile from a life of sensual decadence. It was something akin to this state of luxuriant apathy that I now realise Larry aspired to. He found it in heroin, of course, but I think he was too French to be surprised by it.

He was born in a medium sized French town, the name of which he feigned to no longer recall. He told me that as a kid, he grew up with the impression that in America, the Big Country of Westerns and modern skyscraper cities full of big cars and crime, everybody spoke the same language as him but *without moving their lips in synch*, which he attributed to the fact that they all chewed gum. Like many of the French people I have met and liked, he had had a Jesuit education, from which he rebelled as soon as he was able.

He came to England on a scooter in the early Sixties, a friend of the two Frenchmen who opened in a Soho basement a branch of their successful new *discothèque*. This, London's first, was called Le Kilt after the one in Paris, and – for reasons lost on the whirligig of fashion – it was decorated in Highland lodge style, with mooseheads on the wall and a Regency carriage serving as the DJ booth. A teenager, he brought with him books of Baudelaire and Rimbaud. He gave these away to impressionable girls and returned to France with Rolling Stones records. It was a significant cultural exchange programme.

Eventually, he was busted. This is more immediately painful for a junkie than turning blue. He had been living with an older woman, a fading aristocratic beauty with magnificent, redundant bone structure. He went to prison and she went to Ibiza.

Screaming metal

THE DEPARTMENT STORE called the FNAC, begun in the Fifties as a kind of co-op for professional people, still has the air of a modern cultural centre with its plain, sans-serif signposting. It is busier than any civic amenity, however, the largest French retailer of hi-fi, cameras, books and records.

Part of the books department in the large Paris store is devoted to something called *Bandes Dessinées*. This section is larger than *Littérature* or *Science Humaine* and almost as big as *Beaux-Arts*. And it is far more crowded than any of these, for the FNAC welcomes browsers, turning it, on Saturday afternoons, into a teenage mecca.

It is difficult to reach the shelves for the people poring over the latest 'albums'. In this department, there is a silence unlike the carpeted, air-conditioned silence of a big store and closer to the hush of a venerable reading library. Books are splayed open in peoples' hands or perched on shelves. On the floors, young readers crouch or sit. Their heads are bowed and they are quietly engrossed in the treasures of a library that even Borges never imagined. Reading across the top of the shelves, the A to Z of authors' names is eerily unfamiliar: Chaland, F'loc, Margerin, Moebius, Tardi. The books ranged beneath are not books like this one but large-format hard-cover albums of comic strips, the literature *maudit* of the 20th century.

Easy though it would be to snub this visual narrative art, in France, manifestly, it has been accepted. In a nation proud of its literary heritage, what seems a degenerate form of literature, at best the last-ditch response of literature to film, is accepted and even encouraged to the extent of having its own national museum. The French see comic books not as a degeneration of literature but as a sort of pre-literature. That this pre-literate phase of the French public should now last well into teenage years and beyond does not dismay them. Better to have the next generation opening any kind of book than no book whatsoever.

The development of the comic book itself in France reflects this progress from a young to an adult audience. Here the comic strip has reached, if not maturity as it likes to claim, at least adolescence. The pages of French comic strip albums are often filled with sick schoolboy humour, or with fantasies as violent and obscene as anything outside of Japan (whose comics are the most lurid in the world).

Characters in the new French comics have come on from the two-fisted archaeologists and costumed crimebusters of the past. They are identifiable, introspective nobodies reflecting the preoccupations of the artist-authors; cowboy existentialists in deep space. So far have they penetrated the mainstream to such an extent that serious newspapers carry regular reviews of the latest albums.

These French anti-heros got their start when a Nazi edict banning American comic characters like Mickey Mouse and Flash Gordon was never repealed, giving a home-grown tradition the chance to flourish. Its most familiar products are Tintin by the Belgian Hergé, and Astérix by Rene Goscinny.

Goscinny knew the founder of the American *Mad* magazine and, with the success of Astérix in the early Sixties, gained the means to transform a boys-own comic *Pilote* into a free-wheeling French *Mad*. The gentle satire of Astérix paved the way for *Pilote* to reach an older readership. Soon weirder, more idosyncratic material began to appear by new artists, betraying the influence of the American underground comics. Among them were Claire Brétécher, whose dry depictions of liberal anxiety even found their way into British Sunday papers.

Pilote liberated the comic artists' spirit, but it wasn't enough for some. They began to produce new comic magazines themselves, including one called *Métal Hurlant*, Screaming Metal. Much of the glory or blame for the eminence of the once greasy kids' comic strip belongs to *Métal* co-founder,

Jean-Pierre Dionnet. Produced by a group of disgruntled if already successful artists, the first issue arrived in 1975, heavy with the proof of lives spent in the thrall of nightmare, science and detective fiction. Lovecraft would have called it 'an hideous tome', Ray Bradbury could have borne witness to its magnificent isolation. Philip Marlowe would have poured himself another drink.

Then approaching his thirties, a boyish figure with the zest of someone whose luck it was not to have outgrown their youthful passion, Dionnet said to the others, 'Let's do a magazine with just regular strong dirty fantasy! Where we can say whatever we want, the wildest nightmares!'

The first issue bore an 'adults only' sticker on the cover and contained a strip by another co-founder, Philippe Druillet, about a spaceship impregnated by a wandering monster, an uncanny blend of terror and mirth.

Druillet's work, full of inhuman perspectives and vast panoramas, was already celebrated. He figured in the national archive alongside artists like Granville and Gustave Doré who had inspired him. He drew his tableaux of a barbarian fantasy world, obsessive in scale, for five years without being published, and went on to enjoy his notoriety, answering those who accused him of squandering his artistic talent by saying he was happy to work in a mass media. 'Through this unassuming art I can say things very hard and very forcefully.'

I asked him what he wanted to say to his youthful French reader.

'Most people don't like it, they don't like to be told that the individual is a mixture of violence and sexuality, savagery and impulse. Uncontrollable forces, those are the things that frighten us, ancient things like death and the night.'

The magazine gave its contributors unlimited licence, which tended at first to unloose raunchy fantasies long held in check. Issue 5 contained a strip called 'Cowgirls at War', a tale of lesbian cowgirls worrying about their relationships in a ranch surrounded by Nazi stormtroopers. Allegorical, fruity, tongue-in-cheek, humourless censors nevertheless decided that enough was enough. Comics were for kids, they reasoned, limiting the magazine's distribution to porno shops. The youth of France was not yet ready to discover what Tintin really had on his mind as he traversed the vast emptiness of space. The notoriety of the magazine was assured.

Apart from its subsequent popularity, what *Métal Hurlant* did was to establish a new conception of the graphic arts. The sheer variety of feelings and experiences delineated in their comic strips, the graphic styles ranging from the realistic to the surreal, served to legitimise the form in France. Dionnet went to the art editors of newspapers with originals of the comic artists' work. He persuaded them that it was art, worth taking notice of. It had a large public for whom it expressed something not being said elsewhere. He recognised that comics had an immediacy that placed them alongside other abbreviated, rapid-fire contemporary media. But they were a disreputable form – cheap, instant, fast and disposable – and as such they belonged essentially to youth. Their potential was second only to rock music to describe the mood of a generation. All the feelings that didn't fit would fit in comics.

Among the French gifts is the ability to quantify style and find substance in images. They gave academic respect to jazz when audiences in most of America were still segregated. They developed an aesthetic of Hollywood B-movies, finding art in the artifice of the *film noir*. 'Somehow we understand the popular arts that are maybe disregarded or exploited in their own country, and we bring them alive and help them,' said Dionnet.

At the height of the contemporary French comic book boom in 1985, there was a new album appearing each day, with sales from tens to hundreds of thousands. Through the prolific zeal of the comic book producers – the artists who are as celebrated in France as pop stars – and the avidity of the readers, the market became saturated. By then it was already too late. The minor art of the comic strip had become a French institution.

Figuration Líbre

EVERY SEASON, WITH the commercial rhythm of department store promotions, the *quartier* comes alive.

I live above a gallery in a courtyard of cabinet makers and furniture restorers. This area is little changed since the Revolution, when the local artisans helped erect the barricades around the ruins of the Bastille jail. Their descendants are among the families who own the furniture shops that still line the Rue du Faubourg St-Antoine.

These shops are gaudy and bright now, changing their names every six months. The latest is called Revolution; someone read that this would be the theme of the year. They employ aggressive salesmen to stand at the doors luring clients, the pace of trade tightened by the new discount furniture warehouses outside the city. In the streets behind, a warren of craftsmen's workshops supply imitation period furniture, though these are closing, transformed into agents for the merchandise that arrives by the vanload from Italy.

Recently, the character of the area has begun to change. There are now more than 30 art galleries in the streets behind the Bastille, most of them opened within the last few years. The area now competes with the Left Bank (where art galleries number in the hundreds) and the nearby Marais for the custom of the modern art client.

They come every Saturday afternoon to browse and buy, placing their names on lists to receive a card inviting them to the local *vernissages*. These are massed openings, when every gallery and artist's atelier in the neighbourhood opens its doors and keeps its lights on through the evening, offering glasses of champagne and a conducive atmosphere to the crowds of visitors who meander from one to the next. The buyers of modern art in France are mostly over 30, professional but dressed youthfully. They might work in banks or advertising agencies. They choose the paintings with their spouses, as they would a sofa or carpet – suggesting that the works are bought primarily for decorative purposes. A medium sized canvas by an artist with a handful of exhibitions in commercial galleries in the US, France and Germany costs upwards of £1,000, depending on its content. Anything naked, figurative or easily decipherable goes quickly. The gallery takes 50 per cent. For the artist and the gallery, it is a competitive business.

Attracted by the artisanal activity in the area, and by its cheap ateliers close to the centre of Paris, artists began moving here in the early Eighties. At the same moment a young Tunisian with a taste for camp jazz reopened an old dance hall, the Balajo in the nearby rue de Lappe, once infamous haunt of *apaches* in the Twenties and still popular with gigolos on Sunday afternoons, who were chased by developers from the *thés dansants* in the salon under La Coupole. With its *trompe-l'œil* murals, redolent of a faded pre-war movie set, the place quickly became the scene of an exotic nocturnal cabaret of the young and fashionable, nostalgic for old Paris.

Unable to afford the rents of St Germain, artists began to flock to this, one of the last 'popular' quarters of the city in the old sense. The immigrants, mostly Italian, came at the turn of the century. After the artists, the galleries followed and the antique shops specialising in the *moderne* period, the postwar era, the fabulous Fifties.

As Postmodern came on-stream – noticeably on every new apartment block built by the Ville de Paris – so the Modern became ripe for recuperation. Early plastic was suddenly chic.

This vogue reached a peak, if the speed of the cycle from fashion to nostalgia can be said to have a peak, when the Beaubourg gallery held a massive exhibition in celebration of the Fifties. The cultural department store devoted a whole floor to that optimistic decade.

Unable to sort it out critically, the objects were piled like heaps of bric-à-brac and the inscriptions were hidden in inaccessible corners.

I asked somebody what it all meant. 'The death of interpretation,' came the answer. The Fifties had been deconstructed. They simply were.

The exhibition, the most popular at the Beaubourg in 1987, was designed by the architect Jean Nouvel, who is eminently capable of thinking out the structure of his work. He also designed the Institute of the Arab World beside the Seine, a university and museum seen architecturally as the final taming of glass and steel, a mysterious, seductive, curved monolith which takes the inscrutable signs of Arabia, mathematical and calligraphic, and holds them up large like a bright mirror to the West, represented by the back of the cathedral of Notre-Dame.

The Institute of the Arab World is regarded as the best modern building in France, if not the world (and in terms of the arts, Paris regards the world as its domain, leaving to a dour London the lesser glories of finance, insurance and shipping). In terms of painting, however, this has ceased to be true since the war, when New York eclipsed a Paris that was still leaning war-weary on the crutch of its Impressionist glories. The Surrealists who had established themselves here found that, as the bombs fell on Europe – a spectacle you would think they might relish – the surreal sums of money were to be made farthest from the real damage.

Despite the tradition of painting in Paris, art was never 'popular' in the French sense of the word. Shaped by the events of '68, making art popular became one of the aims of the Socialist Minister of Culture, Jack Lang. When the appeal to French cultural pride is insufficient, he justifies this in terms of economic investment in the wealth of the nation, pointing out that over half of France is employed directly or indirectly in the culture business.

An individualist, and thus irredeemably bourgeois pursuit, art in France was always appreciated privately. The divine relationship between the work and the client (mediated by the gallery and the critic) was unquestioned by any of those involved. But after '68, there began to appear a communal spirit, the result of a political critique of art. Working in co-operatives rather than as rivals, artists like Cristian Boltanski and Annette Messager wanted to say things too about the collective life of society.

French galleries in the Seventies came to be full of aggressive uncompromising art, confronting the clients with the limits of their narrow bourgeois taste. Bourgeois art was consigned to the dustbin. There were to be 'no more frames, no more constraints'. The result was very good conceptual art that fewer and fewer people came to see.

At the same time, there was an upsurge in the popular art of the *bandes dessinées*. The French tradition of illustration and the free interpretation of the sex-and-drugs American underground school combined to produce a new graphic art, figurative in that it departed from the comic strip basis of a storyline. Towards the end of the Seventies, young artists, inspired by comic books, cartoons, record covers, movies and TV, began to produce work for a young audience, clients who were their peers, who shared the jokes and the visual sensibility. Part of the thriving popular comic book market, these were not paintings nor even comic strips but books of drawings and artwork, stylised and personal, illustrating themes or playing with iconography. Like the punks of the time, they wanted to blow away their identities and shock the institutions. They imitated rock groups giving themselves collective names like Bazooka, whose members included Loulou and Kiki Picasso and whose work took a savage, colourful look at fallen idols: a sinister de Gaulle shaking hands with children, a Maoist heroine in fragments.

It was a kind of after-Pop art, like Pop but warmer, more Latin. It came to be called *Nouvelle Figuration*, since it depicted figures. It was art, the imagination acting on people and events, with results somewhat less profound than, say, a heap of dead leaves. Finding it difficult to shift piles of dead leaves, galleries turned to it in the early Eighties with relief. The Yvon Lambert gallery, which before had shown mainly conceptual art, presented the work of Hervé Di Rosa, Combas and Jean-Charles Blais. These were young artists who shared the sensibility of the comic book artists but, with a fine art training, often from the Ecole des Beaux-Arts, confined their work to single canvasses.

The *Nouvelle Figuration* gave way to *Figuration Libre*, 'free figuration', coinciding with a revival of interest in the human form among artists in Italy and New York. The media seized on this because it was easy to understand and easier to live with than a pile of dead leaves. Closer to the comic book artists, Di Rosa invented a series of cartoon characters, a family of cyclopses who go on holiday and chat with the concierge. In the comic book spirit, he markets these as figurines through art museums, while Blais, in his early thirties, has become in financial terms the most successful French artist of the Eighties. His paintings, spidery jottings of a kid facing pop culture pandemonium, already change hands for up to £15,000.

Calling themselves the Steaming Muslims, another group of young artists followed with less seriousness. Coming together to party and paint, they have developed vivid, personal themes. As their work became fashionable, they held court in nightclubs squandering their fees like the Parisian painters of old, except they wore leather jackets decorated with each other's quirky symbols. There were Tristram and Waty and Franky Boy, who painted giraffes at the wheels of racing cars in a modern mannerist style he never explored. They were surrounded by record producers and pop video directors. Eventually they realised that that was where the real cultural significance lay and gave up manipulating paint for pixels.

The hopeless candidate

COLUCHE WAS A French comic, chubby and vulgar. A sad chump with a hangdog face. His paunch protruded between the tops of his lurid shorts and the bottom of his T-shirt. He was hugely popular in the French sense of the word, one of the people. He told stories about himself and his *potes*, his mates, a collection of everyday human tragedies.

He came from Montrouge, where his father was a house painter. At 17 he got engaged to Annie, whom he had met at the age of 12. He was looking forward to 'having a fridge, starting a flower shop where my mum could work behind the till, getting married and so on'. Then he became the candidate of the *nuls*, the hope of the hopeless, the dumb, the dispossessed.

'I don't know,' he said. 'Me and my mates in Montrouge were just looking for a bit of a lift in life. We dreamed of holding up the cashier at Prisunic with a toy pistol. We didn't, of course. I wanted to be a rock singer. We even started a group. Then I thought I could become a movie extra; you know, the ones that run around behind the stars? Ignorant as I was, I remember asking the cashier at the local cinema how you became an extra.'

They thought of sport . . .

'There was a family of boxers near me, the Valignats. All of them used to box because one of the brothers was a champion of France. They all wanted to be champions. Mistake. What's more, the champion of France went back to the factory on a Mobylette.'

Success calmed Coluche, though he remained a megalomaniac, as every good comedian must be. As a youth, he was thin, introverted and sometimes violent. Later he mellowed, growing plump and sullen.

'You know, when I was 16, I was sure that I was dumb. I hadn't read anything. I knew nothing. I looked for intelligent people, people who knew something. At the time, I thought they would be playing chess somewhere. So I went to a chess club that met every Wednesday night in the bistro opposite where I lived. I met a pharmacy student, a Communist, who said if you want to know what's going on, the best thing is to go away and read Marx. And he lent me *Capital*. Three years it took me to get through the two volumes. When I got to the bottom of a page without understanding a thing, I started again. Finally I learned the essential thing about capitalism. A man will always try to get somebody else to do the job for him. Later I read Freud and because I worked in a florist I liked Freud a lot. He helped me understand the sicknesses of the people that came into the shop.'

In '81, Michel Colucci, Coluche, decided to present himself as a presidential candidate. It was like John Belushi running for the White House. It set in motion events that the best gag writers could not have conceived. The French must have needed to laugh at themselves, and he let them; the savage laughter of release.

'Look at me. I came out of the suburbs without even a certificate and now I have 10 per cent of the votes to annoy the four big parties! It's only normal that I'm a bit proud!' he boasted to the international media. They were fascinated by this comedian who had upset the sacred totems of Republican, or any other, politics; who suddenly and unexpectedly found himself with a powerful block of votes. He liked to joke that these were the votes of tramps, illiterates, motorcycle trash, etc. But they comprised 10 per cent of the vote none the less. And whoever they belonged to, these votes were regarded jealously by the other candidates.

The first person to arrive for a discreet word was a fellow from the Communist Party. He didn't say anything specific, exactly. He had come to the Théâtre Gymnase to see Coluche's show, and just knocked on the door of the dressing room – to make contact, as they say. 'I don't know. He wanted to know if I would march with them. He didn't ask for anything else. Those political types never ask for anything. They put the question in a roundabout way to see if I want something. I don't know what they want me to want.'

The funny thing was, there was usually more than one from the same party. They came individually, thinking that if they could persuade Coluche to endorse their candidate it would be good for the party, and good for them personally.

Eight months earlier, Coluche had broken his Olympian silence. 'Yes I will be a candidate. *Le candidat Nul!* My slogan: I fuck the Left all the way to the Right!' Ah well. Humour doesn't always translate.

As usual, though, the good buddies of Coluche laughed on cue. Jean-Jean was in charge of the cigarettes. Dany was pouring the drinks. Bouboule, changing the discs, was the oldest of them, one of the gang from Montrouge. The actor Patrick Dewaere was taking a dip in the underground pool.

If I don't run this time, thought Coluche, when will I? Where will I be in seven years? I want to be on my island. I've done enough. It's daft to work.

It had been a while since anyone around him dared blow the whistle on Coluche. They wanted the show to continue. The whole of France spluttered with them at the comic nerve of Coluche, the sarcastic humour, the off-the-cuff utterances, the loaded barbs that exploded to release the pent-up embarrassments of the French. If, by running for the presidency, he was going to end up looking ridiculous, so what?

'That's my profession. Looking ridiculous.'

The campaign, he judged, was the perfect arena for a showbiz coup. The politicians were so preoccupied with themselves that you could get away with anything. He might even get some of the votes! In his mind he ticked off the groups ignored by the big parties: the abstentionists, the unemployable, the immigrants . . .

His campaign began in October. Although the election was not until the following year, the media was already thirsty for comic relief when candidate *Nul* announced: 'One arsehole more or less, what difference does it make. You might as well vote for me. If Giscard wins the election, France loses. There's no danger of me deceiving you because there's no danger of me being elected.'

He didn't think anyone would take him seriously. The first to do so were the intellectuals. As a rule, *chez* Coluche, intellectuals were not the typical guest. The milieu was French showbiz. Johnny Hallyday and Eddy Mitchel were occasional visitors. There were Coluche's actor friends from the Café de la Gare, the theatre where he had had his first break, half of whom had since become stars themselves: Miou-Miou, Dewaere, Gérard Depardieu. Together, they would play the video machines or billiards, laughing and drinking, talking about motorbikes. Coluche had that modern French vice: he liked to race motorbikes.

The first intellectual to invade this scene was Felix Guattari, hero of the Italian Autonomists and co-author of *L'Anti-Œdipe*, the refutation of psychiatry. For him, Coluche was the fusion point of molecular social revolution, the Degree Zero of politics revealed. But the popularity of Coluche needed to be anchored on the Left. Helping him would be the least that the post-'68 theoretician could do. He organised the support of his political and intellectual cohorts. Coluche, beer in one hand, cigarette in the other, was treated to a series of impromptu seminars. They explained the magistrature, the Constitution, the *Loi Peyrefitte* and article 16. They organised petitions and began collecting the 500 signatures from worthy citizens that Coluche required to become a candidate proper. Through him, they were hoping to subvert the political process. But it was not exactly what Coluche and his manager Paul Lederman had in mind.

'Our methods were more showbiz and "celebritarian" than proletarian. We just wanted to cause a fuss.'

Every French candidate must have public meetings and Coluche's meetings were held every night in the Théâtre Gymnase, where he was playing a run of sell-out shows. At these shows, wearing overalls and a flower in his hat, Coluche sometimes recounted 'his' *mai '68*. He was just emerging from the proletariat, he recalled, when he found himself trapped in the neighbourhood by wagonloads of CRS. It was then that he discovered 'ideas', becoming a member of the CRAQ, *Comité Revolutionnaire d'Action Quelque Chose*. 'Their idea of revolution was blocking the Boulevard St-Germain, forcing people to go round and round.'

Like everyone else, he went with his mate Bouboule to the Sorbonne. 'We borrowed some flowers from my old boss and gave them away to people coming in so they could lay them in the corridors. Give what you can, we asked. Afterwards we collected the flowers up and took them back.'

Coluche's campaign began well. After three weeks, he found himself on the cover of *Nouvel Observateur* with the results of the first poll. The candidate *Nul* had an astonishing 10 per cent.

'With that, I thought I could just go and present myself. That shows just how little I knew about politics.'

And then the letters of support started arriving. A motley postbag of the disenchanted, the cynical, the crazy and the joke-starved, from all parts of the country and all walks of life. Coluche's showbiz coup was going to work! All that was necessary was to exploit it to the hilt and for that, Paul Lederman was an expert. He had previously managed Claude François and Michel Polnareff. These were French pop idols. Claude François, the nearest the French have come to a great country singer, attained immortal pop status when he was electrocuted in the bath while changing a light bulb. Forty-year-old divorcées buy his records religiously.

Two years before, Lederman had sold Europe One the idea of Coluche's weekly radio show. Coluche's popularity was growing from film appearances. He had appeared in a handful of French comedies, playing downbill from his heroes like the frenetic Louis de Funès. The radio show broke listening records with his invectives about national service and his invitations to listeners to write in with tales of local police buffoonery. But though they were accustomed to the showbiz media, neither Coluche nor Lederman had any experience of political journalists.

On 25 November, Rene Gorlin, Coluche's road manager, was murdered. No motive or culprit has ever emerged. At the time, *France-Soir* speculated that Gorlin was Coluche's political fixer, the brains behind the scheme. Next, Coluche received a threatening letter from a group calling itself *Honneur de la police* who were not amused by his performance in *L'Inspecteur la Bavure*, an action comedy in which our hero is mistaken for a police cadet and taken hostage by a deranged transvestite hoodlum played by Depardieu. The title translates as *Officer Dribble*.

The Leftists who had come to his aid earlier now proved less than useful. 'You're worried. We can see that you're worried,' they psychoanalysed. Finally he went to the police, who at least proved their sense of humour by taking neither the letter nor his film seriously but still posting guards on his house.

Pacing anxiously inside, Coluche learned that Radio France-Inter and the main TV station TF1 had decided to boycott Coluche's campaign. Invited onto a variety show, Coluche had made a speech as the candidate *Nul* in front of ten million *telespectateurs* – ten times the audience for a political debate. Next, on the top-rated Colaro Show, he was scheduled to perform a sketch showing the candidate *Nul* taking his first ministerial meeting. The channel bosses suddenly scrubbed the item. The media was closing ranks against Coluche.

Political staff found his candidature undignified – a clown pretending to the highest office in the country and using it for self-publicity! The station chiefs, whose jobs were political appointments, were not about to disagree. Political journalists did not appreciate the joke either. *Le Point* accused him of wanting only to line his pockets, which he himself admitted in boasting derisively of the 700,000 copies he had sold of his latest comedy album. He was compared by his new-found critics to everyone from Caligula to Poujade. 'Who?' puzzled Coluche. With his chubby tired face perhaps the figure he resembled most was Ubu, the corpulent character created by Alfred Jarry to fart in the face of respectable opinion.

In the Socialist party (which was closest to Coluche's real loyalties) there were two camps. Some favoured a direct attack, joining in the Republican condemnation to isolate the beast. Others, more aware of the significance of the Candidate of the Lost, wanted, if not to win him over, at least to see him come out openly against their opponent Giscard.

All along, Coluche had been careful to attack only the *office* of President. 'He's responsible for all the shit, *non*? He and a few others could do something about it.'

He was amazed, however, by the hive that he had disturbed. 'I realised that three-quarters of the press is controlled by the Right and even the journalists of the Left didn't want me making fun of the institutions. They were rare, the ones that weren't implicated in politics. It made me sick. Only the foreign journalists put the real question to me.'

By what strange phenomenon, they asked, could 10 per cent of the population be ready to vote for someone who didn't want to be elected? They described it as an 'electoral hole'.

The Right, meanwhile, was hoping that the Socialists would fall into this hole. Coluche might cost Mitterrand votes. The RPR invited him to dinner but Coluche declined. Two self-appointed delegates from the UDF, supposedly responsible for television, made suggestions to Lederman about a future TV channel. Jacques Attali came for a quiet word on behalf of the Socialists, and found to his dismay that Coluche had been doing his own thinking about some major issues. Attali had to explain the pitfalls of abolishing social security charges or disbanding the Army and replacing it with American bases.

'People said he was all right but I got on badly with him. He didn't think I'd have my signatures but said if I did, would I call for my supporters to vote for Mitterrand in the second round. So I asked if he'd be prepared to give me my signatures. He said no. I said I would have nothing to do with someone who didn't abide by the rules of democracy (*sic*). It was a stupid discussion. Because of my percentage, I found myself mixed up in things I had no business with. I voted once to see how it felt. It's like having a fishing licence, you use it once and that's it. And what's more I never considered that my percentage belonged to me. I just though I could represent the marginals, because I resemble them. Most of all I wanted to fuck everyone up as much as possible!'

He had his effect, certainly in the media. He was attacked in *L'Express*, accused of leaving hotel bills unpaid and swindling sanitation companies, in addition to being gross and vulgar and unfit for public viewing – let alone public office. In fact he had been locked in the hotel one morning when he was supposed to be on set and the toilets had never worked so he refused to pay. But it was true that he had a criminal record. He had spent one day in prison 16 years earlier for breaking a shop window.

Even Europe One, the radio station where he had achieved his break-through, invited him on *Club de la Presse* but retracted after invitees from the Socialist and Communist parties wouldn't appear with him. Such was the pressure from the Elysée that, while candidates with lower standing in the polls were appearing on TV, Coluche was being ignored. He responded by calling a press conference and treating the French journalists as the butt of a series of jokes for the amusement of the international press.

Refusing to back down from his lampoon of democracy, Coluche announced, 'I'll stop meddling in politics when Georges Marchais stops making me laugh!'

Meanwhile, his shows were selling out at the Théâtre Gymnase. There he presented his silent minority: gays, immigrants, bikers, alcoholics. One evening the candidate *Nul* addressed his supporters stark naked, wearing a *coq gaulois* on his head and with three feathers, red, blue and white, planted between his buttocks. He declared that he would go on hunger strike unless he was invited onto *Club de la Presse*.

'I wasn't kidding. The signatures had to be in in two weeks.' To be eligible to run he needed 500. 'Because the big parties had told all their lackeys not to endorse me I only had seven.'

He actually did go on hunger strike.

'The diet did me good. I lost 11 kilos. I held out fifteen days and I continued the shows at the Gymnase. It was hard, fifteen days. I drank only water. By the end of the first week, you get really, really hungry. But I realised it was no use because no one was talking about it. They would have let me die. And I had no intention of doing that.'

The presidential aspirations of the candidate *Nul* ended in hospital, producing just one photo in *Le Matin*. The dispossessed were again dispossessed with no one to vote for. The electoral hole had been safely covered over.

Coluche returned to his *hôtel particulier* near the Parc Montsouris, to his pinball and video games, his collection of sunglasses in glass display cases, his basement swimming-pool and his elegant walls repainted by the Steaming Muslims. The voluminous American cars he owned blocked the road outside. Inside, Coluche entertained the gang from Montrouge to fine French bourgeois meals prepared by his live-in cook. Sprawled on a leopard-skin chair after one of these feasts, he reflected on his political adventure.

'I knew nothing about politics. What I learned, talking about economics with all of them, was that they all want to keep the poor that they represent. I think as soon as you get to the head of a country you no longer have any idea what's going on inside it. And Karl Marx was wrong. You mustn't take away from people the chance of succeeding for themselves. In France, the enemy is the boss, the state.'

After the hunger strike, Coluche became a recluse. He was grief-stricken by the suicide of Patrick Dewaere. When he appeared in public again it was in the serious role of a sullen garage attendant who befriends a young drug dealer in *Ciao Pantin*.

Beneath the sarcasm and derision and his sometimes fatuous, sometimes liberating vulgarity, was the generous spirit of the founder of the Restos du cœur, now a huge charity. He liked to race motorbikes. It was on a motorbike that, in 1986, the candidate of the hopeless met his final demise.

The defeat of thinking

THE LAST BOOK I ever shoplifted, at the age of 14, was Sartre's *Nausea*. Stealing it at random – it was filed in an opportune corner of the books section in the department store – marked for me the end of adolescent rebellion and the beginning of a phase of intense morosity.

It was the Penguin Modern Classics edition with the serious grey spine and, on the cover, one of Dali's soft clocks draped over a dead branch. On the train to school the next day, I became engrossed in the story of a man disaffected with objects, made queasy by everyday life. He withdraws slug-like into a shell of obscure literary endeavour at the local library, unrelieved by occasional perfunctory sex. With the zeal that only teenagers are capable of for the sullen or hideous, I decided that Existentialism was for me.

Inspired by Sartre's novel and by the TV adaptation of his slow-moving and seemingly profound trilogy *The Roads to Freedom*, I was convinced that I wanted to become an intellectual. But how? Among the pamphlets in the school hallway, there was no careers advice to be had on the subject. Apparently Britain had no need of intellectuals the way it needed engineers and nurses.

Opening a newspaper in Britain, you find on page two the Home News: pools-winner sprees, suburban murders and Roman ruins under new civic projects. In France, page two is headed instead 'Ideas'.

On one such page, Jean Baudrillard, an intellectual but with a fatal sense of irony, suggests that Millennialism will be a tiring phase. He proposes a referendum to abolish the calendar for the rest of the century, and with it the twelve dull years of debate to come. He wants to move forward directly to the year 2000. *Twelve years of debate?* The mind boggles. *Move the calendar forward?* Unthinkable! The British, on the whole, would prefer not to disturb the calendar or better still, move it back.

The next day, more ideas. Laurent Joffrin gives his verdict on the designer decade: 'Frantic, soft, superficial, lazy, image-saturated, media-crazed.' He too wants to move the calendar forward. 'It is no longer sufficient to be modern to be valid,' he concludes. 'One must be valid to be modern.'

What is he so concerned about?

It was the French who, with their speculations on the meaning of meaning, first coded the language of images. Could it be that the Modernists – frantic, soft, superficial etc. – have begun to communicate in some supraliterate way that ignores validity, goes beyond making sense? Is a pair of boots, in short, equal to Shakespeare?

Alain Finkielkraut poses this question, the title of a chapter in his new book. *The Defeat of Thinking*, a meditation on the nature of culture, is a bestseller in France. Finkielkraut worries that the notion of culture has been devalued – and intellectual France worries with him. Britain remains free of such worries because it doesn't trouble with ideas. Move the calendar forward? Oh dear. Shakespeare, surely, will never be just an interruption between commercial breaks.

Most of these troublesome ideas were to do, at first, with man in relation to God, and later, to his fellow men. It took a while for the Gauls to sort out their relationship with the Roman God, nearly accepting the Reformation, but not finally separating Church and State until early this century. But it is a timid state, uncertain of its power, that imposes a civil marriage ceremony immediately before church weddings. After the Reformation came the Enlightenment: Belief was obscured by Doubt out of which Descartes asserted the primacy of the individual, bathed in shining Reason.

Ideas spring from the reinterpretation of facts; turning the world upside-down. Elusive, chimerical, ideas are thus the enemy of the status quo. And upholders of the status quo are the enemies of ideas. Ideas were the domain of progressives; hypotheses of freedom, of social justice and equality, even the redistribution of property. Feudal, conservative, booming Britain, with a commercial empire to safeguard, preferred to keep the usual prophylactic distance of about 22 miles, the width of the English Channel, from the turbulent, revolutionary ideas of the French.

Luckily, this is no longer necessary. Britain need not fear ideas crossing like mice in the tunnel. Commencing with the Chicago economists in the Seventies, the Right has fought back with ideas of its own, based on the primacy of the free market. Like most good concepts, this is an old one, but it was given new force by the recession in the West. It has become the guiding economic principle of Western governments, some of whom, like Britain, have elevated it into a social principle; and soon it may become a cultural one too. As there is already in Britain a new masculine ideal – money-macho, reachable only by cellular phone – there will be monuments to the new harsh, ruthless, dog-eat-dog ideal of civilisation; breathtaking, slippery monuments, I hope, crowned with gaudy neo-classical pediments.

As the American Right was perfecting the theoretical model for paying less tax, the French Left was well advanced in its search for the universal theory, the theory that eats all theories; that welcomes them all to the cathedral of Structure.

Renowned for its upsurges, infighting, immobilism and ideological mania, the French Left was, by the Fifties, approaching a new quandary. The great age of anti-Fascist commitment, of fellow-travelling in the International Brigades that shaped André Malraux and Jean-Paul Sartre was drawing to a close. Among politicians, Pierre Mendès France was talking about the revolutionary potential of the middle class. In philosophy, a new tool was beginning to be used in the search for place, a parascience that set out to measure the relativity of concepts.

This process, Structuralism, a way of seeing relationships, had roots in the writings of Karl Marx. He held that society had an economic infrastructure from which sprang the political and cultural superstructure – a theory with all the ponderous beauty of 19th-century engineering. Sigmund Freud, too, believed that there was a structure to the unconsious. And the linguist Ferdinand de Saussure, in lectures given in Geneva in 1906, later reconstituted and published by his students, suggested there might be a common structure to languages. Language was a system of signs that express ideas, like military signals, symbolic rites or the deaf-and-dumb alphabet. He conceived of a science that studies 'the life of these signs in society' which he called 'semiotics' from the greek word for 'sign'. And he began to elaborate on this science that he saw as a kind of social psychology, encompassing linguistics. To proceed required a basic principle: the 'signified' (concept) and the 'signifier' (sound or image), which together make up the sign.

During the Twenties, Italian Futurists, interested in the form of modern chaos, applied semiotics to poetry, analysing form rather than content. Concerned at first with the interpretations of words, semioticians soon found their new communication gauge registering like a geiger-counter wherever they pointed it. Minute, mechanical, it removed sensibility from analysis. An art critic might look at a painting, but a structural art critic would look at the critic looking at the painting. Claude Lévi-Strauss, founder of Structural Anthropology, looked at himself and us looking at early societies – and found himself looking at our society. His comparison of the workings of myth and music on the human spirit in *The Raw and the Cooked* is the single most astonishing product of Structuralism, from the greatest French (actually Belgian) mind of the century. He hoped to uncover deep structures in the unconscious of society. For his intellectual opponent Sartre, as for Descartes, society was a product of the individual. For Lévi-Strauss, as for Marx, the individual was a product of society. But unlike Marx, and closer to the psychologist Jung (who noted that as the churches emptied, his waiting room was filling up), Lévi-Strauss felt that this was based on a spiritual rather than economic infrastructure, and it was this that he tried to classify.

Structural Anthropology made the divisions between the humanistic sciences seem arbitrary. Myth and table manners, religion, art, literature and fashion were all seen as ways of social expression, structured by similar unconscious processes. The universal solvent was in reach.

Lévi-Strauss's studies of the Brazilian jungle became models for the study of an urban jungle of neon signs. As Structuralism seemed to span disciplines, so it seemed to have the power to recombine them. Interdisciplinarity, a lovely word but unstable, was the new intellectual order. Louis Althusser hosted a seminar in 1964 by Jacques Lacan; the structural Marxist welcoming the founder of the Freudian school of psychology in France. In their systematising, they were both now Structuralists. Everybody was a Structuralist. Michel Foucault claimed he wasn't but in his book, *The Order of Things*, an 'archaeology of the human sciences', he too was concerned with epistemology, language, classification.

Literature was an early candidate for Structural interpretation. The critic Roland Barthes, born in Bayonne in 1915, a self-confessed Structuralist (although by the Fifties he thought it was already an overworked term), looked at structure in Racine and classical theatre and in the *nouveau roman*. Analysing literature in *Le Degré Zero de l'Ecriture*, he found himself asking to what it referred. Before literature could express the nature of sex or death – historical and psychological questions – it had first to agree on describing the mundane textures of life. He applied semiotics to pop phenomena in *Mythologies* and to fashion magazines and styles of dress in *Système de la Mode*. Easy to grasp, these textures were his point of departure. Like the new information flow itself, he mastered that subtle shift of register between the profound and the banal.

Who killed Roland Barthes?

ROLAND BARTHES DIED in 1980 after being hit by a milk van. A curious fate, it seems to me, for everybody knows that the French don't drink milk. The chances of him being hit by a milk van therefore appear remote.

In fact, he died after being struck by a 'milk van', a signifier for something that was not what in Britain would be conceived of as a milk van – a small open-backed vehicle rattling along on three wheels in the early hours of the morning with crates of pint-bottled milk. The *significant* 'milk van' was part of a sign like those he spent his life decoding. This sign was travelling too fast, or else he simply didn't see it in time.

But there are other ways for a writer to die. I am having lunch with the man who killed 'Roland Barthes'.

I decide to avoid a direct approach and begin by noting that he orders *hachis Parmentier*, French shepherd's pie. Did he know that it was Parmentier who introduced the potato to France?

He did. Oddly enough, he is related to him. Parmentier was one of 17 children, and had numerous nephews and nieces.

A journalist and founder of *Actuel*, my companion is conscious of his heritage. He has a country house in Savoie where he grew up in a Catholic family, the son of a bank official, and spends his summers there arranging his library, with its 17th-century bibles.

He has a classicist's interest in the intrigues of politics. He tells me the story of the assassination attempt on Mitterrand in the late Fifties. It was a hoax, he says. A right-wing deputy mixed up with the OAS was ordered to assassinate the minor anti-Gaullist politician. In a scene that a French dramatist could never invent, the deputy came to Mitterrand to tell him, and to ask his complicity, so that he could appear to carry out his mission and not lose face. Instead of calling the man a lunatic or phoning the police, his intended victim went along with this scenario, leaping over a wall just before the machine-gun tatooed his car. He was a mite precipitate, however, leading to the suspicion that the whole thing was staged.

It seems improbable to me, but Michel-Antoine claims to have heard the taped confession of the deputy.

He shrugs. 'It shows you how ambitious Mitterrand was, and what the Algerian war did to France. It was as if it took 25 years for the English to decolonise from India, a long guerilla war with the Sikhs on the British mainland.'

As a teenager, he was interested in philosophy and read Sartre. Later, he did *Science Po* at the Sorbonne, becoming a journalist through his involvement with the student Left. In the Seventies, he co-authored a book called *Barthes Without Tears*. It was a great success. It demonstrated the accessibility, shall we say, of Barthes's style. It was tantamount to character assassination.

'Did you kill Roland Barthes?' I quiz him.

Michel-Antoine Burnier is not ruffled.

'I was very, very sad when Barthes died. I really loved his style. I never laughed as much as when I read his books. What amazed me was that it was ever taken seriously!'

Barthes was at the height of his fame. His philosophy of the everyday, the apparent and the transparent, was easily assimilated by undergraduate philosophers who, if they couldn't get to the bottom of a page of Husserl, knew at least what a soap bubble was and were thrilled to find that it had 'significance'.

Distinguishing Foucault and Lacan, who he feels had something useful to say, or at least a sense of the relative value of their observations, my companion regards Barthes, Baudrillard and Jacques Derrida as an unholy threesome of contemporary French philosophy.

'Barthes created a philosophy of daily life and objects; analysing what he had for breakfast in search of the significance lurking beneath the shallow surface of life. Baudrillard's brains exploded in '68 and he is still trying to untangle the mess. And as for Derrida . . .

'No doubt there is a profundity in the fact that, for instance, I have spilled some coffee, but it's for a Proust or a Balzac to render it interesting. They philosophise because they are afraid of literature. They say things in the most complicated language, like Molière's *précieuses ridicules*. They theorise to death to say anything at all.'

Structuralism, at first invigorating, soon began to warp those who came into contact with it. Apparently sincere, but with a tinge of Buddha-like amusement, they appeared on French TV and on the stages of American universities, talking about the newest cars and movies. Instead of a critique of society – a theory of how it works with suggestions for improvement – they were delayed by interpretations of its busy, ephemeral surface.

They had been enlightened by the zen of Structuralism; they had begun to Deconstruct.

What value have my observations if what I conclude depends on my history, my environment, my unconscious prejudices, as well as the interpretations of others and of a society which is only one of many?

Nothing is absolute, everything is relative; subjective, unsystematic and quite possibly deluded. It was a very 18th-century dilemma which met with the very 20th-century response of badly co-ordinated blanket shelling. Employing a combined arsenal of psychology, economics, sociology and semiotics, the French intellectual turned to look into the very eye of modern civilisation, and here did not miss the mark in that it was indeed relocated in the newly opened hypermarket on the edge of the new consumer town.

Around these aisles of roses danced the free-associating, interdisciplinary, apolitical pop Structuralists. Looking at life with the critical stare of a security camera, they offered, if they were good, sublime insights into the product galaxy. Semiotics was a fascinating gauge for evaluating the sexual curves of automobiles, the textures of soap, the brilliance of phenomena; it delighted in wordplay, juggling with words that, freed of objective meaning, lost their gravity and floated between concepts, forming affective connections like children in a nursery – or dangling between quote marks like severed nerves.

The central role that someone like Sartre could once play in the conscience of a nation, tackling in novels the great issues, expounding Existentialism, taking up causes such as the torture of prisoners in French Algeria, was no longer possible. Such a role was merely part of the structure. The French Left was no longer armed but abandoned by the intellectuals, who lost their subjective emotional drive and humanistic clarity – coinciding with the advent of television and, more importantly, the rise of the new human science of marketing. Business boomed in France in the new hypermarkets created by consumer evangelist Edouard Leclerc where, used to interpret and satisfy desires, psychology, sociology and the rest worked a mysterious, neglected miracle.

Concerned with 'meaning', then, Structuralists turned on the TV to see what other people were meaning. Deliberately or not, their attention became attuned to the flickering surface of television, and, unnoticed, was still flickering when they turned away to look at life. They were like the person who steps from a juddering train and, unobserved by Einstein, continues to feel the vibrations.

Having lost faith in an objective, real world, they began next to interpose TV with experience.

In this respect, they were a lot like the rest of us; for whom there are two kinds of reality, the one you can touch or smell or feel or taste, and the one that flickers in 98 per cent of homes. The beauty of it is, there is no longer any need to distinguish between them; indeed, many people already don't. TV, film, advertising, photographs are not a reduction of reality but another reality, stronger than the first in many instances. This is what Jean Baudrillard – who, you will recall, wanted to abolish the rest of the century – calls hyper-reality.

Travels in hyperreality

I PAY A visit to Jean Baudrillard, the modern French philosopher. In over a
dozen books, beginning with *Towards a Critique of the Political Economy of
Signs* in 1972, through *Forget Foucault* and *The Ecstasy of Communication* –
marvellous titles that have endeared him to fans of French intellectual
frippery – he has attempted to come to grips with a new consumer society
whose superstructure is primarily televisual.

His critics accuse him of being as confused as a Postmodern building,
taking bits of psychology, sociology, philosophy and pasting them into
dizzying constructs in an effort to analyse a world in fragments. They do not
deny, though, that the world is in fragments. It is one of Baudrillard's
precepts that the world has fallen apart, doesn't work, has grown unwieldy,
straggling, tangled and confused, and isn't getting any simpler. In his terminology, it is 'ruptured'.

This doesn't, however, prevent the world – objects, images, concepts and
people – reproducing and multiplying, an uncontrollable mutation.

Two examples of this. It amuses Baudrillard a lot to reflect on the stock
market crash-that-wasn't of '87 and on the poisoned computer Xmas card
sent to IBM in Paris the same year, which, once lodged, began to erase the
memory of their computer network in Europe. After three days of failed
efforts to control this bug, the system had to be shut down. It was a costly,

alarming prank; but to Baudrillard a symptom of the modern world's incapacity to understand and control itself. The crash was a financial nebula that exploded – or imploded. For Baudrillard, we live in a world that expands as it shrinks.

His own environment is more stable. He is 59 years old, a spry, gnomic fellow who lives on the fifth floor, without a lift, in a medium-sized bourgeois apartment, furnished without noticeable tastes. The Ansaphone sits on the mantelpiece. There are modest chairs and a comfortable sofa. The large photographic prints on the wall were taken by him.

He was born in Reims, the champagne district, in what he describes as the remains of a peasant family. He is pleased to be asked what his father did. 'That's always a good identifier.' His father was a gendarme and his mother worked in the post office.

He was interested in philosophy and studied German because he wanted to read Nietzsche and Freud in the original. He did not start writing 'theory' until he was 35.

A teacher of German, he was invited in the early Sixties to join the sociology department at the new university of Nanterre. 'It was a pilot university,' he says. 'I was between disciplines.' Cohn-Bendit was one of his students. Those were: 'fusional years. We were in rupture with sociology. It was antisociology.'

He was given the title *Maître de Conférence*, which he dismisses. He is not a professor, but accepts the title when it is mistakenly accorded to him by foreign universities who invite him to lecture. 'The hierachy exists but I played that game to do what I liked: travel, write. I never wanted a career. I'm not a teacher. I never wanted to impart things. I always thought of what I was doing at the time as a test for me. The essential thing was always the shock that I could give to the students. After that they could sort themselves out.' He quit the university two years ago, feeling he had been there long enough and missing the feedback that he once got from the students.

In 1979 he wrote *On Seduction*. His concept of seduction was the dynamic flow, the magnetism between things and people, between the subconscious and the inert. He employed the term at 'a moment of rapture with theoretical terms'. He recalls with amusement that he immediately saw his sales bottom, and has since found an audience among the public at large. But his academic public was wary. He was attacked from various sides for departing from the orthodox terminology. 'They thought I was doing . . . whatever, falling into frivolity. In France it was difficult. There is an intellectual mafia – philosophers, psychoanalysts, sociologists – and it fitted with none of them. I've done my classes in the different subjects, but I found myself alone. I criticised Foucault.' He states this as though it were a clerical heresy, but dismisses it. *'On oppose, on s'oppose.* It was a way of talking about the ideology of desire and sexual liberation, a way of relating to that in a warmer way. The feminists especially were against that.'

I ask him to describe hyperreality.

'Generators of hyperreality are the media and advertising. I have difficulty explaining it in specific terms but it's easier to grasp in terms of objects. The position is *objectal*, which doesn't say a great deal. But I never had a doctrine. It works in spirals rather than opposites; it's neither true nor false. The processes of the modern world interest me; but that doesn't stop you having Nietzsche in the head too.'

Is hyperreality dangerous?

'All that passes for morality today belongs in a kind of museum. There are no more values, in the same way that there is a political scene, but it doesn't function any more. People don't relate to it in the old way. It has passed to hyperreality.'

Is it the hole in the ozone of philosophy?

'When you talk about an object,' he muses, 'you are accused of inventing it.' He rocks back in the chair, his small frame curling into a ball, and laughs. He didn't invent confusion after all. He has bushy grey hair and wears thick glasses that amplify his blue-green eyes. He has a busy mind, and takes three phonecalls in the hour I spend with him. He returns to the subject of morality, and of being perceived as part of what you describe.

'In semiology at the start there was an idea of alienation. Semiology attempted to save meaning and reject nonsense. But signs evolve, they concatenate and produce themselves. Reality is an effect of signs.'

And hyperreality too.

'TV is not subject to laws, it has total liberty. One image can succeed another. It's an aleatory movement. The screen is the new surface of reality. And images have a mode of production, images have perverse effects. They have their own life; that escapes the professionals. There is an irony that perverts the strategy. There is more than one level. All the strategies were lost completely in the crash, for instance, but it wasn't a catastrophe.'

His own TV doesn't work very well. The aerial is falling off the top. 'I have a barbarian use of it,' he shrugs. 'I watch it like anybody else.' It's what everybody, especially intellectuals, says about TV. 'I like American TV,' he adds enthusiastically.

He doesn't have a Minitel, but notes that he has seen friends intoxicated with it. 'Is it,' he ponders, 'an integral circuit — sexual, affective — of people? Not really. What is it, communication?' He is thinking aloud, with an infectious enthusiasm for the conceptual, for bridging concepts. 'Communication is a kind of enormous prosthesis, a kind of simulacrum. It was an ideal wasn't it? Transparent communication, information networks? The IBM virus was a pathology produced by the system. It's not a radiant utopia, communication.'

Recently, he was invited to judge a competition to design a Pacific monument on the theme of Communication. A very French project, like the donation to the US of the Statue of Liberty. One of the other judges is the actress Cathérine Deneuve. Baudrillard is not sure if the winning design will ever be built. And it seems the Japanese don't want it anyway, since they don't have any word for 'communication', so the monument would mean nothing to them. This, he agrees, is no reason not to build it.

It amused Baudrillard to learn that there is no Japanese word for 'universal' either. The concept doesn't exist. He holds his hand up as though turning an invisible cup. 'What is your universal, they puzzle ... Your universal is relative!'

Is philosophy a game?

'I think it's a game that plays with reality. You have to look for the rules of the game. There is no more alternative, revolutionary solution; no more reference, no more ideology. The habitual mental food is gone.'

The vanishing object

AND WITHIN THE cathedral of Structure there is now a dilemma of interpretation; a dilemma of meaning, a vault of mirrors. The Structuralists have begun to analyse the cathedral itself. Led by Jacques Derrida, they have begun to Deconstruct.

It was as though, pointing at the moon, the philosopher became fascinated by his own finger.

Structuralism assumes there is a structure and tries to uncover it. Deconstruction – Structuralism applied to philosophy – says your view of the structure depends where you stand. Like the physicist Niels Bohr, who at the turn of the century opened the Pandora's box of modern physics by remarking that data is not objective but depends on the point from which it is viewed, this has wrecked the old consensus of meaning. To even describe the effect, the Structuralist is obliged, like Bohr, to give more than one set of coordinates. Literally, what I mean is not straightforward. There is what I think I mean, what you think I mean, what we are referring to, and the word or picture or sign normally attached to it.

The problem is: I will never be understood since any word I use will mean different things to different people. The same goes for other signs and for images. Each viewer will have their own interpretation. The accumulated and ever evolving languages of society – linguistic, pictographic, gestural, visual –

are thus deprived of meaning. I don't even know what I mean. And what I write may unconsciously express something else.

Derrida was a pupil of Paul de Man, the Belgian philosopher. A biographer of de Man, digging out his wartime articles in Flemish, discovered that de Man, as well as being a Structuralist, was also an anti-Semite. He had written a series of articles supporting Nazi ideology. Derrida, who studied under de Man for 12 years and adopted his theories of the inconsistency of text, was stunned. He is himself Jewish, and his family suffered under the Nazis. Could it be that the inconsistency of the text, the theory that, because meaning is relative, one can never write what one means, was all along a smokescreen for de Man's former Nazism? Fans of tight ideological corners were thrilled to read Derrida's new book, *Mémoires pour Paul de Man*. In the final chapter, Derrida admits that he is forced to interpret events the way they present themselves, according to his emotions. It is an irony worthy of literature.

It was worse than the fact that Heidegger, the founder of Existentialism, accepted a university post under the Nazis, a personal lapse which was always known about but periodically overlooked. Lately, there has been much agonising over whether Heidegger's dubious politics discredited his theories. The British are right. Ideologies are not to be trusted. Table manners are far more important.

Recuperation of the sentimental object

JACQUES DERRIDA TACKLES the problem of meaning in relation to objects; how we perceive the world; the meaning-giving activity that is consciousness. He asks what sort of minds we have to have the experiences we do. And as he does, meaning goes into flux; objects begin to vanish. Alienated from their rural past, their Republican ideals, censured for their carcinogenic pleasures, reckless driving and second homes, the French now risk alienation from things themselves.

The Beret. Basque in origin, made of lambswool, blue or blue-black, with a knot at the centre, the Beret is a recent French fetish. It was created in the 19th century and became popular after the First World War, when Claudel and Hemingway both wore them, as well as Michèle Morgan and Greta Garbo. During the Occupation, they were worn in Alsace as a sign of loyalty to *la Patrie*. The baguette under the arm and string bag containing a litre of red wine are optional.

Hermès. On 90cm squares of silk, over 800 designs have been created by the artisans at Plat, near Lyon, where a trade in the warm, diaphanous fabric originally came from Italy. The motifs are often equestrian, and a Hermès scarf is sold every two seconds around the time of the Xmas Derby. Scissors and flowers that prick, signs of bad luck, are never depicted.

2CV. It had one headlamp and the side-window flew off at speed, but there was a waiting list of six years for the 2CV or Deux Chevrons when it was unveiled in '48. The nickname 'deux-chevaux' come later in reference to its not-so-stunning performance. Going around corners on two wheels but fulfilling the government's brief of carrying two people and a sack of potatoes at 60km/h, the car designed by the team of André Lefebvre was economic but sordid, ugly but useful, a sign of the inconvenience of modernising France.

Gauloises. Comprised of a blend of 20 tobaccos, the Gauloise cigarette was launched in 1925, when the state tobacco company, nationalised by Henry IV, changed the name of the Hongroise and repackaged it in a light-blue pack with an image of a winged helmet, signed by the artist Jacno.

Michelin. Originators of the pneumatic tyre, the roadsign, the map and restaurant guide, the Michelin brothers of Auvergne did not tarry in getting the 20th century rolling. Inheritors from a Scottish great-uncle MacIntosh of a patented process for moulding rubber, they produced the first replaceable bicycle tyre in 1891, and the first automobile tyre in 1895. They invented the radial tyre in 1946 and facilitated the motor tour of France by paying for the system of yellow, enamelled roadsigns, as well as publishing maps and the famous restaurant guide. The Micheline, the red and yellow panoramic bus-train that used to glide between provincial stations is also a Michelin creation, after André arrived in a bad mood from a noisy Paris–Cannes journey in 1929 muttering, 'We ought to put some kind of tyre on the thing.'

Moulinex. After 200 tries, Jean Mantelet perfected his invention in 1932, a simple device for puréeing vegetables. An aluminium bowl with a handle that turned to press food through a strainer, the *mouli* was a sign of liberation from the hard manual labour of the kitchen. The firm Moulin Légumes changed its name to Moulinex in the faster Fifties, introducing the electric coffee-grinder.

Vuitton. Born in 1821, the son of a miller, Louis became a suitcase maker during the Second Empire, thriving in that era of leisured elegance. His initials, printed on what was once leather but is now an ugly brown plastic imitated or pirated the world over, have become a sign of luxury, synonymous with travel, that distraction of the idle rich, equally at home on the steamer *Mauretania* that crossed the Atlantic in five days or the Concorde that crosses in three hours. Though the firm is now part of the Moët-Hennessy-Vuitton combine, the Bureau-trunk created for Leopold Stokowski in 1936 and requiring two porters to transport it is still available to order.

Opinel. Balanced and graceful in the hand, growing sharper with use and thus in the affections of the user, the Opinel knife is a small French treasure. Like Russian dolls, the raw steel blade and wooden handle have the same proportions no matter which size. The No. 6 suits a woman's hand, the No. 8 a man's. It will open everything from oysters to window latches. Designed by Joseph Opinel at the turn of the century there is one in the Museum of Modern Art in New York and in the Victoria & Albert in London, as well as in every French kitchen or garage. It has a rough practicality, a sign in the French mind of *paysan* values; the greying, untempered blade will complement ripe camembert and cut greasy chunks of *saucisson*.

Dim. In 1962 Dimanche created the first seamless stocking. In 1965, advised by the agency Publicis, they changed their name to Dim. In 1968 they introduced tights, the secret sign of the sexual revolution. French men, never confused by the concepts of sex and sexism (since they were only interested in the former), noticed the miniskirts and the legs, but not the tights.

SEB. Cooking under pressure, a method invented in 1680 to 'get the meat out of the bones', was a tamed culinary miracle offered in the Fifties by SEB, the Société d'Emboutissage de Bourgogne. A heavy bar screwed down the lid of the steel tub and a pressure gauge warned if the *boeuf Bourguignon* was about to explode. Allaying the fears of French housewives, the president of the company went around demonstrating with a hammer the sturdiness of the new design. Twenty-five million have since been sold, the design unchanged in 25 years, a sign of its sturdiness, economy and convenience.

Chanel. In the first there was too much jasmine. The second was very tender, rather weak. The third, a mixture of the two, seemed right but wasn't stable. The fourth was quite wrong. Coco Chanel sniffed the fifth perfume mixed by

Ernest Beaux and gave a sign of coquettish pleasure. Rose, jasmine, iris, lily of the valley, hawthorn, daffodil, patchouli, amber and musk. 'It smells like a woman,' she opined, lending it her name and her lucky number five. The bottle with the lozenge top and sober typography is in the Museum of Modern Art. The contents were drunk by Marilyn Monroe in *The Seven Year Itch*.

Paraboot. The French equivalent of the Doc Marten, the Paraboot is the functional shoe on which generations have trodden. Invalided during the First World War, Remy Richard-Ponvert returned to his native Isère, known for shoemaking, with an order to restitch the soles of Army shoes. The French had shoes but the American troops had boots, a sign of their invincibility. With a local chemist, he formulated a supple, resistant rubber. The latex came from the port of Pará (now Belém) in Brazil, and the Paraboot was born, transport of soldiers, firemen, postmen and meatpackers. The Morzine model, unchanged since 1919 and still made by Remy's grandson, has the chunky grace of a jeep and recently rediscovered schoolkid appeal.

Velosolex. Conceived in 1942 by the engineers Goudard and Menesson, the Solex motorised bicycle which, like the Model-T Ford, you could have in any colour you wanted as long as it was black, was a premature miracle of eco-engineering. Mounted above the front wheel, fired by pedalling hard to start, the motor gave 100km of comfortable riding for one litre of Solexine. It was the sign of country priests and provincial professors. By 1964 380,000 had been sold and it was bought by Motobecane, creators in 1949 of the Mobylette, a slightly better-weighted version, in that the engine was mounted below and drove the rear wheel. This was the sign of students and intellectuals. Surprisingly, 2,700 Solexes were still being sold last year, when Yamaha, who now own Motobecane, decided to retire the model.

Lacoste. Rene Lacoste had a pet crocodile that he took for walks in the gardens of his villa. The top tennis player, a champion at Wimbledon and Forest Hills between 1925 and 1928, also wore a crocodile crest on his blazer. Passing through London, he had some sleeveless shirts bearing the crest made in lightweight cotton suitable for the court. They were available only in white until 1951 and everybody wore them, a sign of leisured, affluent lives. In the relaxed Sixties they walked off the court and didn't bother to change. Most people wear them with the top button open; the French lorry driver wears his unbuttoned entirely; the French Minister of Culture wears his with all the buttons done up; the French stylist tears the label off.

Duralex. Wine glasses without stems, sturdy, durable, on every bistro table since 1939, when they were perfected by Saint-Gobain. Scuffed and scarred they serve, hopelessly unbreakable in the affections too, a sign of the futility of change.

Rossignol. The first French ski manufacturer, opening in 1907, was Abel Rossignol. The victory at Squaw Valley in 1962 of Jean Vuarnet (who sold his name to the Skilynx glasses) helped make the marque worldwide. The once expensive, esoteric leisure sport has since expanded; a sign of the homogenisation of society. Whole valleys of Savoie have been turned into ski hotels, and ski lifts lace the snows of the Alps.

Bic. In 1947, Marcel Bich started making ball-point pens, invented by Reynolds in the US in 1880, and made popular by visiting US troops. But these were leaky and unreliable. The clear plastic Bic Biro, a sign of the universal sign of writing, represents a third of the world market of pens. Accessories of a hurried, inconvenient new lifestyle, they were followed by the throwaway lighter and – what else can you sell in the *tabac*? – the throwaway razor.

Perrier. Louis Perrier was a doctor and also the mayor of Nîmes. Just outside the town, at Vergèze, he owned a mineral water bottling company, with rights to a source known since Roman times. He was more interested in devising an electric signalling device for trains, however, and sold the company in 1903 to a young Englishman, the brother of Lord Rothermere. Keeping the logo, he created a new pear-shaped bottle and proceeded to sell the gaseous fine water initally to an élite of thirsty polo players. The company was sold back to the French after the war; nobody then could have foreseen bottled water becoming a centrepiece of the modern English table.

Secrets of the successful Frenchwoman

FRENCH WOMEN DID not win the vote, it was given to them after the war, and even then only because de Gaulle surmised (correctly) that they would vote for him. 'Why else would anyone give somebody the vote?' a Frenchwoman once reasoned to me. So much for emancipation. But then, how can the perfect coquette ever be the perfect equal?

Frédérique is 28 years old. Between mature adults, I put the crucial question to a Frenchwoman: 'Do you prefer to be an equal or a coquette?'

There is barely a moment's hesitation.

'*Rester coquette.*'

She is quite confident. 'I have no problem being an equal. But if you have to struggle for a post, I would be a coquette too. *Il faut profite de ça. Jouer de ça!*'

But there are nuances. 'It's not that you don't want access to the privileges and the power that men have. Or that you can't do the same jobs as men. I think that's not the issue any more. The one doesn't impede the other. It's a bit frivolous, the word *coquette*. Women can work, we can do all the things men do, but we like to be desirable at the same time.

'All my friends around 25 to 30 have had children; they all do interesting work, not jobs reserved for women, and they all enjoy buying clothes and being beautiful.

'It's a post-Seventies thing. Our generation of women live a lot better and are much happier than the generation of the Seventies. We didn't live through the trauma of '68 like the older generation, and so we didn't have to deal with the negative consequences. They worked so hard to be equals that they ended up "out of their shoes". They have a hard time reconciling themselves with the fact that they are women who want to be beautiful, to be desired and to have children. What they did was so enormous that they were a little deranged by it. They feel they still have a score to settle with men. Thanks to them, though, I have the choice to be a woman in a traditional role and to have a job that interests me that was once the province of men.

'It's important. We want to *assure*, but not at any price. Not at the price of rivalry and jealousy – which is what the older generation have paid by competing with men on their own terms – but in another way.

'But it does depend where you are in society. Things have not changed that much. You would still have a lot of difficulty getting respect if you were working with a lot of old-fashioned men. If you were a nurse, you would probably see things in another way. There are still a lot of jobs where women are paid less than men despite the legislation for equal pay.'

The imperfect lover

CONNOISSEURS OF EVERYTHING – including women – fastidious, attentive and charming, do French men make better lovers? I ask some women in a position to compare.

Maria, 28, is Swedish. She works in advertising and has lived in Paris for ten years. She is still enchanted by the art of the *drague*; the French pastime of chatting up.

'I think it makes a good accessory to the day. It's the first sign of spring. You're chatted up everywhere, by shopkeepers, in cafés. It's not really chatting up, its just people passing the time of day. But the serious *drague* – that's horrible; guys who lie and try to impress you. That you get all over the world. What's very French is the little daily *drague de charme*. And even that's not as heavy here as it is in Rome for example. In Paris it's lighter. But I missed it enormously in London. It was as if the days would never end. That's what it's like in Sweden and Germany. And in Japan too. There they only try to chat you up when they're very, very drunk, and it becomes grotesque. In France the way they escort women is very particular. But you can't stay friends with guys; you think you can but after two years or so you find out that you can't. They want to be surrounded by beautiful girls, no matter what the price; even if it makes them unhappy.'

Connie, 27, is German, a translator who has lived in Paris for five years.

'Parisians more easily come up to a girl and just start chatting her up. The only problem is that they think they can always chat you up the same way. Sometimes they try to think of roundabout ways, playing on your vanity or your weaknesses, trying to put you down or make you less sure of yourself. The funniest thing is that they think that is what will interest you. Usually it's not aggressive, it just lacks imagination. But then maybe French girls always want to hear the same things?

'My impression is that the average length of affairs here is two or three months, compared with nearer six months in Germany. Anyway, the average sentimental age of a French guy of 25 is that of a boy of 16. It's impossible for them to get deeper than a certain level. It's just having fun, having the girl as an ornament, a status symbol, a sex toy. The faster you get interested in the guy, the faster he will break off with you, because he feels he's not ready to get involved – until he decides that he has to get married. And then three months later he marries a girl, though she might not correspond to his type at all.

'I know a man who had a number of very heated relationships, always very sexually charged but never lasting very long. He has just turned 30 and has decided he wants to get married. He will probably marry a girl who is nice and with whom he can get along in bed more or less – less rather than more because he will always have girls on the side, but not with whom he would feel able to have children. They wouldn't please his mother.

'Frenchmen are not really at ease with women. They see girls as girls and not as other human beings with whom they can build a friendship. They expect women to be coquettes. They are victims of the idea that women are not equal to men, that you can't have a normal relationship with them.

'And in bed they are no better than men anywhere else! Sometimes you have the impression that they put more effort into getting you into bed than into what they do once they have got you there. The thrill for them is in the chase.'

Caroline, 30, is British, a photographer married to a Frenchman.

'I left London when I was 20 and I lived in the States before I moved here five years ago. Men in London are much more down-to-earth. There's no dream, you aren't given a dream – even if it is a false dream. I never really fell for anyone in London. I met a few people but that was all through work or things like that. I was never swept off my feet in London the way I have been in Paris. I think Parisians are basically more charming. I think they do have a facility for seduction. It may be superficial, but the impression is overwhelming – hotels and champagne and so on – which I don't think you get in England.

'But Frenchmen don't make such good friends. Englishmen are harder to get to know but once you do they make a solid friend. In Paris if it doesn't work out, things go from hot to cold. Here you never see them again. I think it's too hard on their egos.

'The basic crux of it is that the French are a much more romantic nation. Sex is a more important part of the dating game. In England it's not only sex that counts. In England you can have a relationship. That makes Frenchmen lonely and one day they realise it. Then they grow up. There's no laws about it. But I don't think it's true that they make better lovers. I'm sure that's something that a Frenchman made up.'

The Europeans

In a small insurance office, the owner is dreaming of expansion. He imagines the teeming future and its lucrative augmentation of risk. He decides with foresight to change the name of his company. He wants to meet the challenge of Europe. He dreams of an insurance empire . . . Europe United! It sounds like a football team. He settles for Uni-Europe, more modern and, he thinks, English-sounding with its catchy abbreviation. His business is growing and he is looking forward to 1992, the date mooted for a great liberalisation of trade within the Common Market.

He is not alone in his anticipation of the Promised Market. No French politician, whether extremist or moderate, of the Left or the Right, would dare to come out against the idea of a united or somehow allied Europe. It is the touchstone of the modern outlook. It would be like being against credit cards. Such a universal precept, something that everybody blindly and wholly agrees with, deserves scrutiny.

What do they mean by Europe and why do they think that it would be a good thing?

Sold alongside the schoolbooks and satchels in department stores there is a map of Europe made of coloured plastic, like the maps of the British Isles that British children trace around for geography classes. What is at the centre of this map?

This is the first lesson in French geography.

The answer is easy: France.

The French see themselves quite naturally at the heart of Europe. Their borders touch on all sides of the European psyche: Iberian, Latin, Saxon, Flemish, Breton. Historically, these borders are unfixed and vulnerable. Squabbles over them have engulfed Europe in war. After the last, the Second World War, it was agreed that something had to be done about this troublesome, different Europe that surrounds France.

From the French point of view, it needed to be harmonised; that is, brought into line with itself – with France naturally at the centre.

It says something of their indefatigable pride, bordering on folly, of the headstrong vainglory that propels them, that amidst all the post-war rubble and recriminations, the French still saw themselves as the dominant élite of Europe. From Charlemagne to Bonaparte, the French have dreamed of extending their frontiers to encompass Europe. Clearly, to impose their rule by force was not in the power of a nation beaten and demoralised twice this century by the same neighbour, but what they lacked in military machinery the French have always made up for in *politesse*. Until the First World War, the language of international diplomacy was French and peace negotiations traditionally still take place in chateaux outside Paris. And so, they set out to achieve their European Solution by means of modern economic diplomacy.

Not for a second time were they going to put themselves in hock to a vanquished nation, as happened after the First World War when inflation made German reparations valueless. The French, even more than the Poles, have been the victims of Europe. The most populous European nation at the time of the Revolution, they have seen their political and economic power decline steadily.

Yet they have been hedged in and preserved by a tangle of regulations and a fortress of trade controls. They practise cultural imperialism abroad and cultural protectionism at home. Obsessed with the erosion of their glory, they institute desperate measures to preserve their identity. In the Seventies they outlawed shop names in English. Every Tuesday, the members of the Académie Français (set up by the Cardinal de Richelieu) gather to compile a French lexicon. But after centuries of effort, they are still only on the letter 'F'. They have been distracted from their noble task by the bother of finding French equivalents for the English words that French kids adopt with such ease.

There are new words every week, like 'compact disc' (*disque audio-musicale*) and 'skateboard' (*planche a roulette*). Their labour accomplished, the academicians send the translation to the Minister of Culture who sends memos to every radio and TV personality advising them not to use, say, the word 'Walkman' any more, but instead, '*le mot typique et approuvé par l'Académie Français – balladeur*'. Other recent additions to the language of Ronsard include *palmarès* (hit parade), *billard électrique* (flipper), *remue-méninges* (brainstorm), *numérique* (digital). And the *video-clip*, the most significant French contribution to international culture this decade, has also now ceased to exist. The French artists and designers at work making pop videos, admired and hired in London and Los Angeles, found themselves overnight the authors of *bandes vidéo-promotionelles*. In the abbreviated world of the *clip*, it just wasn't the same.

The French see Europe as a great republican franchise, and the business challenge of the age. From behind the tariff walls that have protected them for so long, they are preparing to launch a commercial offensive on 320 million consumers. They imagine a tariff wall large enough to envelop the whole of Europe. And within, a self-sustaining European economy.

If this goes against all the fashionable tenets of laissez-faire government and is sure in any case to be thwarted by bureaucracy – as the complacent British would like to think – the readiness of the French to look forwards, to dream and build on a grand scale, is not to be underestimated. It is the legacy of the republican project. Never forced to consider the future as anything but a continuation of the present, the British trust in old ways, old pals, old schools, and old families. Yet, if they undertake the correct plan, the French might just succeed.

For the supposedly anarchic French do not hanker for the frisson of a society motivated by competition, a life of selfish, grasping, material satisfaction in the market-place jungle, where everyone is your enemy, waiting to do your job for less; a pyramid of alienation, against which (although supposedly a nation of individuals) they have opposed the concept of brotherhood, of fraternity.

Gallic individuality is a well-known cliché. Everyone who has studied them from Britain thinks that the French are incurably individualist, though I think this only reflects the level of conformity among the British. The French are far less individual than supposed. They are greedy and vain, yes, vying angrily to be first away from the traffic lights; no concept of queuing, extremely reluctant to pay taxes (though this last is mainly a class problem, since it was the peasant who bore the brunt of taxation while the aristocrat was able to arrange his affairs). But apart from these spontaneous instances of selfishness, the French are possessed of social, communal and fraternal considerations, not least those embodied in the Napoleonic Code, which seeks merely to arbitrate between devious people inclined to cheat one another.

Travelling on a sure ticket of British parochialism, my own representative in the Euro-parliament is a Labour man who, before the referendum in 1968 that brought Britain into the Common Market, published a pamphlet proclaiming that the best interests of British working people were, of course, their own. He urged us to stay out but promptly became a Euro MP because he feels that as long as we are in it, we should get the best we can from it. Such are the exigencies of storefront politics. But I do sympathise. In France, much of the support for the *Front National* comes with dismal inevitability from disgruntled Communists. Similarly, among the British, there is a seam of narrow self-interest – tapped to great success by Tory policy in the Eighties – that is manifest not least in the popular xenophobia of the tabloid press. Insular, smug and claustrophobic, Britain languishes, haughtily ignorant of her stately decline into a tinpot democracy under American patronage in which the phones no longer work.

De Gaulle was reluctant to admit Britain to the Common Market because he felt she was too closely allied to the US. Anyway, one strong power at the centre of Europe was enough. Under the charter of the Fifth Republic, foreign policy and defence were portfolios reserved for the President. The newly instated President Mitterrand soon faced the fact of one of the Community being invaded by a foreign power. France sent prompt messages of support to Britain over the Falklands, while Ronald Reagan dithered between conflicting US interests. With disputable far-flung territories of their own, the French could easily sympathise with the UK, and saw the chance to demonstrate European faith.

This faith was shattered, however, by a French device called an Exocet, a potent missile which blew a large hole in a British warship. Had the Argentinians been able to get and launch enough of them, the course of the war might have changed. Thus British and French spies scurried around Paris trying to buy up, or pretending to sell to the Argentinians, every spare Exocet.

Despite this little mishap – and the plight abhorrent to the French Left of Republicans (Irish) dying in British jails – the present heads of the two states are known to find it easy to forget their differences at international conferences. Something to do with Gallic charm and British phlegm. But like Jean Monnet, the planner of Europe, or de Gaulle, its builder, Mitterrand has a difficult time imparting his own Eurovisions to the British, those reluctant Europeans. They face a jolt to the national psyche when and if the Channel tunnel is completed, a breach of the national hymen that has been so primly fenced and tended all these centuries. Being physically penetrated by foreign trains will probably be painful to the nation at first. Finding it difficult to reach a satisfactory climax, Britain should in time become accustomed to, and even come to enjoy, the agreeable sensation.

Ann

WE ARRANGED TO meet in the café on the Left Bank where, she tells me, Paloma Picasso comes for breakfast.

'She sits under that painting over there and drinks hot chocolate. You can recognise her by the eyebrows. You can't tell how old she is.'

I have ordered the same hot chocolate, but it is too sweet to drink and the swirling surface reflects the ornate mouldings on the ceiling, greasy with a hideous scum. The painting under which Pablo's daughter sits has faded from the smoke. The bright red roses daubed by a painter who couldn't pay his bill have turned brown and queasy. Picasso was smarter. He passed dud cheques knowing his signature alone was worth more. Sometimes I feel there is an underside to the charm of Paris: green mould under the *tarte Tatin*; dark brown stains under the sheets.

Maybe our meeting wasn't such a good idea.

Ann frets about growing old, wondering about the quality of her skin and what she might have missed. The first thing she notices now about other women is how old they are.

She looks at me to see if I have noticed her remark. I must have smiled. In the mornings – when she used not to care – she used to tease me about the younger man.

'It's all right for you,' she jokes now, 'you're still young.'

Despite my age, I feel as if my shoelaces have been tied together. It's a familiar uncertainty.

I haven't seen Ann for seven years. I walked by the house where we both lived in separate rooms and found it had become tidy and acquired a strong iron gate. The creeping vines had been clipped around the newly painted shutters. Embedded in the post next to the gate was that new French article of electronic security, a Digicode.

Patrice was still living there. His daughter now slept in my old room. When his father died, he took over the family business, a chain of pharmacies, and married a woman his mother liked. 'Did you know that the French consume more tranquillisers than any other nation?' he asked. Since the spate of terrorist bombs began exploding in Paris that year, his sales had gone up. 'I think the French, all of them, whoever they are, get on each other's nerves.'

He told me that Ann had left with Alain and gave me a number. It was an old number, and since then the phone company had prefixed all Paris numbers with a 4. Maybe I could add a 4 and try it.

The last time Patrice had seen the two of them was in 1981 after the elections. The Left which they had argued and wrangled over, marched beside and betrayed like a dull, steady spouse, had won. 'We didn't think so then but it was a hollow victory,' said Patrice. 'Giscard had already brought the social clock forward in matters like the age of majority and the right to an abortion and there was nothing much for the Socialists to do apart from abolish the death penalty and nationalise everything.'

Still, Alain had called and they went out together to celebrate. Patrice came alone because the baby was only four months old.

His eyes brightened as he described their night together. The streets were filled with a spontaneous carnival. It was during the pirate radio boom. Some of the pirate stations just set up their record players and microphones at one end of the counter in the local bar. There was music everywhere, all kinds of music, and it seemed that everybody was drunk for days, intoxicated with the prospect of change and radiant from a flitting glimpse of liberty and justice. It meant different things to all of them. But in the excited crowds Patrice found he could no longer recognise himself.

'It was typically Parisian. The sort of popular celebration that Parisians traditionally indulge in, part of the cycle of repression and release. After-wards, the Left tried as usual to institutionalise this spirit. Jack Lang inaugurated the Fête de la Musique and the rest. But it doesn't work. It's just a hellish din all night and everybody is too bad-tempered and exhausted the next day to get anything done.'

Ann told me later that the day after, Patrice took a suitcase full of cash to Geneva to avoid the currency export restrictions and capital tax that came down like a curfew on the traditional liberties of wealth.

'He read Bernard Henri-Levy and the *nouveaux philosophes* in the late Seventies and was relieved to find intellectual support at last for his bourgeois selfishness. He had been ashamed to obey his basic impulses without guilt. A Jew trying to be a Catholic. That's France. Did you meet his wife? *Vraiment.*'

She pronounces evenly the word 'Jew'. 'I have nothing against the Jews,' she adds, a typical conversational rider as the wave of anti-Jewish terror continues.

'Did you hear the joke Coluche told on Canal Plus? Do you know why God invented Catholics? So the *grossistes* would have individual clients . . . At least Coluche makes a point of offending everybody.'

I tell her that the innate anti-Semitism of the French always startles me. They know all the best Jewish jokes. Sometimes, their contempt surfaces unbidden, a polite monster. Prime Minister Raymond Barre once described as 'innocent' the non-Jewish victims of a bomb outside a synagogue.

'It's the Catholics who have all the problems,' Ann shrugs.

Behind the wrinkles, her rancour has not subsided. Her black hair no longer glistens. It has become matt and sombre, but the lines are not as serious as she thinks; at least her knees are still smooth. The first thing I recognised about her was the walk: in flat shoes and a loose skirt, it was still brisk and tight.

'The last time Patrice went on a demonstration you know what it was for? It was in '84 at Versailles of all places when hundreds of thousands of bourgeois like him stopped the closure of private schools.'

Ann got her *bac* and took evening classes in law, where she met a man, a metal worker from Rennes who was being sponsored by his union. They married and she gave up the classes.

'I was a fool to do that really but I thought it would help him. Instead, it all became too much.'

They lived in an HLM, the French equivalent of a British council flat, sometimes equally cramped and dingy, but theirs was new, large and bright.

'It was really the suburban life, but that wasn't the problem. I didn't mind that. I wanted to have children and he wasn't ready. Anyway, we were divorced two years ago. Alain was a big help then. He persuaded me to go to a therapist.'

She reflects for a moment. 'I've built my life around nothing much.'

'It's OK,' I mutter.

'I thought it would be good for me to get out. That's why I agreed to come and meet you. I don't go out much any more. What for? I feel kind of *désengagé*. Even last year, in the middle of the rally for SOS Racisme in the Concorde, I was surrounded by all these people, and I realised I didn't care about any of them.'

She lights a Marlboro, lifting her head to blow the smoke sideways, and smiles at herself, the former Red Cross worker and feminist.

'Everybody was there, even Alain. It was important, yes, now that the Front have deputies at the Assembly, but it's not the same. Something like the Restos du Cœur that Coluche started. You know, he started buying food and distributing it to all the tramps in the street. But he's so cynical. He says he did it rather than pay taxes. So now it's a big charity and there are more donations than there are tramps.'

She sips at a glass of Badoit.

'It's just not the same feeling. I think you must help yourself first, before you can help others. I realised from the therapy that I had been negating myself. Maybe that's why I don't really like crowds any more.'

'What happened to Alain?' I ask. In the recession disco of the Eighties, I can't imagine the fate of someone like him, an ascetic Trot, other than to be enfolded in the spine of an old paperback of social analysis.

'He went to the East and there he was seduced by Oriental mysticism a decade too late,' laughs Ann. 'Well, he fell in love with a Chinese woman and now he organises tours there. He was always pragmatic, you know. He's out there at the moment. You should have seen him dancing last year at SOS Racisme. His glasses fell off and broke, you remember, the oval ones? *Tant pis*, he said. I think he took it as a sign.'

Tonight is 14 July and we have planned to go to the Bastille. I didn't know about her new aversion to crowds. 'It's OK,' she says. 'I don't mind. If you've never been we should go.'

As we approach from the rue de Rivoli I hear what sounds like machine-gun fire, firecrackers exploding in rapid succession. The street is filled with smoke, obscuring the crowd, though from the noise I sense that the whole of the wide *place* is filled with people. Above the smoke I can see the lights of a Ferris wheel set up in the car-park.

As we come into the Place de la Bastille, a firecracker explodes suddenly beside us, jumps and explodes again a few feet away. The crowd parts and dodges. There are laughs and screams. People light the twists of blue paper and toss them nonchalantly into the crowds, their expressions full of mischief. They toss them from café terraces and passing cars. The object is to frighten others and be frightened too.

Africans in long robes who might have just arrived from a bazaar in Senegal stand beside paper carrier bags full of firecrackers strung together in little bundles, which they sell to passers-by. They seem to understand the requirements of the celebration but do not share in the emotion. Their eyes are red and heavy-lidded; they are unconcerned at the danger of a stray spark striking their wares.

There is a foreign, proto-revolutionary fervour in the air. There is a smell of anarchy, blue and heady, in the smoke from the fireworks. It is a potent charade of danger and excitement. The whole city has joined in a gleeful mêlée, enacting a war with itself.

'Paris really is a Latin city,' says Ann.

Her observation is like a charm to preserve us from danger. I cannot help starting from the firecrackers that explode unpredictably around us.

She is saying that I must dispel the danger from my mind, like someone walking on coals. She is reminding me of the sensuality of danger. My fear will, if I allow it, touch itself off like a firecracker. In the flash of the firecrackers, I can see her excited face.

'Tell me about your ex-husband.'

'He was from a family from the north. His uncles were all Communists. They plotted to gain control of the *mairie*. His name was Jean.'

I picture him with a trim moustache, wearing a leather blouson, at the wheel of a Renault.

'When the Socialists made their big U-turn in '83 and closed down the steel works, just abandoning all those workers, I think he felt betrayed. He used to sulk and go to the bar just to argue. He stopped studying after that. I haven't seen him in a while.'

We walk through the people who are drunk and laughing, towards the centre of the *place*. The firecrackers seemed to have been exploding mainly at the edges of the crowd. Ann says this is typical of anarchists. We ride the bumper cars and as we stumble off, I say that there is something I have always wanted to ask.

She stops.

'Will you have dinner with me?'

Giggling, she entwines her arm with mine.

'You don't understand French women,' is all she says, leading me away.

Bastille day

ON 14 JULY 1789, at half-past five in the afternoon, the people of Paris, seized by revolutionary fervour, began their assault on the Bastille. Rapidly overcoming the few guards left in the old prison where the man in the iron mask was reputed to have been chained, they set about demolishing the walls and giving rise to the founding myth of the French Republic. Except that it wasn't the people who demolished the walls. The causes and effects of the French Revolution have since been much discussed, but little has been said of the shadowy figures who scurried out of the nearby Faubourg St-Antoine carrying hammers and pick-axes, or of the role played that fateful day by a certain Pierre-François Palloy.

The actual business of dismantling the Bastille – a job for professionals, since even the hungriest, most frenzied mob would have a hard time dealing with three feet of stone – was carried out by a real-estate developer with an eye for a prime property. Palloy, an *entrepreneur des bâtiments*, had in fact already submitted to the King a scheme for the demolition of the little-used fort at the Porte St-Antoine. He had plans drawn up by the architect Corbet for a new palace and gardens. He would be able to part-finance the operation by re-using the old stones of the Bastille. All he needed was the King's approval, but the papers sat unattended on the desk of the ineffectual Louis XVI, who had other things on his mind.

At a meeting in the *église* St-Antoine of the Rosicrucian circle of which he was a 'sovereign prince', the disgruntled Palloy heard talk of the growing complaints of the people of Paris. There were even rumours of a plot to storm the Bastille. Losing no time, Palloy returned to his office. Go to the prison tomorrow with some men, he told his chief mason, and if anything happens, get in there and set to. It was the thirteenth of July.

As night fell the following day after the onslaught of the mob, shadowy figures in the hire of Palloy began swinging at the stones of the prison. Below, the master masons began hurriedly to organise the *chantier*. Notes from Palloy discovered later tell of the difficulties. 'It will be necessary to equip seven hundred men, and I don't have enough picks and shovels.'

But Palloy never saw his great scheme through. Carried away with events, he styled himself a hero of the Revolution. He renamed himself Patriot Palloy and from the stones that he recuperated he had miniature Bastilles carved for sale as mementoes in the provinces. From the proceeds he flooded Paris with inflammatory tracts. He joined in the arrest of Louis XVI, got thrown in jail, was left there to rot and died penniless under Louis Philippe.

Pyramitterrand

USUALLY, THE WEATHER has brightened by May but this year it is uncertain and today it has turned violently grey and cold. A sudden, whirling snow is falling over the Pyramid.

Photographers huddle under their coats and camera crews try to shield their lenses, as the wind snatches the wet flakes and whips them in the faces of the officials gathered in the *cour Napoléon*.

In this courtyard in front of the palace of the Louvre – once the greatest house of France, but abandoned after the construction of Versailles and in disrepair by the time of the Revolution – a podium has been mounted on a scaffold overlooking a sea of yellow mud.

In the centre of this sea, rising with obscure, luminous mystery, is a huge glass pyramid. Enfolded in the neo-classical embrace of the wings of the old palace, it shimmers in the rain, a seductive mirage.

Lifting their chins, despite the driving rain, to give the occasion its proper dignity, the officials on the podium are forced to grab at the collars of their raincoats. They are here for the inauguration of the Grand Louvre, the refurbished museum which, it is intended, will become the greatest art attraction in the world. At the front of the group, his face wet but transfixed, seemingly oblivious to the blustering elements, is a short man in a dark rain-coat.

As he prepares to perform the ceremonial opening, the President of France gazes sphinx-like at the enigmatic pyramid he has created.

The pyramid is four storeys high, made of a special glass, clear as crystal and without the usual green tint of industrial-grade glass, for a green tint, caused by the presence of iron oxides, would not capture the honey shades of the surrounding stone. The glass had to be of industrial strength but of artisan quality, as strong as it was pure; but glass so pure would transmit high levels of heat, and so a new method of homogenisation had to be used. The 793 lozenges and triangles had to be precisely cut and pieced to a tolerance of one centimetre over the 30-metre high surface, forming a translucent skin over the 95-ton steel frame. As well as providing a central access point to the old and confusing museum that contains over 250,000 works of art, the purpose of the pyramid is to diffuse light down into the cavernous new basement galleries, which are lined in a new kind of concrete with the pale sheen of ivory.

Surveying his design from behind round glasses, his small eyebrows arched in satisfaction, the Chinese-born architect Ieoh Ming Pei pronounces himself pleased with the work. The pyramid is a kind of living organism, he feels, that reflects the constantly changing moods of the Parisian sky. The greatest challenge of his career, more important to this naturalised American than the extension of the National Gallery in Washington, it was a design problem that involved the history of a nation, touching the social, political and economic life of that nation. And so the fantastical pyramid is also a symbol.

For the President, whose writings consist of elegant, unrevealing replies to his critics and reflections on literature, painting and nature, the transformaton of the Louvre, with only three million visitors a year compared to the Pompidou Centre's seven million, into the premier cultural attraction in this city of culture was a paramount project. At almost the same moment as he gave his autocratic accord to Pei's design, his rival, the mayor of Paris, Jacques Chirac, was signing a permit to construct, on a site one-fifth the size of Paris, a mere 32km to the east, the new EuroDisneyland.

Whether in competition with Disney's 'imagineers' or in homage to Bonaparte's celebrated military foray of discovery in Egypt, the President chose to leave as his *imprimatur* on the city an inscrutable heiroglyphic. Commissioned by him in 1983 without consulting French architectural bodies or even the governors of the museum, Pei's design beautifully surmounts the golden

proportions of the old palace. I try to imagine the scene in the Elysée as the
model was unveiled. Did it light up, a beacon for tourists from the next
century? It forms the vanishing point of a kind of flying saucer runway that
extends through the Egyptian obelisk of the Concorde, up the Champs-
Elysées, through the Arc de Triomphe and out through a new arch, twice as
big, at La Défense. Based on ancient geometric truth, executed with awesome
faith in the future, my most fervent wish, if I were the President, would be to
have my mortal remains preserved beneath it.

At once lucid and opaque, the pyramid is for the French symbolic of the
character of the President himself. And today, peering into the murky glass
where the President's features are reflected, calm and unperturbed against the
darkening sky, the press tries to interpret the mood of the republican
monarch – especially in connection with his undecided or as yet unannounced
candidature for a second term of office. His jaw is set in a characteristic half-
grin, the clenched smile of a cunning opponent who divulges no more than he
needs.

He guards his reasoning to himself, and is careful not to give himself away,
rewriting his answers to even the most casual of interviews in women's journals
lest they arm his opponents. By Tories, Social Democrats and Communists
alike, he is regarded abroad as one of Europe's foremost politicians. The
French, for their part, admire style but will only forgive passion. He wonders if
he didn't master his style too well, forgetting the passion that took him into
politics; diverted by his own cunning. It took all of this cunning to become the
first Socialist president of the Fifth Republic. If, as his opponents on the Left
accuse him of doing, he betrayed the workers in the steelyards of Lorraine in
'83 when hopes of reflating the economy went flat and he had to condone a
quasi-monetarist policy, cancelling support for unprofitable industries; if he had
to relinquish his dream of affluent, abundant social justice, well, at least he has
left his mark here in the courtyard of kings and emperors.

Not just providing a new point of entry, the pyramid stands between the
two long galleries added by Louis Napoleon to join a restored Louvre to the
Palace of the Tuileries. It is a moment given to him by history and he is
savouring it, notwithstanding the elements that circle and howl reminding
him of the vanity and the sacrifices – the broken Right whose shards threaten
to rip the fabric of French society, and the embittered unemployed.

Although the full reconstruction of the palace is not finished and the public won't be admitted until the autumn, the major elements are in place and the pyramid can be viewed. If nothing else, it represents presidential achievement, an important statement in the run-up to the next election. It says something too of his temerity in restructuring the sullied, creaking, archaic institutions of France.

He is a mercurial and cautious fellow who now regrets not having gone further, faster in his aim of creating a modern social democracy. He has lost a lot of time playing his shrewd political game. He was one of the handful of politicians who rejected de Gaulle's new Republic in '58. Judging his motives occult, political commentators were suspicious. They looked for a rationale in his strategy and found only the pragmatic, considered gestures of the manager and diplomat. Estranged from de Gaulle's centre-right, he had no option but to try to build a power base for himself on the fragmented Left. People attribute to him too much cunning and too much patience, and fail to acknowledge the enormity of what he achieved. It took 25 years and all his powers to organise finally a successful *cartel des gauches*. First the Communist party cautiously agreed not to field a candidate alongside him in the presidential elections of '65, and then in 1971 agreed to a historic joint programme.

Fifty years earlier, with the aim of creating a loyal, ruthless core, Lenin had presented the French Socialist Party with his terms for membership of the Third International. The pro-Communists carried the day by three to one, gaining control of the party apparatus and daily paper *L'Humanité*. Henceforth, the Communists would trumpet themselves as the party of revolution, with emotive appeal to French national history. The first targets of this new party were not the bourgeoisie but the Socialists, those insipid fellows in Parliament who remained loyal to what was now the party of reform.

If Mitterrand was a reformist, so be it. He did not need to climb to the top of the revolutionary house to be moved by the cries of the people. He was nostalgic about France, but impatient with it too. He was born in 1916, the son of a Catholic station master with a son who went into the military and another into business via the *Ecole Polytechnique*, while François came to Paris to study law. It was the time of the Popular Front, the two year alliance of Communists, Socialists and Radicals that won power in '36 after an attempted coup by ill-sorted monarchist mobs and Fascist leagues such as the venomous *Action Française*. In the midst of the great Depression, the appeal to 'bread, peace and liberty' did not immediately rouse the political spirits of the young student. He was late also to officially join the Resistance, but quick to become a junior minister in de Gaulle's post-Liberation government. Over the next decade, he was a minister eleven times in what the General called the 'shadow theatres' of the Fourth Republic. To survive on their treacherous stages, it was necessary to acquire habits of subterfuge and bluff, to juggle principle with expediency. *'L'Algérie, c'est la France,'* he once declared, and his tenure at the Ministry of Justice coincided with vicious anti-terrorist measures against the FLN. Later, his tenure as President coincided with the sabotage of the *Rainbow Warrior*, the Greenpeace boat protesting against French nuclear testing in the Pacific, in which a photographer on board was killed. Mitterrand did not become a Socialist himself until '71, and ten years later became President riding on the crest of a social wave that had been rolling since 1968.

The chief nemesis of any king is always his finance minister. Two centuries ago it was to secure the resignation of Necker that the mob gathered at the Bastille. The price of bread was spiralling and Louis XVI's Minister of Finance was unable to stop it.

Overlooking the President in his moment of glory from the windows of offices in the Louvre, the current finance minister is enjoying the irritating effect of a measure worse than any austerity budget. After the Right regained a parliamentary majority in '86, Mitterrand was forced to 'cohabit' with a new finance minister, Edouard Balladur, who refused to vacate offices in a wing of the Louvre, thereby delaying the completion of a project which, along with columnists in *Le Figaro* and the owners of small, coiffured dogs (representing a sizeable lobby in France), he found to be a lunatic affront to the taste and sanctity of the nation.

Declaring himself dissatisfied with new offices not far away in an urban redevelopment zone, he complained about the noise of the construction work and had a soundproof wall built. But the wall was ineffective and so work had to go on only at night. Public opinion, which was at first hostile to the pyramid, turned against him. Loving an aesthetic argument almost as much as a political bunfight, the public didn't stop enjoying themselves. Though he didn't care for the pyramid either, the new Minister of Culture, not wishing to appear a philistine and seeing no sense anyway in going against public opinion, tried to persuade Balladur to back down. Having squandered some 30 million francs on these various caprices, he finally agreed to move, but still wouldn't go to the new offices, saying he would find somewhere more central.

The monumentality of kings

EMPERORS, KINGS AND politicians, like the merest of us, want to leave a mark. The public funds and projects of a modern state allow plenty of scope for this, from the damning of rivers to the planting of flags on the moon. For the predecessors of Mitterrand, urban renewal was a priority – revitalising the quaint but often sordid city that was post-war Paris. As late as 1963, crowded shanty towns housing 10,000 Italians and 15,000 Arabs squatted on the fringes of the city at Nanterre and Bobigny. Skyscraper suburbs like La Défense were planned to alleviate this shameful congestion.

It was de Gaulle who decreed the uprooting of Les Halles, the old food market that Zola called the guts of Paris, where the beau monde supped onion soup at the Pied de Cochon alongside burly traders who handled one-fifth of the nation's produce. It left a gaping abscess in the centre of the city. His successor, Georges Pompidou, agreed to the construction of a conference centre – that panacea for urban delapidation – with the inevitable offices, shops and underground parking. It was to have been a glass edifice to the power of commerce like the tower at Montparnasse across the Seine. Victor Baltard's wrought-iron market building was retired to a hill in the suburbs and the market itself moved to a new industrial hangar.

In the meantime, between the gaping hole of Les Halles and the old district of the Marais that Malraux, as part of his job of cultural refurbishment, had rescued after the war from its slum landlords, a new arts centre was planned. It was envisaged as a library, museum and centre of artistic activity, a lively modern cathedral of the arts after the creed of Malraux. A selection committee was appointed and from 681 entries chose a design by the Italian-British partnership of Richard Rogers and Renzo Piano. It was not what Pompidou, a banker fond of art, had anticipated. The new building resembled an oil refinery or the brightly-coloured toy of an overendowed child. It was self-explanatory, its visible structure appealing to modern French Marxists and older French Rationalists alike. It was as if it had turned inside-out to attract the public who, lurking in the narrow 17th-century streets alongside, looked on as it grew with suspicion that turned to awe and finally pride. With exposed green water pipes, yellow electricity conduits and blue air-conditioning ducts – as on architects' plans – the building has all the qualities of French engineering folly. Like the 2CV or the Eiffel Tower (too expensive to dismantle after the Paris Expo) which the Pompidou centre reflects with its metal exoskeleton, it is both ugly and beautiful, serene and ghastly, but now ubiquitous.

I saw it rise – a bright, bold monolith above the dingy streets – and leapt to its defence, enthusing over the diagonal exterior staircase and the Kandinsky paintings inside. It represented a monumental public victory of the future over the past that seemed impossible, almost irrelevant to Britain. I think it got built because no one knew quite how to efface its pop confidence. Once it was conceived, no one knew quite how to stop it; like the Revolution, it was carried away by the delirium of ideals. Colourful and unabashed, it defied the preservationists, the angry councillors and the qualms of the new President Giscard by its very audacity. It affirmed the democratic warmth of plastic and the sexiness of steel tubing. It was all that the Seventies should have been.

As the Seventies closed, it became a natural magnet for back-packers, runaways, oversensitive suburbanites, abused children, clowns, casualties, squatters, tramps, pickpockets and hash-peddlers. They fill the wide plaza behind the building with a modern medieval circus, from acid-racked minstrels sworn to the memory of Jimi Hendrix to fire-breathers and religious fanatics in orange robes. And with them each year come over seven million other visitors.

The Pompidou centre was well under way by the time the more progressive Giscard came to power. Aware of the arguments of ecologists and the women's groups – he boasted ministries with more female members than any other in Europe – he cancelled the conference centre planned for Les Halles and gave the project over to the new mayor of Paris, Jacques Chirac.

A new Métro intersection was opened and the hole above it was turned into an inverted atrium, lined with a waterfall of glass allowing the light down into the underground shopping centre. Above, a garden was created along the lines of the Tuileries. And so the refurbishment of central Paris was complete. What opportunities for a republican monarch of the Left to leave his mark? One who knew that the struggle for the soul of a nation of aesthetes is as much cultural as political.

Mitterrand commissioned the best-known contemporary French designers to redecorate the private apartment at the Elysée, to which he moved in '83 after flooding from the Seine forced him to leave his house opposite the cathedral of Notre-Dame. Each item of furnishing was an original by Andrée Putnam and other contemporary French designers. Philippe Starck created an all-black television room. Next to the former bathroom of the Empress Josephine and the gold-panelled room where de Gaulle made his appeals, there are now modish three-legged chairs and matt-black desk lamps. It was a statement but not a public one.

He announced soon after his election in '81 that he would evict the ministries from the palace of the Louvre to provide more space for the collections piled in the basement or cramped together in the galleries. The pyramid he proposed seemed at first too absurd to ever come about. A folly of the first rush of power that would be quietly cancelled. This was in addition to rehousing the Impressionist collection from the Jeu de Paume, the two-storey wrought-iron house at the corner of the Tuileries which for its light, its geniality, its harmony with its subject was, despite the ever growing queues, everybody's favourite museum.

The Impressionist collection was transferred to the new Musée D'Orsay, the museum of the 19th century converted from the old railway terminal across the Seine. Seeking fashionably to group its treasures by fresh cross-reference as well as by traditional schools and chronologies, it is the favoured museum of Postmodernists thrilled by the death of interpretation; the perfect environment for basking in a barrage of conflicting information and experiencing the high anxiety of taste that comes from obsessively switching channels and being just around the corner from another senseless car-bomb. It amuses me no end that the museum of the European century has black trellises dividing the space like those in Japanese houses. Was it by coincidence that the design brief entailed stylistic obeisance to the mighty Yen just as a Japanese insurance company bought Van Gogh's flowers for a record sum?

There was one other vacant site that the Socialists could not ignore: an old railway station at the Bastille. An opera house was proposed – a belated reply to Louis Napoleon's cultural centrepiece of the *ville lumière* – commissioned from a Canadian architect after an international competition. The building with its grand hall and smaller experimental stage is a cathedral in the tradition of André Malraux's provincial *Maisons de la Culture*; though Malraux thought music a secondary art and once said as much to Stravinsky. It was encouraged by the composer Pierre Boulez, supported by Minister of Culture Jack Lang and approved by the President. Nominated Prime Minister in 1986, Jacques Chirac tried to reverse it. The right-wing moderate, a middlebrow who felt more comfortable with a management study and preferred his opera light, was determined to halt this blatant piece of monumentalism on the part of his adversary. And in his own domain of Paris too! But it was too late. The international musical reputation of Paris was now at stake. The Opera at the Bastille would go ahead.

Delayed by union problems it was half ready for the Bicentennary. Nobody can decide whether the programme should be radical or reformist. Nobody is even sure why it's there, next to the site of the old Bastille jail, a fortress this time of culture.

The house that Jack built

'YEAH JACK! JACK *revient!*'

Jack doesn't even turn around, but turns his head slightly and smiles out of the corner of his mouth. The two teenage girls suddenly feel embarrassed. Here they are in the Place des Vosges, which just happens to be where he lives, up in Paris on a Saturday excursion and they saw Jack Lang! He's really tall, with thick black hair, they tell their friends. And handsome, they confirm.

'*Jack revient!*'

Jack Lang used to be the Minister of Culture. One of his first acts was to change the rating of the movie *Christiane F* which told the true story of a suburban German girl who became a drug addict and prostitute at 13. He lowered the category, overruling the censor, because he wanted 13-year-olds to be able to go and see it, accompanied by their parents, and talk about the problems of drugs afterwards. Did they go? Did they talk?

Something happened. In the *lycées* of the big cities now, *Moi, Christiane F,* the autobiography on which the film was based, has become cult reading. Mention Rimbaud, who explored the romance of fatalism long before it sprouted in urban tower blocks, and they think you're talking about the American movie muscle man.

That was Jack Lang's doing.

'Jack revient!'

Jack lived in the same boring, stultifying officially sanctified tourist-trap as the rest of them. But the difference was that he seemed to know it. He seemed to know that the endless TV diet of *variété* broadcast from a spangled, fur-lined palace of kitsch in the Champs-Elysées was as indigestible, as gross as any five-course meal in a five-star restaurant in Lyon.

His name was spelt Jack the Anglo-Saxon way because he was born on the day Britain declared war on Germany and his parents were proud to endorse the *entente cordiale*. While studying law at Nancy, he founded a festival of experimental theatre. Joining the Socialist Party, he became close to Mitterrand, and helped stage his campaign appearances. The new president was a cultured man pledged to doubling the arts budget. Lang was well qualified to become his legislator.

'The French have crossed the frontier between darkness and light!' he proclaimed.

This was one of the first things that Jack told the new Parliament in 1981. Even the French thought he was going a bit far.

He was in his early forties, and a little elated at the time. But he was serious. He spoke ominously about the 'cultural imperialism' of the US, hinting at the need for French cultural protectionism – a kind of nationalisation of the arts. But Lang had little interest in protecting a staid, institutional French culture. He had the evangelical fervour of Malraux, but he was a modern community priest. In keeping with the ethos of the post-68-ers, culture was to be a group activity. The individual artist had only bourgeois value. Among small groups throughout the country, he avowed the aim of letting a 'creative disorder' reign.

The former manager of the Théâtre de Chaillot in Paris dispensed a doubled arts budget with an infectious vigour. It was a kind of nationwide 'happening'. The purpose appeared to be to get the whole country to express itself, the way the technocrats of the Fifties wanted to encourage the modernisation of industry. Broadening the church of culture, he created a museum of fashion in the Louvre, a school of photography at Arles, a gastronomic institute at Lyon, a museum of *bandes dessinées* and a school for circus performers.

He inaugurated the *Fête de la Musique*, encouraging musicians of all kinds to go into the streets and perform. Once a year, for a whole night, creative cacophony fills the streets. There are chamber quartets and rock groups at every crossroads.

What about the groupies, Jack?

'They do exist.' He sounds embarrassed but not surprised. 'I get some letters.'

He put money into traditional craft industries and avant-garde performing arts, into rock music and into *variété*, into contemporary music and amateur film. If it was popular or if it encouraged participation, the chances were it would get a grant. In the new cultural playpark, creative disorder reigned. By the time of the elections in '86, Jack Lang had become such a popular figure that the likes of Samuel Beckett, Graham Greene and Arthur Miller added their names to a petition approving his policies. Naturally, the Right took a teeth-clenched dislike to this popular largesse with public funds. Even if they *were* French, they were managers and economists and they saw no use-value in creative disorder.

Jack Lang didn't say, 'Paris should be *en fête* every day.' He must wish he did. But he did say that intellectual investment is the most important a country can make. 'Did you know,' he asks, 'that cultural activities employ four per cent of the active population, more than car production and chemicals?'

We didn't, Jack.

'More than ever: culture and the economy are the same battle,' he stresses.

It bothers him that television was never brought under the control of his Ministry of Culture, but rather became a political prize in the hands of the Elysée. He almost resigned over the President's decision to hand out licences for two new channels to businessmen.

He calls TV a cultural supermarket, guided by the law of prime-time profit. If the artistic history of the 20th century had proceeded 'under the sign of that terrible law', Ionesco would have been thrown in the dustbin and Alain Resnais would have been holding the lid open. He bemoans the lack of opportunities for French televisual artists like Jean-Baptiste Mondino, who won fame nevertheless via advertising and US pop videos. While others await their turn, they could do with a commission from the new channels but these have become faucets for cheap American soap, to which Franco-Italian genius has added a lather of soft porn.

So Jack came back, with the Socialists, to sit again in the original Mies van der Rohe chairs at the ministry in the Palais Royal. He says he would like to see French TV become a controlled commercial environment but his immediate problem is the Bicentenary. He has been made the minister responsible for staging the biggest popular fête the country has ever seen. It's a big headache in a country that prefers its fêtes to be spontaneous.

If he finds himself running out of inspiration – and he runs his own cultural think-tank just in case – from the windows of the ministry he can once again contemplate his most controversial effort, a piece of modern sculpture by Daniel Buren. It was this that provoked his very own cultural row: a series of truncated black-and-white pillars laid between the 17th-century columns of Richelieu's Palace.

What came to be known as the Liquorice Stumps were a typical piece of preposterous public monumentising, in the tradition of the Eiffel Tower which, built on the centenary of the Revolution to exemplify the technological dynamism of the age, at least had some reason for being absurdly tall and ugly. The work of a bridge builder, it seemed to set the standard for public monuments. If there is a controversial design around, then rather than be accused of *petit-bourgeois* conformism by building something simple and harmonious, the French, those skilled engineers of folly, will certainly build the controversy.

It is the Citroën syndrome. Neither ugly nor illogical, the Liquorice Stumps in the Palais Royal are primarily controversial. They served the immediate purpose of annoying a furious Chirac. Like all modern public sculpture, they have become a magnet for homeless punks and BMXers looking for a new challenge.

We love you, Jack, they say.

Le maire-soleil

IT WAS JACQUES Chirac who said, 'Paris should be *en fête* every day.'
Smiling, baby-kissing Jacques Chirac.

He cleaned up the squalid Paris of the Seventies, razing the junkie squats in
the east of the city and rebuilding the unsafe and still teeming tenements.
Clean, Postmodern public housing sprouted alongside new private develop-
ments, and a new sports complex opened at Bercy to help revive the east of
the city. Attempting to build a presidential machine out of an old party of the
centre-left, the RPR, Chirac never missed a photo-opportunity. A US-style
mayor-politician in an open-necked shirt, he sent armies of fluorescent-clad
roadsweepers out into the streets of the capital. He used his position as
mayor of Paris to place himself on the national stage and in 1986, with a
majority in the Assembly, Mitterrand had no choice but to nominate him
Prime Minister. His first test was the anger of students, many of whose
parents had voted for the RPR, and whose hard-won access to study was not
going to be easily revoked. Huge demonstrations that allied with the fledgling
anti-racist movement forced Chirac to reconciliate.

After two years of 'cohabitation', he threw himself into a presidential fight
with all the speed, co-ordination and one-word messages of an American
campaigner. Still, he found himself trailing behind a candidate, Mitterrand,
who had yet to announce that he was in the race. Chirac offered to reduce

VAT on pet food. He offered to fund France's next bid for the World Cup. The presidometer barely flickered. Allowing his opponent to wear himself out, the wily veteran Mitterrand proposed nothing, he was simply there, while Chirac floundered.

The Prime Minister made a last, desperate effort. A few days before the final vote, French hostages were suddenly released from the Lebanon after nearly three years. According to a Syrian diplomat who was instantly expelled from the country, it cost the French government a million dollars. In New Caledonia, a French colony in the Pacific, nationalists had taken hostage some policemen and were hiding in a cave. The Army proposed to resolve the situation with acceptable losses. These hostages were freed too, but the 17 Kanaks who staged this rash showdown were all killed. Still, Mitterrand refused to budge in the polls. After seeing his votes snatched on the Right by Jean-Marie Le Pen in the first round, Chirac was beaten in the second round by a haughty Mitterrand.

It was a testing year for Jacques Chirac. I think his mistake was to smile too much, to be too ingratiating. My mother once told me that she didn't trust people who smile a lot, which I think is a general rule for the French. If there was little idealism in the re-election of President Mitterrand, there was even less enthusiasm for the ubiquitous charm of the *maire-soleil*.

Night rally

THE STADIUM AT Bercy in the east of Paris, near the old goods yard and the crumbling squats that have almost all gone, is an efficient new sports and concert hall about the size of Wembley Arena in London. Tonight it is hosting a *Front National* rally.

On sale inside the doors is the usual array of key-rings, flags and mugs, speeches on cassette and the songs of the Paras. There is a Catholic Action stand distributing religious tracts. The 8,000 seats are nearly all taken at 30 francs each, most of them by middle-aged Parisians and their wives – not all of them taxi-drivers as popular myth supposes. They are *petits commerçants*, *petits fonctionnaires*. The men are casually dressed with gold teeth and cravats. They don expensive spectacles to view the distant stage. Their wives are coiffured and made up as though for a night out. The mood in the giant auditorium is that of a jolly picnic. People munch on sandwiches and sip beer from plastic cups. There are no skinheads with flaming *tricolores* tatooed on their foreheads. Instead, there are many younger *Front National* supporters, well dressed in the style of the BCBG (*Bon Chic Bon Genre*), the Parisian Sloane Ranger. These are the people you brush past in the big, plush department stores. They are at the next table in the brasserie. I imagine them at home, eating *foie gras* at Christmas, watching the eight o'clock news and the old black-and-white French movie on Sunday evening, reading *Le Figaro* and walking the dog around the block, growing increasingly fearful at each immigrant face they pass.

Would the British Right not also stoop to hatred to battle a powerful Left? Ordinary, decent, these people want their children to get a *bac* and have a good job in a country they can be proud of. They hate the internationalism of the Left and its concern for minorities. What about us, the majority, they wonder? Most of all I think they hate the fact that the Left has formed a new aristocracy, before they had a chance to ascend to the old one.

All political shifts in France can be interpreted as attempts to disband the old aristocracy and constitute a new one. This was the aim of the revolutionaries, who loved their king and plotted only to overthrow his court. Le Pen would create a patriotic new republic, a Third Empire, replacing Liberty with Order, Equality with Might and Fraternity with Fear, putting himself and his henchmen in charge.

For the political show, the stage has been covered with wide expanses of red, white and blue cloth. To the side are three chairs and a vase of flowers. Jean-Marie Le Pen sits in the chair nearest the centre. Next to him and the first to speak is Jean-Pierre Stirbois. Twenty years younger than Le Pen, he was convicted of hoarding arms in '71, a young member of the fascist leagues that spread in France in the Seventies in response to de Gaulle's call in '68 for 'civic action' against 'international Communism'. He was involved in plots to bomb the Tass news agency in '74 and the Paris–Belgrade express in '77. A cool tactician, he has refined the vulgarity of his boss. His phrases are precise and effective. He calculates the strategies of his gruff mentor and bides his time, the natural successor, and, because of his glibness, more dangerous. Le Pen would never pass in polite society other than like a bulldozer – and along comes Stirbois distributing leaflets and organising committees behind. While Le Pen poses in parachutist drill and makes racist jokes, Stirbois wears a dark blue suit and polished shoes, a short man, lifting his chin to speak. He rises to give a polished but deferentially shorter version of the speech I saw him make at Vaison six months earlier. He grips the lectern and leans forward, his phrases resounding in the arena. Banners wave and flags flutter. To the sarcasms of Stirbois, his intimation that they all know what's really wrong with the country, but only the Front dares utter it, there are roars of amusement – derisory, contemptuous guffaws that sound as if they have been stifled in daily life – and to his exhortations of the Front's rightful due, the chorus of gutteral cheers. There is a palpable sense of anticipation. Stirbois smoothly conjures the nightmares of the audience. He describes a France of shadowy foreign danger, its hospital beds full of pregnant aliens without a *carte de séjour*. The themes of the Front are constant: insecurity, unemployment – and their cause? – immigrants.

The lights are still bright in the hall and around the walkways stand ushers who are part of the DPS, the Front's self-drilled potential goon squad. DPS stands for *Défense, Protection, Sécurité*. They keep watch at meetings, at rallies and in the neighbourhood. Stirbois and Le Pen envisaged a network of them, on every street. In their twilight France, the DPS would watch for and denounce 'anti-French' action: socialising with immigrants, being even brusquely courteous to them. Ghettoisation would be followed by deportation, leaving the long-promised security; a simple equation for a new order. Security is a primary fear. For now, the DPS keeps watch for muggers, pushers, sero-positives. The Front campaigns aggressively for the return of the death penalty.

Le Pen and Stirbois have been hard at work since the spring of '83, when the Socialist government, placing exigency over principle, 'abandoned' the French worker. To these dispossessed workers and to the ever disgruntled bourgeois they offered a principle – France first – tarnished but durable as the armour of Joan of Arc, around whose statue Le Pen and his followers gather each year. That July, in the Paris suburb of La Courneuve, a young Maghrébin named Toufik was murdered in an apparently unprovoked attack by a neighbour. Friends took revenge on the assailant. In the following months, race hatred simmered, lit by the new red-white-blue flame of the *Front National*. Before the end of the year, thanks to a deal with the local Right, the party won its first municipal election. At the European elections the next year, they won 11 per cent of the French vote. At the legislative elections of '86, they entered for the first time as a group into the Assembly. Marching and fly-posting, drumming their consistent beat of danger and insecurity, they have built a national organisation that meets in civic halls and in the front rooms of flats in tower blocks where the wind howls like a dog outside and next to the bar that has closed is a mosque. The members plot local politics, or just get things off their chests. They know when vacancies are coming up at the factory and can sometimes get new TVs for half the price. They ponder what to do about 'anti-French' shopkeepers, those who serve Arabs . . . because there are no other clients.

As the lights dim in the hall, 8,000 of them rise excitedly from their seats chanting *Le Pen Le Pen Le Pen*, as though at a football match. Le Pen rises from his seat too and the cries are drowned in a burst of music – *Also Sprach Zarathustra*. The leader hesitates, not sure of whether to wait until the music has finished. The cheering flounders. He sits down again. Finally, he walks to the lectern. He wears a dark blue suit and a radio mike. Above him on the giant video scoreboard a *Front National* emblem flickers.

Having secured 14 per cent of the vote in the first round of the presidential election, this should have been a night of triumph for Le Pen. His party has gained a measure of respectability. There have been no violent scuffles 'provoked' by Leftists to make the Front look like rampaging thugs. There have been no unguarded remarks – like the one he made on TV the year before about the gas chambers being a 'detail' of history. Instead, the founder of the *Front National* appears nightly on TV to give his views alongside the representatives of the major parties. He is zealous but controlled, relishing the role of the *grand perturbateur*, the articulator of the unspoken, his glass eye malevolently static. He claims to have lost the eye in the war. His estranged wife Pierette thinks it was in a brawl in a bar.

And now, having found the courage of his convictions, having accepted and even rejoiced in his immediate fate of political leprosy (at least martyrdom was a destiny he could share with Front icon Joan of Arc), having built the party, meeting by meeting, speech by speech, on a euphoric crusade of in-dignation at the plight of a bedraggled France; after a decade of plotting and organising and marching, on the verge of winning third place in the presiden-tial polls, he has been frustrated by those eternal *magouilleurs*, the crooked, conniving politicians that he has always so contemptuously denounced.

This has been playing on his mind, causing him to ball his fists. He is distracted. As his image plays above him like those of the pop stars and sports figures who usually fill the arena, he raises his tone angrily. He accuses the media of playing down the importance of the *Front National*. He calls on members of the Right, the centre and the Left to unite with him. He derides President Mitterrand as 'the Ayatollah of the Left!'

Having been re-elected with a clear majority, the President has, as he promised, taken this as a mandate for fresh legislative elections, rounding on a beaten, divided Right to try to fill the Assembly with Socialist deputies. By deciding – as is his right in the Fifth Republic – that the election should be by majority scrutiny, which disfavours minority parties, he is threatening to 'laminate' the *Front National*.

The very announcement, it seems, has already put the Front into check. Le Pen responded by announcing his own candidature for a predominantly white seat in Marseille beside a large immigrant district. 'They have the problems to which I have the solutions,' said the unstinting Normandy-born candidate. But he seems to have misjudged the xenophobia of the Marseillais, who according to early polls seem more uneasy about this immigrant from the north of France turning their neighbourhood into a political showpiece than they do about the immigrants living next door. His seat in the Assembly is now in jeopardy. The porcine leader of the Front has also been told by his doctor that the strain of the last few months is telling on him. There are rumours of cardiac problems.

Lamination is one of the nicer expressions thrown up in this political spring on the eve of the Bicentenary. There was also Immobilism, which Mitterrand was accused of when he refused to budge in the polls, or even to announce himself as a candidate. Examples of lamination include Chirac's perennial smile set in anguished, frozen failure on TV at the news of his defeat after the last-minute military action in New Caledonia and the final *coup de media* release of French hostages in the Lebanon. Voters on the right found themselves in agreement with Le Pen's condemnation of the cynicism and corruption of politicians. They either endorsed Le Pen's belief that it is in him alone that the three-coloured flame of a pure ideal burns; or else, repelled by the anti-democratic logic of this conviction, they gave their votes grudgingly to Mitterrand.

Having wrecked the unity of the Right with the by-now infamous 14 per cent showing of their leader, the Front is now bidding to ally itself with the demoralised fragments: Chirac's RPR and the older Gaullist party led by Raymond Barre, the UDF. The conservative Barre has already declared that he would prefer to ally with Socialists than with the *Front National*. He is manoeuvring himself into a position at the head of a potential new centre-right group in the Assembly. Chirac, little heard of since his humiliating defeat, has so far refused to accept the cold and, for him, probably fatal electoral handshake extended by the *Front National*.

As his voice rises and falls, Le Pen has difficulty stirring the crowd. Do they know of his uncertainties? I wonder. Looking forward to next year's anniversary, he ends with a stirring call for his supporters to 'rise up against the tyranny of the *classe politique*, that *ancien regime*!'

It is an appeal to insurrection but the moment has slipped from his grasp. An old man next to me complains cheerfully to his wife that his hands are sore from clapping too hard.

For the most part, this applause has been perfunctory, and frequently off cue. Le Pen is a little too florid and long-winded for his audience. They are amused by his mention of a politician's 'magic baguette' but not by Le Pen's considered, debating chamber, leader writer's style. He uses formal, quasi-legal terms to accuse Mitterrand of duplicity. His attacks only hit home when he plays on favourite fears, and even then phrases like 'the revolutionary theory of Islamic fundamentalism' (when he means Arab terror) fall with an empty thud across the vast hall. He consistently misses the pulse of the crowd, whose grasp of political terminology is not as pseudo-sophisticated as his own has fatally become. He has not mastered the stadium effect. His niceties don't cross the huge spaces. His assonances echo and fade off the long walls. He's not as abrasive or vicious as his cheering fans would like. And the cheers die down.

What is wrong? What has happened to the *grand perturbateur*, the Outsider?

He has become one of the politicians he feigns to despise, one of the politicians he has schemed against and secretly envied all along. And in doing so, he has been disarmed.

His supporters drift away, back to their discontented lives.

The fourth world

BEYOND THE THIRD World is the Fourth World, the world of the poor and the immigrant, scrabbling at the feet of the uncaring city.

On my way to Marseille, the port that marked the entrance to this kingdom for generations of the new French citizenry, I stopped in the small town where I spent my summers two decades ago.

The TGV now slices through it, refusing to stop; time passing by. The gates of the old level crossing have been replaced by the fences of an underpass. In the bar by the station where I drank lemonade and played table football with Phil, I sit quietly, uncertain if I am the ghost or the town itself. It seems that nothing has changed. In the *boulangerie* whose prices have been fixed by the French government since the Revolution, the towns-people still greet each other politely on entering. The cost of bread in the cities – where, two centuries ago, people consumed three kilos a day – was a safety valve of French revolutionary fervour. A few weeks ago, the prices were deregulated. French bread has been thrown to the open market. It is an important psychological break. The *boulanger* is free to compete but, like a chicken released into the yard for the first time, he does nothing yet and returns to the coop.

The talk in the bar is of the coming elections and the situation in the Bouches-du-Rhône region, which includes Vaison la Romaine and the city of Marseille. Polls show that the *Front National* faces losing many of its deputies in what has hitherto been a stronghold as, aided by the effects of majority scrutiny, the French seem set to recoil from that disturbing part of their nature, the infamous 14 per cent of presidential votes for Jean-Marie Le Pen.

His provocative stand in a suburb of Marseille has also been upset by the surprise Socialist candidature in a nearby ward of Bernard Tapie, the debonair businessman. An ex-TV presenter, among other things, Tapie has eclipsed the Front leader in media terms. His is a fresher story than the Front's in Marseille. Between them, they seem to represent the two poles of France: young, progressive, open, streamlined; ageing, reactionary, enclosed, baroque.

In the bar in Ambérieu, a railway official stopping for a drink on his way home says that Tapie can't be trusted. 'How can a millionaire also be a Socialist?' he scoffs. 'At least you know where you are with Le Pen.' A ticket inspector, he lives in a new house on the outskirts of the town where my grandfather once owned land. He moved from Lyon because of the violence in suburbs like Les Minguettes, where immigrant kids stole cars for crash-and-burn demolition derbies. 'They have no respect for France,' he complains. As the SNCF men talk, the barman maintains the circumspect silence of all barmen. But I don't remember him and he doesn't remember my friend Phil. The pinball machine no longer clangs but talks to itself in a synthesised American voice.

As the Rhône drains southwards, there is a marked transformation of the landscape from green valleys to stony olive groves. Within the medieval walls of Avignon is the one time seat of the Pope that has given French Catholicism a sense of destiny ever since. This year, Archbishop Lefebvre ordained four priests into a new fundamentalist Catholic sect. It was the first serious schism in the Roman church for almost two centuries. Up to the last minute, the Vatican tried to dissuade him. There was a car waiting outside the cathedral to take him to Rome for an eleventh-hour recant. He didn't go. Now France has a hardline faith to meet what she perceives as her most dangerous ideological threat, Islam.

Approaching Marseille, the landscape changes again. Flat, rectangular new warehouses spread across the river delta, with no character other than their commercial logos. A huge gleaming, belching refinery, designed to relieve some of the employment problems of the area, sits on the banks of the river.

It was completed as the oil crisis hit and has been underused ever since. Imperceptibly, the city begins, sprouting from the rocky hills in that organic way of Mediterranean towns, which never struggle to dominate their surroundings but yield like the inhabitants to the hot afternoons. Beside the ports to the north, the houses are little more than shacks: two rooms with red-tiled roofing and whitewash faded yellow.

My first impression of the city is in the faces of poor and transient Algerians. They are not tired and furtive faces as elsewhere in France. Descending the hill from the railway station towards the harbour where the Phoenicians landed 2,500 years before, I traverse side streets with washing strung between the windows. Rows of faded hotels bear witness to a once thriving commerce and the ebb and flow of humanity across the tideless Mediterranean. There is *Front National* graffiti everywhere, machine-gunned in dripping black letters across shutters faded grey from the smog and the heat. The residents of this Arab quarter no longer even notice the violence of the insults.

A young Tunisian pauses as I stop to photograph a graffiti-covered statue.

'You like that?' he asks drily.

'No.'

He looks at me, wondering why I should take a picture of something I don't like. And then he relaxes. Once obscenity has lost its force there is only absurdity. For him, I am obviously adding to it.

He tells me Le Pen only came to Marseille so that he would stand out. 'Nobody would notice him anywhere else in France!'

I ask him where the Front's constituency is. Down the street, he points. 'You can't miss it. There are flags outside. *Super!*' he says sarcastically.

He walks along with me. His name is Bernard. He is 19 years old and works in a bakery.

'Le Pen wants to have a war,' he says, having reasoned with the absurd. 'They don't remember the last war.'

'Who?'

'*Les fromages.*'

That's what immigrant kids call the French: *les fromages*.

We turn into a bustling avenue with elegant Second Empire buildings black with grime.

Bernard is happy to leave the rest of France to *les fromages*. He has been to Paris, but prefers Marseille.

'I came here at the age of two and fell in love with it,' he says. 'I've been in love with it ever since.' Soon he will have enough money to leave the two-room house he shares with his three brothers.

'It must be a lot like Algiers,' I offer. Except that the magazine kiosks are full of pornography.

'I wouldn't know. Marseille is my home.'

To the Maghrébin, Marseille represents liberty. What is the first thing he sees as his ship docks at La Joliette? A Moorish cathedral, its huge spire rounded like the earthen roofs of his homelands. The smell of La Joliette, the port district, is the smell of Tunis, Algiers or Tangiers: roasted *merguez* and boiling couscous, grilled fish and hot car fumes. The view is now obstructed by a motorway that cuts across the waterfront, concrete flyways obscuring the faded signs in French and Arabic of the import/export houses. In the bars are posted the timetables of ships, long out of date. High security walls now enclose the jetties and customs houses, with barbed wire fencing above and police checkpoints at the gates.

To the French, Marseille represents the underworld, a dangerous, libidinous world, a passage open to Arab and African sensuality, spices and sweet fruits. Maurice Tourneur made *Justin de Marseille* in 1934, before he went to Hollywood. The film begins with the sound of screeching tyres and gunfire and a reporter phoning in a story: 'France's second city is turning into Chicago!' Justin, a wide-lapelled, heavy-lidded gangster, strolls along the waterfront, with real-life flower sellers and fish vendors greeting him warmly in a hotch-potch of Mediterannean accents. An innocent girl from Avignon is seduced by a black pimp and driven to jealous revenge with the flash of a knife in a cobbled alley. Eating *oursins* in a restaurant, Justin gesticulates at the police chief on another table. 'We're all the same, police or thieves.' In the course of the film, the policeman does nothing to disprove him. This is the Marseille remembered by the old men playing *boules* in the squares, the Marseille of businessmen with white hands and French boxing champions, of the old Corsican families who controlled the ports, dividing up the vice and the rackets. The film was based on a real mob war between two gangs, led by a pair of characters named Spirito and Carboni. The film supposes a genial amity between them, a thieves' trust betrayed for a woman.

Bernard is on his way to meet his girlfriend. He invites me for a drink. 'Have a *pastis*.' Marseille is the home of *pastis*.

His girlfriend is called Maya. She is 22 years old, with brown eyes and thick curly black hair. She is studying for a diploma in public relations. She was born in Algiers and came to France at the age of 13 to attend a cardiac centre in Aix.

'I wasn't happy. In the hospital I felt like a stranger.'

She returned to Algiers for a year but was advised to move back to France for continuing medical treatment.

'People had a certain apprehension towards Algerians,' she says. 'I wouldn't say it was racism . . . There's this prase: "We like you, you're not like other Arabs".'

Bernard scoffs. 'She doesn't look Arab, but she is.'

Maya frowns at him.

'People think of them as thieves, dirty.' She says this with no emotion.

'I've not had any direct experience of racism – apart from jobs but that's normal. If there's not much work around it's to be expected that they give it to the French.

'How do you see yourself now?'

'Me, frankly, I think of myself as French. I have my friends and my way of life here. I'm not concerned about what's going on over there. I feel like a stranger in Algiers. It's changed even in ten years; all the people from the countryside who've come into the towns. It's dirty and there's a lot of un-employment.'

She seems unaware of the irony of this.

Bernard reminds her that they are not French. As immigrants, Bernard and Maya have no vote, despite the length of time they have lived in France and the fact that they pay taxes. Her mother, with whom she lives in the prosperous southern part of the city, was a secretary in the colonial administra-tion. She was offered citizenship at the time but declined. Maya tells me her mother says it's understandable that people vote for Le Pen. Her mother was mugged two years ago. But who would she vote for?

'Why are there no Arabs active in local politics?'

'They don't feel it's their business. They prefer to hide themselves to avoid problems.'

'There's Harlem,' says Bernard.

'He's not Arab.'

*

Harlem is Harlem Desir, the son of a provincial schoolteacher who heads SOS Racisme. After the success of the *Front National* in the local elections at Dreux in '83, Harlem Desir, then still a student, set about organising a national march. He had been instilled with the values of republican democracy by his father. Among his friends he sensed a fear and anger that, provoked by events like the murder of Toufik that same year, threatened to combust into violence calculated to play straight into the hands of the emerging Front, handing them their trump card of insecurity.

He was determined to channel the frustration of what the French perceived as dangerous young 'immigrants', who were more often the second generation, French-born, of immigrant parents. Their families, contrary to statistical myth, were starting to integrate into French society; intermarrying and having fewer children. The first wave of these children were then just coming into their majority.

They had grown up chiefly in the suburbs of provincial towns, in the shadow of prosperity, during a decade of recession. When the local factory laid off or closed, it was their fathers who bore the brunt. 'French' workers after all could claim a longer tenure and somehow were always first in the queue. A French queue is always a crowd with someone pushing to the front. Behind the counter at the social security office, the clerk decided who to attend to next. Harlem Desir saw that it was vital to enfranchise the young inhabitants of the TV suburbs, estranged from the family traditions of Islam and not accepted by French society. They resembled the youth who break-dance in shopping malls all over Europe. It was in La Courneuve, a new town outside Paris, that Toufik was murdered. And so it was through the new towns, the suburbs like La Courneuve and Les Minguettes where the Front distributed their tracts, that Harlem Desir passed with his marchers. By the time the first march arrived in Paris, they were 60,000 strong, not just 'immigrants' but their *potes*, their mates, and a slogan of fraternity, *touche pas à mon pote*, Leave my mate alone.

Two years later, there were 300,000 marchers at the Place de la Concorde. Diplomatic, reasonable, always polite, Harlem Desir, their leader, did not deny his role. He was rapidly drawn into politics, becoming a guest at the Elysée. By now he represented a sizeable block of young voters, whose loyalties were most likely to be with the Socialists. He appeared on TV panel discussions, calm under the studio lights in a brown suede bomber, informed and intelligent, describing the threat to democracy and articulating the hatred of hatred. That's what Maya meant. Desir is not an 'immigrant'. He has been integrated. Arabs too want to keep their distance, jealous of their own identity.

What he did took courage. In France, bombs explode in the offices of magazines that attack the Front. The *fromages* should be grateful to him. It took an 'immigrant' to articulate the revulsion that many French people felt at their rise. While it was perhaps only someone like Desir, who by giving his mates a voice, a figure on TV that was not one of fun or fear, could deny the Front their fodder of insecurity, it is significant that it was not a French person who broke the sinister circle of discreet acceptance.

That night, with 48 hours to go before polling starts, I attend a meeting held by Bernard Tapie at a sports hall in the suburbs of Marseille. It is taking place in front of the faithful for the television cameras. There is Spanish guitar music playing as 1,000 of Tapie's supporters find their places. They are youngish and dapper; entrepreneurs. Dynamic new business people who can identify with Tapie.

It was Bernard Tapie who introduced the enterprise culture to France. It can't have been easy, but in the Eighties the field was his. His father was a worker in a suburb of Paris. An electrical engineer in the Young Communists, he now resides on a yacht in the bay of Marseille. He bought for one franc a bankrupt printing company that had been occupied by the workers. He offered the bank a repayment schedule and offered the workers co-ownership. Then he brought publishers down and appealed to their emotions. Tapie moves quickly, playing on the subjective. In 1979, on a plane for Abidjan as his printing empire grew, he read in a poll that 90 per cent of French people would be favourable to the seizure of property in France belonging to Bokassa, then involved in a financial scandal with President Giscard. Tapie was in front of the emperor the next day. He showed him the poll and offered to buy the lot for 12 million francs. Bokassa accepted. He introduced time-share ownership of second homes and sold space on the skis of the French ski team to Benson & Hedges. From coup to coup, Tapie has barely paused. He owns a brace of diverse enterprises, often bought knock-down, stripped and made viable. He has the gift in French industry of being able to talk to workers and bosses, and has become an aspirational figure for both. Handsome,

dashing (he races cars) Tapie's message is: you can make it too, let's make it together.

His message in Marseille is slightly different. 'I'm here to win,' say his
posters, alluding to the unabashed title of his autobiography, *Win*, 'and I'm
here to stay.' This last refers to the mistrust of the proud Marseillais, who
regard their city, for all its sullied and sordid history, as nobody's property or
political platform. Tapie has been here for two years now. His first strategic
move was to buy Marseille Olympic, the football team in whose performances
every Saturday at their home ground, in front of the new owner, is measured
the virility of the city. It's a bold move. The team has nearly ruined at least
five fortunes since the war, and has been for its owners an impassioned
gamble. Last season they were improving.

Things are going well for Tapie. The campaign manager apologises for him
being late. He says he's read the papers and finds the image a bit cold. 'He
has "front", and the Marseillais like "front".'

Tapie's arrival, just a little late, brisk and mediagenic, as cameras roll in
time for the eight o'clock news, is greeted with a strong handclap. There are a
lot of women in the audience. The men all look like they are succeeding,
nouveau riche. In a dark suit, Tapie sits on a tall stool on the empty stage.
Square-jawed and smiling at the applause, he perches with one foot on the
floor like a cabaret singer or television host. He speaks quickly and without
formality.

He says he is here where the boats landed from the South because he was
invited. 'People talk about crime, prostitution, drugs . . . Marseille is not
ahead in any of those things. But when people talk about the *Front National*,
Marseille is ahead. And I'm here to beat them,' he says with bullish certainty.

He is frank, inspiring faith. He explains once again his credentials, his right
to be representing the people of Marseille. 'The Left said to me' – he nods at
the old Party leaders standing at the side of the stage – 'you know things we
don't. We're of the Left. You're not anti-Left. You're a Socialist because
you're generous. We're in a real crisis, it's not an invention. We need to
make, build, sell. We need to open our arms to people who can make things
happen. In the schools, the housing estates, the supermarkets we need help.
"Will you help?" asked Mitterrand. I said yes.'

He talks about the 100 best companies that make the most money. 'They
bring profit, but also a social profit.' He says the class of entrepreneurs is not

a shame, it's a necessity. 'The Arab world counts a billion people who represent a billion consumers. Isn't it better to ask the Arabs among us to help us? You know the market – let's do business! It's certain that Le Pen will be beaten. I know it,' he insists, balling a fist. 'But we are at 50/50 and there are only 48 hours left . . . Let's throw Le Pen out and give an example to France!'

Le Pen lost his seat, but – by only a few hundred votes – Tapie didn't win his. At the town hall he was told he had, but by the time the ballot papers reached the city hall, the result had mysteriously changed. Tapie cried fraud, saying that packets of votes had been deliberately mislaid. There were a dozen other suspicious results elsewhere in France but the President said no replays. Instead, he gave the traditional amnesty to parking fine offenders.

Towards the end of the summer, Jean-Pierre Stirbois who, like his boss, had also been squeezed out of the Assembly, was driving home late at night. For 15 years, since the Front started in 1972, he had been criss-crossing the country. He had organised the activists who fly-posted the small towns where the Front scored their first municipal victories. It was he who made the secret deals with politicians of the local Right. He spent evenings and weekends canvassing in the housing estates which the Socialists had grown too lazy to visit. He imagined his time would come. Weary, he fell asleep at the wheel and spun off the road into a tree. By the time the ambulance arrived, he was dead.

FIN

Shropshire Walks by the Waterside

David Gregory

EXPLORING SHROPSHIRE

with Shropshire Books

EXPLORING SHROPSHIRE

SHROPSHIRE WALKS BY THE WATERSIDE forms part of a series
of books and leaflets on walking published by Shropshire Books known as
EXPLORING SHROPSHIRE. For other titles in the series see page 80.

Front cover photograph by Gordon Dickins

ISBN: 0-903802-74-0
© David Gregory 1998
Cover and Book Design: The Graphic Terrace
Illustrations: Kathryn Green
Managing Editor: Helen Sample

The maps in this book are based on the 1992 Ordnance Survey 1:50,000
mapping with the permission of the Controller of Her Majesty's Stationery office
© Crown Copyright.

Published by Shropshire Books the publishing imprint of
Shropshire County Council's Community and Economic Services Department.
Printed in Great Britain by Precision Colour Printing, Telford.

CONTENTS

———— ✦ ————

INTRODUCTION

———— ✦ ————

The life-giving properties of water are too well known to warrant any description here. However, it is hoped this book will enable walkers to enjoy the therapeutic benefits of walking close to water while exploring some of Shropshire's quiet and alluring places.

Streams, rivers, canals, pools and lakes feature significantly within the various walks but waterside is not exclusive. There is also ample opportunity to wander through the sort of fields, woods, lanes and villages which help shape the county's unique landscape.

Some of the walks entail the climbing of gates or fences, others travel through places which can become very muddy during wet weather. I have tried to indicate these problems as appropriate in the preamble to the individual walks.

I am grateful to the many people who have willingly given me help and information during my travels on the walks, and also to Nigel Jones of the County Council Countryside Service and Helen Sample of Shropshire Books. Last but not least, my thanks go to my wife May for her forbearance and help with many aspects of the work involved in getting the material ready.

Dave Gregory

January 1998

KEY TO MAPS

◆

- - - -	Route of Walk
═══	Road
= = =	Track/Unmetalled Road
┼┼	Railway
～	River/Stream
❶	Route Information
S	Stile
G	Gate
Sp	Sign Post
W	Way Marker
FB	Footbridge
PH	Public House
～	Bridge
P	Parking
●	Pond/Lake
⬠	Buildings
♣ ♠	Woodland
✝	Church
☀	Viewpoint
▲	Triangulation Point

Rights of Way

Every care has been taken to ensure the accuracy of the maps and route descriptions. If a right of way is obstructed the facts should be reported to the Countryside Section of Shropshire County Council.

Cantlop Bridge - Betton Pool - Bomere Pool - Allfield - Condover - Boreton - Cantlop Bridge

◆

O.S. Map 1:50,000 Landranger 126. Starting point: GR 518063.
Parking: Lay-by at Cantlop Bridge off Shrewsbury - Acton Burnell Road.
Distance: 6¹/₂ miles.

A fairly easy walk on lanes and paths through gentle countryside and beside some attractive pools. Cound Brook is also crossed at various locations.

Cantlop Bridge

Cantlop Bridge spans Cound Brook which passes through a shallow valley beneath the former Shrewsbury - Acton Burnell turnpike road. Alas, the cast iron bridge is no longer able to support the weight of present-day traffic, and stands beside a modern structure as a proud monument to its early nineteenth century designer, Thomas Telford. Then Shropshire's County Surveyor, Telford had the bridge built in 1812 and it gave

7

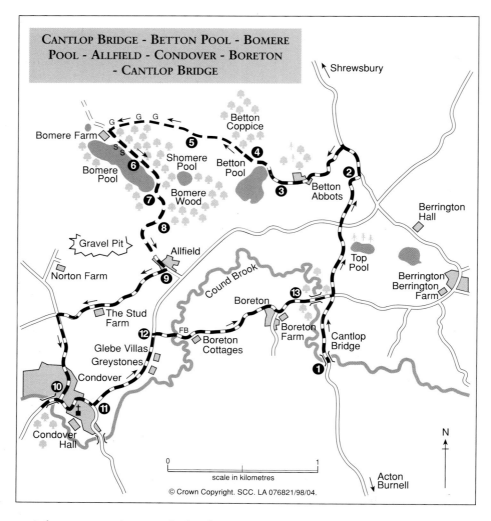

satisfactory service until the late 1970s. A section of the old road is now a lay-by and picnic area.

1. Begin walking along the lane in the direction of Shrewsbury. The lane twists and also gradually climbs. At the first cross-roads keep straight ahead as the lane climbs more steeply, between hedges. At the second crossroads, (King Street), keep walking straight ahead (signpost 'Shrewsbury').

To the rear, lie views of the Lawley and Caer Caradoc hills. To the left, the low ridge of Lyth Hill overlooks the nearby fields, and there are sweeping,

8

distant views of the Stiperstones, Longmynd and other hills above Church Stretton. As the lane levels out, the Wrekin rises up on the right, while Haughmond Hill, the town of Shrewsbury and its surrounding flat countryside together with the wave-shaped Nesscliffe Hill complete the panoramic view.

2. At a road junction (Betton Abbots), follow signpost to Shrewsbury. Soon after passing a gabled house on the right, leave the road by turning left along a metalled lane, passing the 'Betton Abbots Farm' sign. The lane continues between hedges, bends to the right then passes some cottages on both sides.

The still waters of a small pool lie to the left, opposite an attractive farmhouse and garden. Reed beds stand at the far side, white mallard and moorhen busy themselves both on and around the pond.

3. Continue past Betton Abbots Farm. The lane then becomes a broad, unmetalled track. After a short distance go through a gap on the left which allows access to the poolside at Betton Pool.

The smooth, mirror-like surface of the water provides a sanctuary for mallard and black-headed gull.

The far side of the pool is backed with mature trees and, in summer, edged with flowering water plants. Betton Pool has the same origin as the Ellesmere Lakes: It was formed during the ice age, and also contains some rare aquatic plants.

4. After enjoying the serenity of the pool, return to the broad track and turn left.

The track curves along the edge of the pool for a short distance and there are views of the water between trees on the left. There are also glimpses of white water lilies whose crown-shaped flowers lie on the surface while yellow iris thrust their heads right out of the water on bare, green stems. Soon on the left is a short wooden platform which affords a closer view of the water lilies and of the entire sheet of water.

Continue along the track for a short distance. Where the track veers sharply right, leave the trackway by turning left and walking across a field, following a line of telegraph poles.

The commuter village of Bayston Hill lies across the fields ahead, while the mass of Bomere Wood stands to the left.

5. Near the end of the field the path curves first to the left then to

the right to run along the right-hand side of the woodland. Look for and climb a small wooden gate into another field. Walk alongside a fence on the left, the woodland also lies to the left. The path veers to the right still running along the right-hand side of the fence. Farm buildings then come into view on a hilltop to the left. In a few yards go through a metal gate on the left and ascend a sloping field towards the farm. Walk over the brow of the hill and descend the other side, walking towards two wide metal gates. Climb the second gate, then the grassy track towards the farm buildings. A few yards before reaching the top of the slope, turn sharp left and walk for about fifty yards to a stile. Climb the stile and walk straight ahead along a grassy path, with the farm buildings on the right. Climb another stile alongside a broad metal gate.

Down the bank to the right lies the impressive, tree-lined expanse of Bomere Pool. The right of way takes you along a woodland path above the length of the water from end to end. The views of the pool are obviously clearer when the trees are leafless. The pool is yet another glacial formation which once covered 60 acres. It is also the subject of legends, including that of a giant fish wearing Wild Edric's Sword strapped to its body. Celebrated Shropshire authoress Mary Webb made Bomere the 'Sarn Mere' of her novel, *Precious Bane* and was known to be a frequent visitor to its then peaceful waterside. Present day walkers seeking peace need to be at Bomere before late morning when the Bomere Water Ski Centre starts its activities, and the wakes of boats disturb the shoreline where tranquillity once reigned.

6. Continue along the woodland path.

The narrow finger of woodland separating Bomere Pool and the much smaller Shomere pool (unseen to the left) is a result of glacial activity during the ice age. The area was later fortified by our iron-age ancestors with banks and ditches.

7. On emerging from the wood, Lakeside House stands to the right. Turn left to join a stretch of concrete trackway.

8. After several hundred yards, the track becomes a metalled lane which descends between fields and affords wide views of the distant landscape. A small

pool to the right is a haven for wildfowl. **The lane curves its way towards Allfield.**

Across the fields to the right stands a gravel pit near Norton Farm. Here in 1986, the exciting discovery of four mammoths took place as a digger driver at the site belonging to the Associated Roadstone Company was burrowing into the clay in search of the gravel beneath. The driver did not appreciate the nature of his find, but fortunately a local resident walking her dog nearby alerted experts who identified the nearly complete skeleton of an adult female and considerable remains of three young mammoths. Until the fifteenth century most of the land hereabouts was owned by the De Aldefield family.

Later, Allfield became a small manor in its own right then a valued possession of the Manor of Condover in the sixteenth century.

9. Immediately after passing some farm buildings, turn right at a T-junction and walk along another quiet country lane. After about half a mile pass by some mature houses. At a T-junction turn left, signposted 'Condover'. There are lovely views of Lyth Hill, Longmynd and the Stiperstones ahead. Soon enter the village of Condover. Walk past the post office and at a junction near the centre of the village briefly divert to the right (following signpost 'Ryton') to a stone bridge above the Cound Brook.

The broad brook has its source in the Stretton Hills and its twisting

Ancient cottages and St. Andrew's Church, Condover

11

course leads to the River Severn near Cressage. At Condover, the shallow waters trickle under the bridge and beneath trees before rounding the grounds of Condover Hall. Here, and at various points along its route, a multitude of snowdrops carpet the banks in later winter.

10. Return from the bridge to the junction and turn right (signpost 'Frodesley, Pitchford, Acton Burnell'). Walk along the pavement as it passes a shop then winds its way through the village.

Condover - whose name seems to be derived from 'Cound', the brook running close to the village - existed before the Norman Conquest and was recorded in *Doomsday Book* under its present-day name. Some of the brick-fronted cottages are thought to disguise their 14th or 15th century origins, including numbers 4, 5 and 7 (the food store) which hide their timber frames beneath a more recent veneer. The lovely Church House was originally 15th century. It is partly of cruck construction and was later remodelled. There has been a church here dedicated to Saint Andrew since before the Conquest, though there are only a few Norman remnants to vouch for its long history. The original nave and transept collapsed in 1660, and the tower was added a few years later. This large church serves several other villages in the parish.

Follow the road as it snakes around the early 19th century boundary walls of Condover Hall, eventually arriving at the road junction near the entrance gate to the hall.

It is worth going straight ahead over the junction, to the entrance gate and taking a distant look at the Elizabethan Hall built for Judge Owen in the late sixteenth century. Mark Twain was twice a visitor to the hall in the 1870s, and Clive of India briefly rented the property. It is now a school for blind children run by the RNIB. Before leaving Condover we should reflect on other famous names connected with this slumbering village. Henry I visited a few times during his reign and a field near Norton is still known as 'The King's Furlong'. Richard Tarleton the farmer's hump-backed son from Condover was talent-spotted by the Earl of Leicester and became the favourite jester at the court of Elizabeth I. Some say he was immortalised as Yorick in Shakespeare's *Hamlet*.

11. Retrace your steps to the junction and follow the lane signposted 'Berrington, Cross Houses'.

Cound Brook flows between trees at the bottom of the field down to the right.

12. After about 3/4 mile, turn right at a road junction and follow the signpost 'Boreton (through ford)'. The lane soon descends to a ford across Cound Brook. Cross over the footbridge.

Near the farm at Boreton the lane passes a small, wayside pool where willows dip their branches into the water and water lilies decorate the surface. There is very little to present-day Boreton bar the farm and a few cottages,

but at Doomsday it was a separate manor which had belonged to the Saxon church of St Peter at Shrewsbury. Roger De Mongomery gave it to his Abbey at Shrewsbury. In the thirteenth century the manor was divided between two heiresses. When one of them died in 1249 the other was said to have held Boreton paying an annual rent of one salmon to the Abbot.

13. About half a mile further on, the lane crosses a bridge over Cound Brook. After a few hundred yards, turn right at a road junction and walk along the lane encountered at the start of the walk. In about half a mile, you will arrive back at Cantlop Bridge.

Brown Moss - Ash Magna - Edgeley Hall - Brown Moss

✦

O.S. Map Landranger 126. Starting point: GR 563 398.
Parking: Car park close to the main area of Brown Moss. Follow the sign to
Brown Moss from the A41 Whitchurch - Newport Road near Prees Heath.
Distance: 4 Miles.

An easy walk initially encompassing the nature reserve of Brown Moss,
then across fields with lovely views to the village of Ash Magna.
Lanes and field paths, a country mansion and farmland complete the journey.

The area of the Brown Moss Reserve which is under water is somewhat smaller in size than its better known neighbours, including Whixall Moss, and water levels are very responsive to climate changes. Hence, during the dry summers of the early to mid 1990s, the water became practically covered by the assorted, encroaching aquatic vegetation. Nevertheless, this remote place consists of about eighty acres of territory not all of it watery, and hosts some rare varieties of plants together with numerous species of bird life. The moss is an area of unenclosed common land now managed by Shropshire County Council.

1. Leave the car park and walk back to the lane and turn left. Soon, you will pass by a large open tract of grassland on the right and a wooden notice board giving information about the nature reserve. **The lane then passes between trees with the reserve behind the trees on the left. After about 100 yards, turn left and join a broad pathway which soon provides a view of the pool through gaps in the trees to the left. Stay on the track as it skirts the pool. Eventually there are fields and a red-brick cottage on the right. After a further 25 yards, reach a black and white cottage also on your right.**

The half-timbered Beehive Cottage used to be the blacksmith's establishment which catered for the nearby community of Brown Moss. The Moss is reputed to harbour more than thirty species of birds, but the one which makes

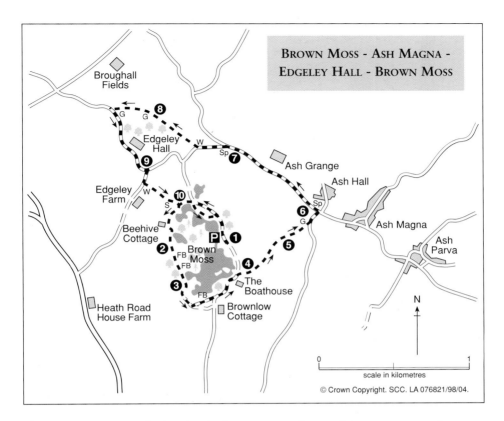

scale in kilometres

© Crown Copyright. SCC. LA 076821/98/04.

the greatest amount of noise is the multi-coloured jay whose ratchet-like cry is often heard hereabouts.

2. Near the cottage is a short marker-post. Follow the arrow leading you straight ahead and along a grassy path (ignore the path to the left leading to the main woodland). The path soon enters a section of woodland.

This part of the wood consists chiefly of oak and birch with plenty of bracken in summer. The Brown Moss woods in general contain both types of birch,

together with rowan, and some oak and holly - some of the oldest species in Britain.

At the next marker-post fork right, following the arrow. Stay on the path as it twists along the edge of the woodland. Follow a further arrow and cross a wooden footbridge over a ditch which disappears into the woodland. In a few yards cross a second, similar footbridge.

The various pools are fed by ground water which percolates through the glacial drift, and

15

this is presumably supplemented by drainage water from nearby agricultural fields.

3. **Follow the direction of the next arrow, bearing right. After about 100 yards, and just before reaching another cottage, look for and follow the marker-post on the left. Leave the main track and take the path to the left. The path, with bracken on either side, soon widens somewhat. Ignore the right-hand marker-post and in a few yards turn left on to a short stretch of woodland towards a newly-fenced area of reeds. This winding path soon brings you to a new wooden causeway and fence beside an open area of the Moss.**

The mosses, as well as the meres, of north Shropshire are a series of water or peat-filled hollows in the glacial drift left by the ice age.

Brown Moss, declared a Site of Special Scientific Interest in 1953, consists of several shallow plant-strewn pools and undulating heathland Beyond the vegetation at this point lies one of Brown Moss's main stretches of water. Tench and rudd are among the fish to thrive in such a setting.

Turn right and walk along the wooden causeway, then bear left on reaching the far end of it. In a few yards follow the direction of the marker-post arrow, keeping the reed bed on your left. In about 100 yards pass the next marker post and soon cross a wooden footbridge. The path continues to meander between trees at the side of the reed-edged lake. Follow the arrow on the next marker-post and soon there is a really clear view of the reed beds and water on the left. The

route now takes you past a narrow arm of the lake. Follow the arrow direction, and quite soon the path passes a bungalow on the right.

You are now leaving the main waterside area of the Moss near a point where oak and beech are gradually taking over from ageing rowan and birch. Nearby mosses such as Fenn's and Whixall saw large-scale commercial extraction of peat until about twenty years ago. However, it is thought that peat cutting at Brown Moss ceased during the Middle Ages. Brown Moss's combination of water, heathland, wildlife, woods and unusual marsh plants makes this diminutive portion of the Shropshire mosses one of considerable interest to scientists and nature lovers alike.

4. Immediately after passing the bungalow, bear right (following the marker-post arrow) and cross a lane before following a footpath sign leading you on to another woodland path.

The dry, acidic soil of this fragment of woodland is ideal territory for bluebells and pink campion. These and other woodland plants create a compelling display, especially during early summer Oak, birch and holly provide ideal cover for a variety of bird species.

Follow the arrows as the path wanders through the woodland. Be careful when reaching the marker-post which points sharp left. Ignore the arrow direction and instead turn right, taking the path which leads in about 25 yards to the edge of a field. Enter the field and bear left.

As you begin walking this section of the field, a view of the shapely ridge of Hawkstone Hill opens up in the distance to the right. The hill is a considerable north Shropshire landmark roughly situated between Wem and Market Drayton, and towering over the flatter surrounding countryside. In the 18th century the woodland, sandstone cliffs and caves were tastefully developed into a pleasure park, and in recent years the site has been re-opened to provide an impressive new tourist attraction for the county. From this aspect the hill's unspoiled wooded length can be enjoyed.

After about 25 yards, turn left and walk along the left-hand side of a field, alongside a tall hedge on the left. Eventually the field path bears round to the right.

Brown Moss

On a clear day an enticing band of south Shropshire hills including Caer Caradoc, Longmynd and part of the Stiperstones lies across the far-off horizon.

5. Look for and go through a gap in the hedge on the left just before reaching three red-brick cottages. Walk straight ahead, climbing up the next field towards a telegraph pole. On reaching the pole, walk diagonally right towards a wide gateway and its accompanying fingerpost.

If you look behind you at this point, you will find that the distant views are even more extensive than before. The hilly country of south-east Shropshire joins the scene to the extreme left, while to the right Long Mountain along the west Shropshire/Wales border, the Breiddens, the Berwyns, the Vale of Llangollen and others seem to disappear into the clouds beyond the north-west of the county.

6. Leave the field path and turn left to walk along a lane towards the village of Ash Magna.

Ash Magna, mounted on its little hill is one of the last rural outposts of north-east Shropshire. It has some surviving black and white cottages and an old smithy. The stone cross of the war memorial would seem to be a suitable village centre. However, in times past the nearby Queen Anne style Ash Hall, a delightful manor house, was at the hub of Ash Magna's social activities including numerous Church Fetes. The hall is now the 'Lady Lambert Exclusive Nursing Home'.

At the T-Junction cross the road and turn left (signpost 'Whitchurch') and walk along the pavement. Soon pass by the Lady Lambert home on the right. After about half a mile of pavement the walkway comes to a temporary end. Walk with care along a short stretch of roadside. Soon the pavement resumes and then takes you past the entrance to Ash Grange.

The late Victorian mansion is now divided into flats, and you should be aware that the ghost of a hooded monk has, on occasions, made an appearance in this vicinity. The most recent sighting was in the 1970s when a young motor-cyclist was startled by the apparition which was apparently suspended about one foot above the ground. Ash Grange was

built in 1884 for Lord Gerald Grosvenor, a member of the Cheshire land-owning family of Cholmondley Castle. It seems the grange provided an eminently suitable bachelor pad for Lord Gerald who also owned several acres of land in the vicinity, including Brown Moss itself.

7. A few hundred yards further on, near Grange Cottages, turn left (signpost 'Brown Moss') and walk down a lane. In about 200 yards turn right and follow a 'Bridleway' sign leading you into a field. Walk along the right-hand side of the field, alongside a hedge.

You will soon have a view to the left of Edgeley Hall and its various outbuildings and accompanying terraced cottages. The present hall was built in the mid-nineteenth century but the Edgeley area was a Saxon township in the Manor of Whitchurch. It is likely then, that an earlier hall would have stood on this site. The existing hall was built for the Churton family, one of whom was a solicitor who became Clerk to the original nineteenth century local authority in Whitchurch.

8. After passing a group of tall pine trees on the right, bear

left making for a small metal gate. Go through the gate and follow a blue arrow sign towards a hedge at the opposite side of a field. On reaching the hedge turn left walking along the left-hand side of it beside a field. At the end of the field go through a narrow wooden gate and turn left onto a lane which climbs gradually for about a quarter of a mile, passing the entrance to Edgeley Hall on the left.

9. After the lane turns sharply left and you pass Edgeley Hall cottage, turn right into a subsidiary lane. In about 100 yards turn left and follow the fingerpost into a field. The field path is at Edgeley Farm and sometimes crops growing close to the field edge make walking difficult. As an alternative the owner is quite happy to allow you to walk along the right-hand edge of the field immediately before that one. The alternative field is entered by means of a wide field gate. You then climb a fence on the right close to the far end of the field in order to join the original field path.

10. At the end of this path climb a stile (often overgrown in summer) and turn left on to the broad trackway at Brown Moss encountered at the start of the walk.

11. Walk along the trackway for about 100 yards, then just before reaching the metalled lane, turn right and follow a woodland path which runs parallel to this lane. The water with its varied vegetation lies to the right. Soon, on reaching a fork in the path, keep ahead on the higher path, then in a few yards bear left. In about another 30 yards bear left again, soon emerging on to an open grassy area beside the lane. Turn right to walk back along the lane for a short distance to the car park.

Coalbrookdale (Coke Hearth) - Loamhole Dingle - Lydebrook Dingle - Leasowes Farm - The Moors Farm - Coalbrookdale

◆

O.S. Map 1:50,000 Sheet No. 127. Starting point: GR 669 049 Coke Hearth, Coalbrookdale, on the Horsehay - Coalbrookdale Road.
Parking at quiet roadside area off main road opposite entrance to Darby Road.
Distance 4 Miles.

A walk of contrasts including an initial stroll beside a pretty woodland brook, then a couple of fairly stiff climbs, a country lane, a man-made pool, an open bridlepath leading to a glorious viewpoint, a short stretch of the Shropshire Way and finally, a descent of historic Darby Road.

The name 'Coke Hearth' speaks of Abraham Darby's renowned ironstone-smelting furnace preserved at the nearby Museum of Iron. When Darby found that coke would do the job more effectively than charcoal, the industrial revolution got underway in earnest. However, for much of this walk we move away from the area's industrial heritage to experience the peaceful beauty of Coalbrookdale's rural surroundings.

1. Walk across the main road and join Darby Road as it passes Upper Furnace pool on the right and approaches a long brick viaduct ahead. Walk under the viaduct (which nowadays carries coal trains to and from Buildwas Power station), and turn right to follow Darby Road for a further distance of about 75 yards until reaching a wooden footbridge on the right. Turn right and walk across the footbridge. Loamhole Brook threads its way through a reed-bed beneath the bridge. At the far end of the bridge the pathway turns sharp left and winds between trees. The stream is down the bank to the left.

You have now entered Loamhole Dingle, often referred to by locals as 'The Lummole'.

21

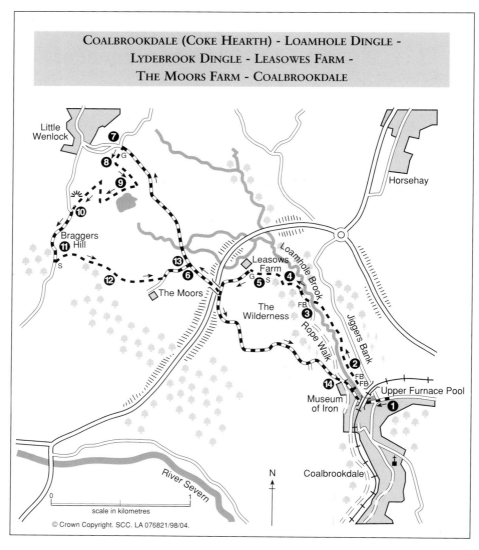

COALBROOKDALE (COKE HEARTH) - LOAMHOLE DINGLE - LYDEBROOK DINGLE - LEASOWES FARM - THE MOORS FARM - COALBROOKDALE

Little Wenlock

Horsehay

Braggers Hill

Leasowes Farm

Loamhole Brook

The Moors

The Wilderness

Rope Walk

Jiggers Bank

Upper Furnace Pool

Museum of Iron

Coalbrookdale

River Severn

0   scale in kilometres   1

N

© Crown Copyright. SCC. LA 076821/98/04.

Despite its unprepossessing title, the dingle is a place of singular beauty where the Loamhole Brook pierces the valley amid trees and wild plants, to the accompaniment of birdsong in spring and summer.

2. Descend some wooden steps and walk along a path of wooden rafts beside the brook. Loamhole Brook, whose source is a spring on higher ground at Huntington, feeds Upper Furnace pool at Coke Hearth. It was that pool which fed Darby's furnace.

22

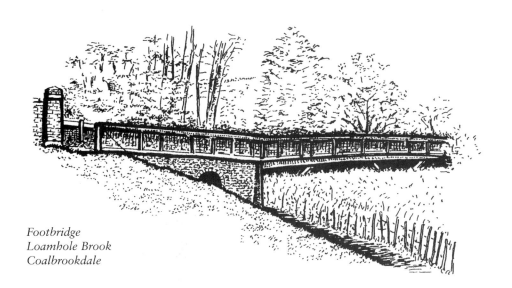

Footbridge
Loamhole Brook
Coalbrookdale

The pathway virtually follows the course of the brook and occasionally runs alongside. At certain stages there are short flights of steps to either climb or descend, and at one point a further small stream tumbles below the path to join the brook which trickles over stones down to the left. Eventually descend a long flight of steps down left to reach the waterside.

The former Telford Development Corporation put the wooden walkway in position about twenty years ago as a leisure amenity. The dingle's charms were discovered long before that, however, as the early industrial workers and their families used to spend Bank Holidays roaming the woodland paths in search of wildflowers (especially primroses) and enjoying family picnics in open spaces. Today the lovely valley still begets a profusion of wild flowers in due season - primrose, bluebell, wild garlic, pink campion, cow parsley and buttercup among others.

3. Turn right, then immediately left and cross a footbridge over the brook. Climb three more short flights of steps, then continue along the path as it climbs out of the valley. The brook is now down to the right. The climb continues towards a final flight of steps and a wooden stile. Climb the stile, then turn right and follow a path which runs beside woodland to the right, and a sloping meadow, backed by woodland on the left.

In early summer a short diversion to the left, having climbed the previously mentioned stile, should reward the walker with a view of an open meadow strewn with wild orchids. The meadow is the site of the former 'Rope Walks'. The path takes you towards Lydebrook Dingle but first passes by placid meadows where ponies sometimes graze. There is also the occasional sound of the trickling, Loamhole Brook, deep in the valley down to the right.

4. Climb a stile which bears the 'Shropshire Way' buzzard emblem, then follow the path as it winds and undulates through woodland. There is a flight of steps to climb at one point.

The climb through the woodland may reward the summer walker with displays of bluebells and wild garlic strewn beneath the branches in some profusion, while the trees provide sanctuary for jays and other woodland birds.

5. Follow the yellow arrow signs as they lead you through the woodland and upwards towards a stile near the exit from the tree cover. Soon climb the next stile bearing the 'Shropshire Way' sign, and enter a field.

Walk straight across the field towards a white gate. The whitewashed farmhouse of Leasowes Farm stands nearby on the right. Go through the gate and turn left into a metalled lane. Pass a bungalow on the left. There is a view of the nestling Wrekin across fields to the right. After several hundred yards, turn right at a junction with another lane. Walk across the bridge which spans the A4169 road at Buildwas Bank.

From the heights of the bridge, the view to the left captures the dramatic variety of scenery of south Shropshire. The richly wooded slopes of Benthall Edge, the peeping summit of Brown Clee and the landscape of Corvedale all combine to delight the eye.

6. Continue along the lane and ignore the 'Shropshire Way' sign to the left. The lane climbs between fields.

In summer Honeysuckle and other wild flowers adorn the hedgerows along this stretch of the lane. Near the hilltop there are impressive views looking back over Buildwas Power Station, Benthall Edge, the varied landscape near Bridgnorth, and beyond to the hills of Worcestershire and south Staffordshire.

Continue along the lane as it passes a pool lying in a hollow, across a field to the left.

This is a man-made pool which now forms part of a landscaped patch near to Little Wenlock. The blemishes left by former coal-mining activity, both deep and opencast, were quite tastefully concealed during the mid-1980s to leave a finer legacy of open fields and clear pathways for the enjoyment of future generations. Soon the ancient tower of Little Wenlock's church and some of the village's roof-tops appear ahead, backed by the sprawling Wrekin. Nearer to hand the hedgebanks are alive with wild plants in Summer.

7. At a road-junction by a signpost to Little Wenlock and Wellington, turn left then immediately leave the road by means of a wooden gate on the left to join a well-made pathway (a bridleway). The pathway runs for several hundred yards between wooden fencing.

8. After a few hundred yards, a short diversion can be made by means of a path to the left, bringing you to the shores of the man-made pool described earlier.

9. Return to the main pathway by means of another path commencing near the pool then turn left to resume walking ahead, with the village of Little Wenlock visible to the right.

10. At a T-junction with a metalled lane, turn left.

After a few yards on a clear day you will want to pause and gaze over a fence on the right. Wenlock Edge's smooth wooded ridge, the conspicuous humps of the Lawley and Caer Caradoc, Longmynd's elongated spread, the jagged-topped Stiperstones, then Earl's Hill, Pontesford Hill, Long Mountain and the Breiddon Hills near the Welsh border are spread before you. The Wrekin also lies, close and large, completing the picture on the extreme right.

11. In about 100 yards look for a stile on the left bearing the 'Shropshire Way' symbol. Climb the stile and join a grassy track.

Wild roses inhabit the nearby hedges in Summer. Ironbridge power station's cooling towers lie in the valley to the right. Beyond them there are open views of Benthall Edge and the distant Brown Clee, the county's tallest hill. The huge wave of

Wenlock Edge completes the unspoiled scene.

12. In a short distance, follow the left-hand path, initially passing between trees, then climbing up to a wooden structure which bears the 'Shropshire Way' sign.

It is worth looking back at this point to view what appears to be a large pool lying in the middle distance. This is not, in fact, water, but fly-ash slurry pumped from Buildwas Power Station. The site used to be a wooded patch known as 'Devil's Dingle'.

Turn right, and walk along the right-hand edge of a field. At the end of the field turn left and walk alongside a fence for about 50 yards. Turn right and climb a stile ('Shropshire Way') near a tall communications mast. Enter the next field and walk straight ahead, alongside a fence on the right and towards some farm buildings. At the edge of the field turn left and walk alongside the farm. In about 200 yards climb a stile on the right and turn left on to the broad driveway of Moors Farm.

13. Turn right at a T-junction to re-join the metalled lane encountered earlier in the walk. Cross the A4169 again, but this time stay on the lane as it curves right and onwards in the direction of Coalbrookdale.

Just before reaching the Sunniside estate, the lane passes the site of the former small settlement of Priest's Wood. Remnants of

Tea-Kettle Row

some of its cottages remained in a nearby field until a few years after World War Two. Some damson trees and part of a pig sty are all that can be seen today, to the right of the lane. The lane passes by some cottages on the left, and then the entrance to the modern Sunniside estate on the right. The name 'Sunniside' is a relic of the days of the Industrial Revolution. A branch of the Darby Family lived at Sunniside House, a name brought to Shropshire from their former residence in the north-east of England. The road passes by some of Coalbrookdale's superbly preserved historic treasures: The Quaker burial ground, The Chestnuts, the entrance to Tea-kettle row, Rosehill House and Dale House.

14. Eventually, you pass the wooden footbridge crossed early in the walk. At the bottom of the hill follow the road round to the left and under the railway viaduct. Once more, pass by Upper Furnace Pool and at the T-junction cross the main road and return to your car.

Marton - Marton Pool - Lower Wood - Wilmington - Marton

❖

O.S. Map Landranger Sheet No. 126. Starting Point GR 286 023.
Parking: Car park at the Sun Inn, Marton Village, on B4386 Shrewsbury -
Montgomery road. First, please inform the licensees that you wish to park here.
Distance 3¹/4 miles.

An easy walk, mostly along field paths and a lonely lane.
The walk includes a close-up view of Marton Pool and the crossing
of various streams and brooks.

One of four small villages in Shropshire bearing the same name, this particular Marton surely lies in the most comely location of them all. It is flanked on either side by a range of handsome green hills and stands among quiet timeless countryside where the extreme western finger of Shropshire points towards the nearby Welsh county of Powys (once Montgomeryshire). The Sun Inn stands at the side of the B4386, opposite the still thriving village shop. The Inn is reckoned to be of the early to mid 19th century, although when alterations were being made by the current licensees some evidence of timber-framing was discovered behind the stone exterior. At some stage in its history part of the building was used as a courtroom, and the Inn also offered stabling for up to twelve horses. In 1862 the shop building was not only a shop but also a dwelling house and bakehouse.

1. Leave the car park and turn right to walk along the pavement for several hundred yards in the direction of the church. Cross the road, pass the Victorian Anglican church of St Mark on the right and ignore a fingerpost on the left. Continue along the roadside towards a sharp bend, but soon cross over to the other side of the road again near a black and white cottage.

The main road through Marton used to be the Montgomery to

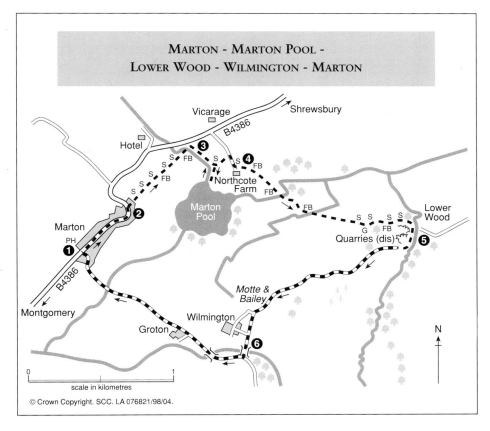

Shrewsbury

Vicarage

B4386

Hotel

Northcote Farm

Marton Pool

Marton

PH

B4386

Montgomery

Groton

Wilmington

Motte & Bailey

Quarries (dis)

Lower Wood

N

0   1
scale in kilometres

© Crown Copyright. SCC. LA 076821/98/04.

Shrewsbury turnpike road. The half-timbered house you have just passed is Yew Tree Cottage. Built in 1634 it is one of a handful of 17th century buildings in and around the village. On its western side the village is overlooked by Marton Hill and Marton Crest, the latter being the birthplace in 1656 of the eminent Dr Thomas Bray founder of both the Society for Promoting Christian Knowledge and the Society for Propagating the Gospel in the USA.

Walk along the pavement towards a grey stone chapel near a sharp left-hand bend. As you approach the chapel, leave the pavement and walk between the chapel and the black and white village hall towards a stile into a field.

The stone chapel was once the local Congregationalist chapel built in 1827 and re-built in 1873, but is now a rural crafts centre.

Yew Tree Cottage, Marton

2. Climb the stile into the field and follow the direction of the yellow arrow to walk towards a further set of stiles at the opposite side of the field. Climb the double stile and walk ahead across a small field to a stile opposite. Climb the stile, cross a wooden footbridge and then climb another stile.

As you cross this series of fields there are pleasing views to the right including the Ganderbeach, Luckley Hill and Whitsburn Hill which has an earthwork near its summit. To the left stand Marton Crest and Marton Hill.

3. Go straight across the field towards the next stile. A group of static caravans can be seen beyond the field edge to the right.

Climb the stile at the opposite end of the field, then cross a wooden footbridge. Turn immediately right and walk along the left-hand side of a line of trees and a stream. Make for a stile at the far end of the field. Climb the stile and walk towards the caravans (follow yellow arrow). Walk for a short distance down the tarmac path, then turn right on to the grass immediately after a bungalow called Sherry Time. Walk past two caravans towards a sand-coloured bungalow ignoring the yellow arrow. Walk along the left-hand bank of the stream, with bungalows and caravans on your left. Follow the yellow arrow. The track soon opens out to give an excellent view of Marton Pool as the stream flows beneath an attractive, stone bridge.

The lake is ancient and once covered over 30 acres. Beyond the water you can enjoy views of distant hills. As evidence of the age of the lake, an early dugout canoe was once discovered at the pool, and a large tumulus on the Marton side may well have been an artificial island for a prehistoric lake.

Leave the pool by returning along the path you have just walked down until reaching the signpost with two arrows. Turn right in the direction of the 'Shropshire Countryside Commission' arrow along the tarmac drive between bungalows. In a few hundred yards turn right at a T-junction, following the yellow arrow sign. Shortly after the reception office on the left, leave the drive by climbing a stile on the left.

Walk across the field in the direction of the arrow towards a wooden footbridge at the opposite end.

4. Cross the footbridge and walk ahead making for a similar structure at the opposite edge of the field. Cross the footbridge over a stream and enter the next field.

In Summer and early Autumn the first two fields lie dotted with puffballs.

Ignore the direction of the arrow and walk diagonally left towards the far left-hand corner of the field. Cross the wide Reabrook by means of yet another footbridge. Initially follow the arrow direction walking slightly to the left of two oak trees. At the second oak turn left and walk through a wide gap between two small beech trees. Walk along the right-hand edge of the field alongside a fence

Marton Pool

beside a small brook. In about 75 yards turn right and climb a stile, then go through a wide metal gate. Follow the yellow arrow sign, walking diagonally left across the next field towards the far left-hand corner.

The hills are now much closer and seem to flow one into the other. The lump of Whitburn Hill and its top knot of trees stands to the left.

At the field corner climb a stile and cross a wooden footbridge over a stream. Climb another stile into a field and walk initially along the left-hand side of a tall hedge (this area can become very muddy after rain). Continue walking along the right-hand side of the field for about 500 yards to a pair of stiles in the far right-hand corner. A detached house stands near to the stiles. Climb the stiles and join a track taking you past the left-hand side of the house.

5. In about 100 yards turn right and walk along a broad unmetalled trackway between trees. Soon a long neglected quarry can be seen through gaps to the right.

Rural Shropshire never ceases to amaze, not only because of its stunning beauty but also its hidden world of early industrial activity in places which seem to have no right to be dabbling in anything so mundane. Soon we see jagged, well-weathered cliff faces, some colonised by trees, bushes and the ubiquitous gorse. Just after passing an old concrete building on the right you will see the remains of a stone bridge beyond the trees to the left. A close exploration among the left-hand woodland will reveal further bridge parapets and two sunken tracks several feet down and divided by a length of hedge. It is thought that quarrying took place here over a lengthy period of time and concluded about the middle of the 20th century.

Continue walking ahead along the lane for about 100 yards. Ignore the fingerpost and stile leading into a field on the left. The lane passes between trees, begins to climb and eventually descends towards a junction with a grassy drive. Ignore the drive which leads ahead towards a farm and follow the original lane round to the left, passing the farm buildings at Wilmington on the right-hand side then a cottage on the left. In about 75 yards reach an old stone bridge.

A stream which has plummeted

from nearby hills now rushes urgently beneath the bridge, then tumbles under tree-cover on the other side. The stream has passed through the village of Rorrington, less than a mile upstream from this point. In the past the village was the scene of one of rustic England's endearing customs, that of the 'Halliwell Wakes'. On Ascension Day a holy well on a nearby hillside was decked with green boughs, rushes and flowers. The locals walked around the hill, urged on by fife, drum and fiddle and danced and frolicked before succumbing to feasting at the well-side. A local ale was brewed on the green to be consumed the following Ascension Day, and there were sweetened and spiced flat buns which brought good luck if kept. Sadly, it all came to an end during the 1830s.

6. Almost immediately reach a road junction with the lane from Rorrington and turn right. The stream runs to the right-hand side. In 250 yards arrive at a further stone bridge over the stream.

Eventually the stream will join Aylesford Brook which, in turn, helps supply Marton Pool with fresh water. There are rounded fields to left and right, including those surrounding the farm at Wilmington. Wilmington's unobtrusive appearance masks a long history. A motte and bailey stood near the existing farm buildings. Even today the motte stands some four metres high at one end of an oval bailey. In 1255 two women, Sibil and Margaret, were tenants paying rent to the Lord of Montgomery. By 1812 there was a valuable estate including a mansion, farm houses and cottages.

In a few hundred yards pass a farm at Groton on the left. About half a mile further the lane climbs up to the village of Marton. Turn right at the junction with the main road, arriving immediately back at the Sun Inn.

Howle Pool - Holy Well - Old Caynton Mill - Tibberton - Ercall Heath - Howle

◆

O.S. Map Landranger 1:50,000 Sheet No. 126. Starting Point GR 692 235.
Parking: Roadside just beyond Howle Pool and Howle Pool Farm on the Tibberton side
of the pool along the country road to Tibberton from the A41 road at Standford Bridge.
Be sure not to block the field gate. Distance: 7 Miles.

*A fairly easy walk using a combination of field paths and country lanes.
The twisting River Meese and the simple beauty of Howle Pool combine
with historic houses and the picturesque village of Tibberton to produce
a walk full of interest and varying scenery.*

Howle Pool

The walk begins alongside Howle Pool, a long and fairly narrow stretch of mirror-like water whose southern edge nudges the roadside opposite Howle Pool Farm. Although man-made, the pool and its surrounding reed-beds and woodland have gelled over many years into a mature and attractive haven for wildlife. An old sandstone windmill tower stands nearby.

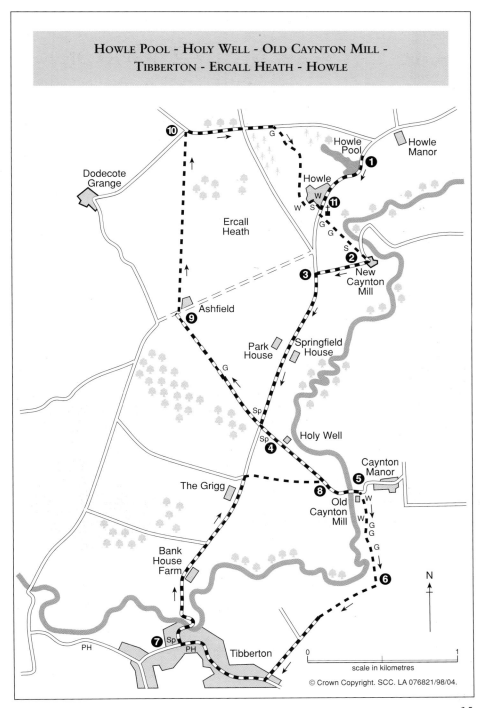

Howle Pool - Holy Well - Old Caynton Mill -
Tibberton - Ercall Heath - Howle

1. Walk away from the pool and along the lane towards Tibberton. Immediately after passing a redundant Methodist chapel on the left, go through or climb a metal field gate and follow a footpath sign past a bungalow walking diagonally to the right across a field. Beware the electric fence in this field. Walk towards and climb a metal gate at the far right-hand end. Descend the next field towards a clump of trees. At the bottom of the slope climb a stile and turn right on to a path running briefly alongside the River Meese.

The river has just snaked through woodland. Soon it rushes noisily under an ivy-covered stone bridge, then over a weir.

2. Turn right on reaching a lane soon passing New Caynton Mill Farm on the left.

The farm was formerly called 'Forge Farm', and it is known that a fair quantity of iron was produced at the location as long ago as the early eighteenth century. In 1954 it was reported that some iron could still be found in the hedge banks, whereas some had earlier been used for road foundations. There has been a mill on the site for several centuries, water being channelled from the nearby river. The present mill buildings were rebuilt in the seventeenth century.

3. After passing the farm, bear right and walk up a metalled lane for several hundred yards to a T-junction with the Howle-Tibberton road. Turn left and walk along the road in the direction of Tibberton for about one mile. At a road junction turn left (signpost 'Edgmond, Newport') and after about 175 yards, and just before Holywell Farm, look for a small gap in the hedge on the left. There is a narrow track between trees. For a brief diversion, follow the track which eventually descends to a brick-encased well.

The water slides out through a concrete channel. This is spring water, and it used to be pumped up to a large tank fixed onto the side of the house at nearby Holywell Farm. When mains water was laid on at the farm in 1972, the main function of the well became redundant, although watercress was grown here (for sale at Newport market) until the early 1980s. One romantic theory has it that long ago, monks from nearby Dodecote Grange took water from the spring.

4. Return along the track and turn left onto the lane. Pass Holywell Farm on the left and continue along the lane for about half a mile. The road descends to a bridge over the River Meese, and then towards Old Caynton Mill.

You have now reached a particularly charming location. The river glides lazily beneath the bridge and between meadows before ambling on towards Tibberton. Meanwhile, a separate water-course has parted company with the river to form a mill-race on the left. At first, the water dawdles beneath overhanging willows. After passing under the road, the mill-race truly lives up to its name by splashing beneath the end of the mill house. It then steadies itself before joining the main river again.

5. Walk past the mill house and make a short climb up a hill towards a Bridleway sign on the right. Follow the direction of the sign which takes you through a wide gap into a field on the right. Take a broad track as it curves around the right-hand side of a crop-field and soon passes alongside Old Caynton Mill house.

The mill house beside the waters is now a private residence. Milling had taken place on the site for a considerable number of years, although the present building belongs to the early nineteenth century. It was at that time an oil mill for the crushing of linseed. Earlier this century Arthur Nock of Sambrook was the miller who took out the waterwheel and put in a turbine. Later an electric motor was installed. The mill became derelict in the late 1960s. There are stories of a secret passage running under the road for some 200 to 300 yards from the original nearby Caynton Manor.

Soon after a red-brick house comes into view, fork right leaving the original track at the 'Shropshire Countryside Commission' sign and join a broad, grassy track which runs along the left-hand side of a wooden fence. The river is just across the meadow to the right. Go through two metal gates and enter a field taking you alongside a curve in the Meese which then funnels its way between steep banks and through crop-fields. Walk along the right-hand side of a wire fence towards woodland. Go through a metal gate and into a short stretch of the wood, using a narrow pathway. The path soon opens out into a broad, grassy track between hedges.

6. Immediately the track opens out, turn sharp right along a broad trackway which runs between crop-fields. After about a mile the trackway ends at a T-junction with a metalled road. Turn right and walk along the footpath towards the nearby village of Tibberton.

There are Duke of Sutherland estate cottages and half-timbered cottages along the way, including the seventeenth century Tibberton House. Despite its small batch of half-timbered properties, Tibberton became better known as an 'estate village' belonging to the Duke of Sutherland during the early nineteenth century.

In Saxon times the place was known as 'Tybrighton', and in the Doomsday book 'Tebritone'. The name is also thought to mean 'The Settlement of Tibbeorht's People'. All Saints church was rebuilt in 1842 on the site of a 12th century church. Among the village's older dwellings are Rose Farmhouse and Sutherland Forge, both half-timbered and of the 17th century.

7. Immediately after the Sutherland Arms turn right (signpost 'Howle, Childs Ercall') in to Mill Lane. Walk along the road which descends past the Rectory and Old Mill Nurseries.

The cottage close to the river Meese was once a paper mill thought to have been the last one in Shropshire. It closed in 1912 due to problems transporting materials between Tibberton and Crudgington

Cottages at Tibberton

Station. Formerly, large horse-drawn wagons were a familiar sight on the road between the two locations. The sandstone bridge over the Meese was built in the 17th century, or perhaps even earlier. It has since been widened with brick on the east side. The iron lock mechanism for the mill pool of the former mill can still be seen.

Follow the narrow road as it climbs away from the village, soon passing a farm on the right. At a road junction keep straight ahead (signpost 'Sambrook, Hinstock'). Pass by a large black barn on the left (at The Griggs Farm) and in a few hundred yards, look for a broad opening into a field on the right (opposite a sandstone cottage standing beside a green lane). Enter the field and walk along the right-hand side. For a short distance there is a hedge to the right.

Woodland, following the course of the Meese can be seen ahead.

8. Emerge through a wide gap in the hedge and turn left on to a metalled lane. This is the lane encountered earlier as you approached Old Caynton Mill. This time, walk in the opposite direction for about a quarter of a mile, passing Holywell Farm and the entrance to the Holy Well again before arriving at a T-junction near some cottages. Cross the road and go straight on down a broad track which soon passes a bungalow on the right, then runs alongside a row of birch trees. Continue along the track as it passes by woodland and crop fields. Go through a wide gate and the path then runs between crop-fields.

9. At a cross roads go straight over a metalled lane and continue along a broad track. Immediately pass by a white cottage, then a farm on the right. There is a large patch of pine woodland across the field to the right.

This area is known as Ercall Heath. It was, in fact heathland for only about 25 years. At the start of World War I, there were some 900 acres of woodland (1000 acres would make a forest) belonging to the Adderley Estate, and consisting of conifers and oak. The woodland was then requisitioned to enable a Potteries timber merchant to fell the trees, some being used for pit-props, some as duck-boards to be used on the Western Front. Two cock-pits were unearthed during the felling process. It is known that cock fights were held here at the turn of the century. Some time after completion of the felling, the land was sold off very cheaply in lots and numerous wooden bungalows were built on the edge of the remaining woodland. In 1939 some of the land was again brought under cultivation, following much laborious removal of tree-stumps. Heavy doses of lime were applied, but later the crops suffered due to soil deficiency. Nowadays the soil is more fertile so that good yields of cereals and potatoes are achieved.

10. At a T-junction near the driveway to Dodecote Grange, turn right and walk along a metalled road which passes between trees. Keep straight ahead at a cross-roads. About 150 yards further on look for a wide metal gate into a crop-field on the right. Enter the field and walk along its right-hand edge with woodland on the right. At the end of the woodland walk straight ahead towards a red-brick house. Make for a wooden footpath sign near the house and walk along the right-hand side of a wooden fence, alongside the house. Leave the field by means of a stile. At another wooden footpath sign, join an unmetalled track which bends sharply to the right and in about 100 yards leads you to a T-junction with a metalled lane.

Turn left and descend the lane for several hundred yards back to Howle Pool.

Aston-on-Clun - Beambridge - Clunbury - Clunbury Hill - Aston-on-Clun

✦

O.S. Map: Sheet 129. Starting Point GR 392 817.
Parking: The car park at the Kangaroo Inn (please contact landlord first),
Aston-on-Clun alongside the B4368 Craven Arms - Clun Road.
Distance: 5 1/2 miles.

*A generally easy walk including quiet lanes, a riverside path,
the peaceful village of Clunbury and a fairly steep climb up Clunbury Hill
to enjoy delightful views.*

For a very small village Aston-on-Clun has enough fascination to cater for a dozen such places. The Kangaroo Inn is thought to have a name unique to this country and its landlord is, not surprisingly, Australian. The building is 19th century. Its next door neighbour is one of Aston's mysterious round houses. There are no corners in which the devil may hide! They are thought to have been built between 1750 and 1830 by a local eccentric. Similar houses can be found in Cornwall. The Forge Garage was once the local blacksmith's premises, whilst in a field behind the village hall lie

Tree decorating, Aston-on-Clun

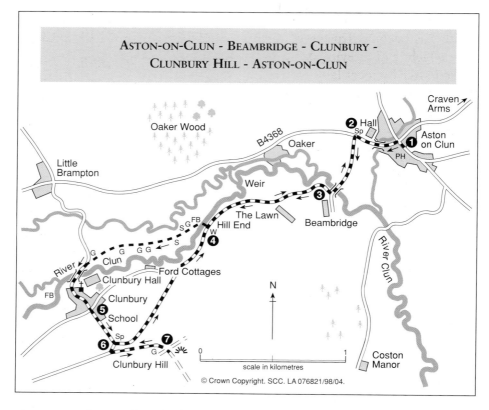

© Crown Copyright. SCC. LA 076821/98/04.

the remains of a deserted village, including the main street and some earthen house platforms. The earliest settlers at Aston were Saxons who were later dispossessed by Normans. The community flourished during the Tudor era but suffered badly in the Civil War.

1. Leave the car-park and turn left to walk along a pavement. Walk in the direction of a flag-covered tree and a two-arched bridge over a stream near the centre of the village.

The tree, a black poplar, is not only the focal point of the village but also the subject of much intriguing study into the origins of the annual ceremony of tree dressing. The present tree was planted in 1996 to replace its predecessor which was finally declared unsafe after watching over the village for an estimated 250 years. On 29th May each year the tree is newly decorated with flags of the home countries and the commonwealth attached to poles, then nailed to the tree.

Since the early 1950s Hopesay Parish has become Trustee of the tree which had previously been looked after by local landowners, the Marston Family. The tree was dressed on 29th May 1786 to celebrate the marriage of Squire Richard Marston of nearby Sibdon Carwood to Mary Carter, Aston's local beauty. The Marstons preserved the custom from there onwards until the estate was sold in 1951. However, the practice of tree-dressing, revived by Charles II in 1660, probably goes back to a much earlier civilisation. It is known that Brigid, a Celtic Goddess of fertility, was worshipped at a shrine which was a tree, and there are records of tree-dressing ceremonies during succeeding centuries. Aston seems to be about the only place in Britain to perpetuate the custom to the present day.

Continue past the tree to where the road crosses a stream which has come down the valley from near Hopesay and later feeds the River Clun at Beambridge. When the pavement ends, walk along the roadside for about 175 yards.

2. At a junction, turn left into a lane (signpost 'Beambridge') and walk for about half a mile to a metal bridge over the River Clun.

Burrow Hill overlooks Aston and has an iron-age hill fort. It is known also that the area was inhabited by bronze-age people.

3. Leave this idyllic spot and follow the lane as it curves sharply to the right. For a while the river parts company with the lane by wandering through fields to the right. Stay on the quiet lane as it gradually rises above the fields to the right.

There are occasional glimpses of rounded hills on both sides of the route. As the lane begins to descend, you will hear, then see the trickling tree-lined river down the slope on the right. A gap appears allowing a clear view overlooking the water as it crosses a rocky causeway.

4. Near the causeway leave the lane by turning right (following the fingerpost) and descend to a footbridge over the river. Leave the footbridge by means of a latched gate at the far end. Walk ahead along a grassy track for a few yards, then climb a stile on the left to enter a field. Walk diagonally right across the field (the river flows

alongside the left-hand field edge). Look for and climb a stile to enter the next field. Walk along the right-hand side of this field.

The view to the left is dominated by the elongated ridge of Clunbury Hill, with a crown of pine trees at the summit.

Make for a small old wooden building ahead. Walk to the right of the building and go through a metal gate into the next field. Walk along the right-hand side of the field towards a wide metal gate in the right-hand corner. Follow the yellow arrow and go through the gate to walk straight across the next field to a gate opposite. Follow the arrow and go through the gate,

St Swithin's Church, Clunbury

then walk along the right-hand edge of the next field. At the far right-hand end of the field, go through a metal gate and turn left into a lane leading you towards the village of Clunbury. Walk along the lane for about 100 yards and cross the stone bridge over the Clun. Follow the lane as it twists through the village.

On the left is the broad square 13th century tower of St Swithin's church. Both the church's nave and chancel are Norman. An intriguing insight into rural ecclesiastical life in the nineteenth century is to be found in an entry in the churchwarden's book, dated 1808: It records that the vicar had agreed with his parishioners 'to take instead of the spare wine at the sacrament, ten quart pottles of good port wine annually to be delivered to him every year at Easter'.

5. Keep walking straight ahead out of the village soon arriving at a cross-roads. Walk ahead (signpost 'Clunbury Hill') and immediately pass the village school on the left.

The Victorian school building is still very much in use as a primary school. Local benefactor

Edward Turner's will, proved in the 1860s, included a legacy of £100 to the Minister and Churchwardens of Clunbury for the use and benefit of a public school at or near Clunbury. The site was then selected, and a contribution also from the National Society ensured that the village school could be constructed.

6. Continue along the lane towards the hill ahead. After a few hundred yards reach a junction with a further lane to the left. Follow the lane which you have walked along as it veers sharply right then immediately afterwards, leave the lane by turning left onto a broad grassy track leading up to the hill. The track soon narrows and climbs to a metal gate about 35 yards ahead. Go through the gate and follow the narrow path as it climbs up to the left. Stay on the path as it climbs between trees. Near the hill's summit go through a metal gate and walk along the right-hand side of a fence. When you reach a T-junction with a track running from right to left, you are virtually at the top of the hill.

Prehistoric man traversed the crest of the hill on the Clee-Clun Ridgeway, a vital trading route which helped oil the wheels of primitive commerce a few thousand years ago. As you might expect, the hill-top views are superb. To the west Clun Valley lies flanked by a ribbon of undulating hills. In an easterly direction lies Coston Hill and eventually the slopes surrounding the village of Clungunford.

7. When you have explored the hill-top, retrace your steps back down the hill as if returning to Clunbury. On reaching the lane once again at the foot of the hill, turn right and walk the short distance to the junction encountered earlier, and this time bear right to join the secondary lane which runs along the bottom of the hill (instead of returning to the school). After about half-a-mile, the lane descends towards the road to Beambridge. Turn right at the junction and walk the one and a half miles or so back through Beambridge to the junction with the B4368 road. Turn right at the junction and walk through the village of Aston-on-Clun and back to the Kangaroo Inn car park.

CLEOBURY MORTIMER - NEEN SAVAGE - MUSBATCH - MAWLEY HALL - CLEOBURY MORTIMER

◆

O.S. Map Landranger 1:50,000 Sheet No. 138. Starting Point: GR 674 757. Parking: Roadside opposite or near St. Mary's Church in Church Street, Cleobury Mortimer. Distance 3 miles and 3½ miles.

Two walks for the price of one are offered here taking in some attractive stretches of the river Rea, and the gently undulating countryside surrounding the historic south-east Shropshire town of Cleobury Mortimer. The latter portion of the first walk includes a stiff climb up a metalled lane leading to Cleobury Mortimer. Some parts may become muddy in wet weather.

St Mary's is thought to be at least 800 years old and stands on the site of an earlier Saxon church. The twisted shape of the spire is caused, rather like that of its more famous Chesterfield counterpart, by gradual warping of its oak framework.

Walk One

1. **Walk along the pavement opposite the church in the direction of Kidderminster, soon passing the library on the right hand side then the Methodist Church. Near the Bell Inn cross the road and walk past the Old Lion Inn. Walk alongside a red brick terrace. Immediately after Peppercorn Cottage, turn left into New Road, then right into** Rockley Bank. **Follow the Public Footpath sign down a sloping path towards a small wooden gate. Go through this gate and descend a narrow path with a grassy bank on the left towards some trees at the bottom of a shallow valley. Walk onto the footbridge over the little River Rea.**

The bridge is an engaging spot at which to make a first encounter with Cleobury's River Rea. To the right the water soon tumbles over rocks, then noisily swirls down the valley beneath over-hanging trees. About ten miles down stream its ultimate destiny will be a fusion with the River Teme not far from Tenbury Wells.

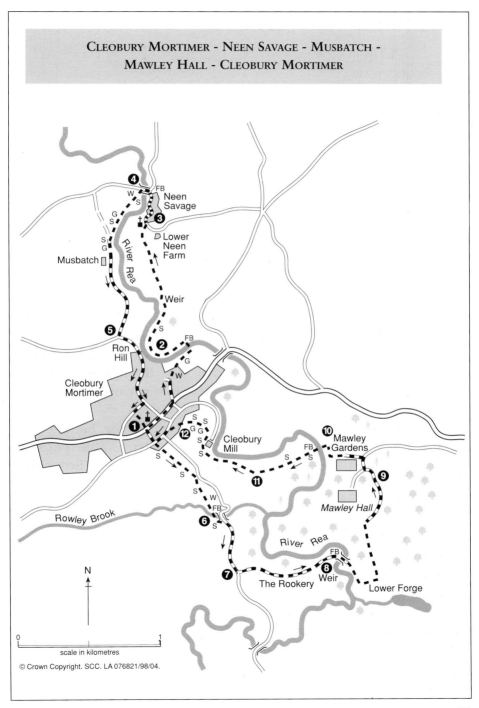

CLEOBURY MORTIMER - NEEN SAVAGE - MUSBATCH - MAWLEY HALL - CLEOBURY MORTIMER

2. Cross the bridge and in about 20 yards, go through a small gate. Turn left and walk along a grassy track between trees.

There is a row of old cottages just behind you and to your left is a broad grassy area including a fairly deep grass-covered channel. This is the site of the former Cleobury Mill. A quite extensive paper mill operated here during the last century until it was burnt down in the mid 1880s. In the 18th century a corn mill had occupied the site. The cottages and the channel (the bed of a mill race) are all that remains of the former riverside activities.

Continue for a few hundred yards along the field path as it curves to the right and leads eventually to a white cottage. Climb a stile and walk past the cottage called W a l f o r d ' s Bridge.

St Mary's Church, Cleobury Mortimer

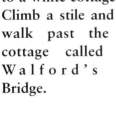

Another paper mill (Walford's Mill) was once situated nearby. Just a few miles further upstream, the river shrivels and becomes merely Rea Brook. Its source is at Upper Netchwood, a mile or two north of Ditton Priors.

Continue walking along the pathway ahead between trees and still beside the water. The path can become muddy after rain. Pass a derelict mill building on the left, and the path then climbs away from the river. Soon you are walking between hedges with undulating fields on either side. Continue along this broad unmetalled path for about one quarter of a mile. At a junction with an unmetalled lane on the right, keep straight on towards the square towered church ahead. In about 100 yards arrive at a T-junction.

At the junction, pause and look up the lane to the right for a good view of an interesting half-timbered house standing on a rise in the terrain. Lower Neen Farmhouse consists of stone and brick with a timber framework. Its origins may be 16th century or even earlier.

3. Turn left at a junction and walk along the road towards Neen Savage Church.

The Church of St. Mary is essentially a Norman building with a sturdy, square tower. There are also some fifteenth century internal features. Near the entrance gateway stands a war memorial to sons of Neen Savage.

Follow the road and in a short distance you will arrive at a ford on the left. Ignore the metalled road on the left and instead, turn left onto a narrow path which leads to a footbridge over the river.

In times past this valley of the Rea (formerly the Neen) rang to the noise of numerous paper mills (from the early 18th century). The twelve mile 'Cleobury Mortimer and Ditton Priors Railway' occupied the valley from 1908 until 1965 and ran some distance to the east of the bridge, later crossing the B4363 road.

4. Walk to the far end of the bridge, then briefly divert to the left onto a grassy bank beside the river.

From the riverside vantage point you will be able to read a notice on the bridge, indicating by arrow mark the height of the flood of the 26th September 1946, as recorded by F.M. Tomkinson of Chilton.

Return to the path, then walk towards a metalled road. Turn right on to the road and in a few yards, turn left to follow a 'Public Footpath' sign leading you into a field by means of a stile. Ignore direction of arrow, instead walk virtually straight ahead across the field. The river and church are nearby on the left, behind the trees. Head for two prominent oak trees and then walk between them, making for the right-hand corner of the field. Go through a wide metal gate to enter the next small field and walk straight across it. Where the field narrows, climb a stile on the right-hand side and follow a narrow path which twists upwards between oak and pine saplings. On reaching the top of the slope, turn around for a final view of Neen Savage Church. Climb a stile and turn left, then go through

a metal gate to walk ahead along a narrow path between hedges. In about 200 yards, the track opens out as it passes Musbatch, a renovated part-timbered old house on the right. Walk ahead along a wide unmetalled track. After a few hundred yards go through a metal gate and continue ahead along a driveway.

After a further two hundred yards or so, views open out towards Cleobury Mortimer and its surrounding countryside to the left. It is claimed that William Langland, 14th century author of the poem *Piers Plowman* revealing the dreams of a medieval son of the soil, was born at Cleobury Mortimer.

5. At a T-junction with a metalled lane turn left and walk down the lane. At the foot of the hill the road curves to the right, taking you alongside a quiet stretch of the river. After about 100 yards, the lane parts company with the river and climbs steeply. Towards the top of the climb, pass a woodland glade on the left. For a while use the pavement as you continue walking ahead. As the lane descends towards the main road at Cleobury take the last right turn. Soon pass the Georgian, former Lacon Childe school on the left.

In 1714 Sir William Lacon Childe, Lord of the Manor, left his personal estate to be used to pay for a master to teach the youth of the parish of Cleobury. The elegant building was completed in 1751, and in 1997 was converted into a private house. The present-day Lacon Childe school is housed in a modern building in another part of the town.

Continue past the old school, and near the Childe road sign, turn left between metal bollards and descend a winding path. In about 75 yards this path leads to St. Mary's churchyard. Bear right, passing by the right-hand side of the church tower.

In the church is a memorial in the east window to William Langland. A nineteenth century vicar had it put there, and among its crimsons, greens and blues lies Piers Plowman with the river and hills as his companions. At a spot near the outside of the church, the body of the young Prince Arthur is believed to have rested on its way to Worcester Cathedral following his untimely death in 1502 at Ludlow Castle.

Continue along the path to arrive back at the starting point in the main street.

Walk Two

Start this section immediately opposite the church and near the King's Arms Hotel. Leave the main street and walk down Lion Lane. In about 100 yards, at a bend leave the lane and climb a stile leading into a field. Keep to the left-hand side of the field, close to a hedge, as you climb away from the town. At the hill top go through a wide gap between hedges and walk ahead along a field path, passing by the right-hand side of some farm buildings. (Beware of an electric fence as you continue ahead.)

At this point a first view of the imposing Mawley Hall presents itself in the distance.

Climb a wooden fence, walk diagonally left and soon descend a grassy slope at the bottom left-hand end of which is a stile.

It is thought that much English and Welsh blood was spilt on this slope during a horrendous battle between the two armies in the 11th century. Certainly, three castles have been built in the Cleobury Mortimer area in early times, only to be destroyed.

Climb the stile and descend a further, fairly steep path between trees. A small brook (Rowley Brook) threads its way below

the path just before you arrive at another stile which is accompanied by a fingerpost. Climb the stile and turn left walking along a broad trackway for about 30 yards.

6. At a junction with a metalled road, turn right.

7. Look for and follow a wide unmetalled driveway on the left, just before a sharp right-hand bend in the road. The drive curves to the right and after about 300 yards, passes by some stables on the left and a green barn on the right at The Rookery. Go through a wooden gateway and walk alongside a stone wall on the left. The broad trackway continues between wooden fencing and past a tree plantation.

8. The path twists downwards, then falls steeply between trees towards a weir. Immediately before the weir, turn right on to a grassy path which leads you in about 20 yards to a green footbridge. Cross the footbridge. Turn right onto a broad trackway taking you over a small stone bridge. Follow the broad track for about one mile as it first winds between trees and grass. The trackway then twists for several hundred yards through a

The Weir,
Nr Mawley Hall

tree covered valley and climbs above a reed-edged pool on the right.

There is a closer glimpse of Mawley Hall through the trees to the left. The hall was built for Sir Edward Blount in 1730, in rustic baroque style in brick and local sandstone. Despite some weathering of the original exterior, the hall still boasts some of the finest internal plasterwork and wood carving in the country. From 1961 to recent times, Mr and Mrs Anthony Galliers-Pratt have developed the former run-down gardens in complete sympathy with the 18th century house. Some mature trees (remnants of the ancient Wyre Forest) still remain.

9. At a T-junction (footpath sign) turn right along a tarmac drive.

At this point there are views down to Cleobury Mortimer and beyond to the commanding height of Titterstone Clee. It was the need to transport effectively Dhustone quarried on Lord Boyne's estate at Titterstone (Shropshire's second tallest hill) which provided part of the motivation for the railway built through the Rea Valley to Cleobury Mortimer.

At a cross-roads, turn left (footpath sign) and descend a slope close by an orchard and walled gardens on the left. The track curves downwards, then turns sharp left. Walk alongside the wall on the left for a further

100 yards, then look for and follow a track on the right which descends between undergrowth. At the bottom of the slope, you will hear the river rushing down to the left. Look for and follow a path on the left which takes you immediately onto a footbridge over the Rea.

10. Cross the bridge and climb a stile, then walk up a grassy slope with fencing to your left. At the top of the slope continue ahead alongside the fence towards the next stile. Climb the stile (yellow arrow) and walk straight ahead along the right-hand side of the wire fence for about 400 yards.

11. Where the fence ends, look for a yellow arrow pointing right on a metal gate on the left (ignore the arrow pointing ahead). Turn right and cross a narrow path which would have taken you straight ahead. Descend a wide grassy track down to the river. Climb a stile at the valley bottom and walk ahead along a grassy track with the river nearby down right. Continue walking along the river. The path runs alongside a stile, then the right-hand side of a stone cottage. Climb a stile just after the cottage and bear left moving away from the river towards a wide gate on the left-hand side of a brick house.

This small settlement lies at the end of Pinkham Lane. It is the far end of Lion Lane which you took at the start of the walk. At this point the road once crossed the river either by means of a bridge or ford. In 1794 Thomas Telford built a new bridge over the Rea to the north-east of the town, thus depriving the lane if its status as a main road to Bewdley. Nowadays the lane terminates at the cluster of buildings you have now reached. The brick house was once the New Inn but later became a mill house.

Go through the gate and walk up a grassy slope alongside the brick house and towards a similar gate about 50 yards ahead. Climb a stile on the left-hand side of the gate. Walk ahead and upwards towards the next gate and stile a further 50 yards ahead.

Down the slope to the right lies Cleobury Mill, constructed mainly of stone and with a tile roof. It has been converted into a private dwelling. A 16ft diameter waterwheel stands on the river side of the building. It is thought that a corn mill stood on the site as early as the 11th century. The much restored mill was in full production until

1974, and there was some activity as recently as 1990. There were three other mills nearby at Pinkham and the surrounding woodland and countryside also contained furnaces and forges, some of them dating back to the 16th century.

Climb the stile and continue walking upwards, through a tunnel of trees. After about 200 yards, reach some buildings at the top of the slope. Turn left on to a track, and walk on the left-hand side of a stone cottage. Continue along the broad trackway past some bungalows. Pass a second stone cottage and immediately turn right. In about 5 yards, turn left onto a narrow path. The path descends to Lion Lane.

Turn left and retrace your steps to the start of the walk.

A stroll along the elegant main street of the town would be very rewarding. There are Georgian houses, old inns, interesting little shops and some charming half-timbered cottages. A town has stood on this spot for at least 800 years and its name is derived from the Clee (clay) Hill which towers to the west. The Norman family of DeMortimer made the town its main dwelling place.

Ellesmere Wharf - Blakemere - Colemere - Lyneal - Welshampton - The Mere - Ellesmere Wharf

◆

O.S. Map 1:50,000 Landranger Sheet No. 126. Starting Point: GR 399 345.
Parking: Small car park near Canal Wharf, just off Wharf Street,
near centre of Ellesmere. Distance: 9 miles.

*A lengthy but rewarding walk including lovely stretches
of the Ellesmere Canal, delightful lakes and some attractive, open countryside.
A slightly shorter alternative is also described.*

The wharf, which has experienced something of a renaissance in recent years as an attractive focal point, was once the commercial centre of the town. The old warehouse and some of the other early buildings still stand, and the whole area has been smartened up to create an appealing waterside feature just off the centre of the town. Ellesmere had some thirty malt houses in the mid-nineteenth century, (much of the malt being transported to Lancashire by fast canal boats), and later became an important cheese-making centre. The wealthy Earl of Bridgwater once owned most of Ellesmere and ever with an eye for further development, he created an iron foundry, brickworks and timber yard amongst other industrial buildings at the wharf-side.

1. Leave the wharf by taking the path along the right-hand side of the water. The canal inlet path takes you out of the town, and after several hundred yards, turn left and cross a bridge with white metal parapets. You will then arrive on the opposite side of the water near the junction with the main canal.

There is a signpost to Llangollen pointing along the main canal, and a red-brick late Georgian house with an unusually rounded end also faces the water. Nowadays called Beech House, it was once the canal office complete with committee room, offices and apartments for the accountant and engineer. When 'canal mania' gripped the country in the 1790s, Ellesmere found

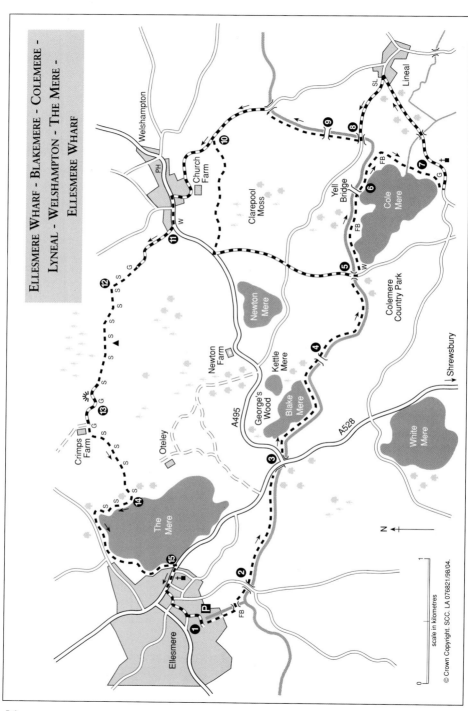

ELLESMERE WHARF - BLAKEMERE - COLEMERE - LYNEAL - WELSHAMPTON - THE MERE - ELLESMERE WHARF

Welshampton

Lineal

SL

Church Farm

PH

Clarepool Moss

⑩

⑨

⑧

Yell Bridge

FB

⑥

⑦

G

Cole Mere

FB

W

⑪

W

⑤

Colemere Country Park

G

S

S

⑫

S

S

Newton Mere

S

S

S

S

④

⑬

G

S

Newton Farm

Kettle Mere

Crimps Farm

G

S

S

Oteley

George's Wood

Blake Mere

A495

A528

S

S

White Mere

↓ Shrewsbury

The Mere

⑭

S

S

③

N ←

Ellesmere

⑮

W

✠

P

①

②

FB

scale in kilometres

0   1

© Crown Copyright. SCC. LA 076821/98/04.

56

itself at the heart of a system linking such places as the Wirral, Chirk, Llanymynech, Ruabon, Whitchurch and Nantwich. Coal and limestone were among the chief commodities to be transported along these waters. This stretch of canal, now known as the 'Shropshire Union Canal', was built by the Ellesmere canal company between 1793 and 1805.

2. Continue to walk along the left-hand side of the canal, along the towpath trod many years ago by horses pulling the barges. In a short distance pass under a bridge. Soon to the left the walk passes the entrance to the newly developed Blackwater Meadow Marina. The towpath then continues for about a quarter of a mile towards a tunnel under the A528 road.

3. The tunnel is 87 yards in length and has a towpath with a safety rail. However, it is quite dark and the path is slightly uneven in places. Occasionally water drips from the roof. For all that, a walk through the tunnel is an interesting experience but there is a diversion for those not wishing to sample it. For the diversion, turn left up a narrow path just before the tunnel entrance. At the junction with the main road, carefully cross the road and turn right on to a footpath. Then, at the junction with A495 Whitchurch road cross the road and join a path on the left-hand side of a small car park. The path descends to join the towpath at the opposite end of the tunnel. Whichever route you have used, continue along the towpath with the canal on your right-hand side.

The canal curves towards Blakemere and the towpath passes beneath a covering of tall trees. Soon, the path slices between the canal and the shore of the lake. On the far side of the mere, the blooms of countless rhododendrons seem to tumble into the water in technicolour profusion during early summer. The shrubs are backed by the mixed woodland of George's Wood which clothes the shapely moraines on the outer rim of the Oteley Estate. In the post second world war period, British Waterways encouraged the leisure boat industry on certain canals as a source of revenue. The process virtually saved the Shropshire Union Canal and, in summer especially, the frequent slowly-gliding boats bring a touch of character and life to the watery scene. Narrow boats often moor at the canal side at this point. There can be few more idyllic settings for a wayside lunch stop than this.

4. **After leaving Blakemere behind go under the bridge and continue along the path.**

Dragonflies often dance above a large patch of marsh marigolds in a tract of marsh land down on the left. A little further on a pool lies to the left. These wet areas are remnants of the same ice-age activity which created Ellesmere's lakeland thousands of years ago.

Soon a wide turning point for boats is passed. Bridge number 55 then comes into view. A thatched cottage stands nearby on the right.

The half-timbered cottage was built in the seventeenth century and in former days, its thatch would probably have been of local reeds.

5. **Immediately before the bridge, follow a steep narrow path up to the left, then turn right to cross the bridge over the canal. Walk ahead for about 50 yards and turn left, just before reaching the thatched cottage (follow signpost 'Yellwood'). Walk along the broad trackway which soon passes some old** workshops and stables on the left, remnants of the heyday of the Ellesmere canal. The track then enters a stretch of woodland and reaches the stone arches of former lime kilns on the left. Ignore a track curving up left and follow the lakeside path ahead. This wide track takes you alongside the broad sheet of water which is Cole Mere whose edges are laced with water lilies at this point. Cross a wooden footbridge were water flows down a slope and towards the lake. The trackway continues between trees and becomes narrower before climbing up left towards a canal bridge.

6. **Return to the path and then turn left to walk along the right-hand side of the canal while the lake is beyond trees to the right. After a few hundred yards, the path leaves the canal side by veering right and descends a short flight of steps. Bear left at a junction and continue through the woodland. After a further few hundred yards, the track crosses a small stone bridge, then emerges on to a field path beside the lake. Follow the path ahead towards the yachting compound.**

After the woodland walk, the stroll along the field path

provides a delightful contrast. To the right, the exciting expanse of Cole Mere's water borders the grass. Yachts idly glide to and fro, while canada geese and gulls also stake their claims to a share of the calm surface. The name 'Cole Mere' relates not merely to the mere itself. Records show that the settlement of Colemere (or 'Culemere') was held as a Manor on behalf of Earl Roger De Montgomery in 1086. Sixteenth century thatched cottages still survive in the village.

7. **Leave the mereside by means of a wooden gate, then turn left across a stretch of grass towards a car park. From the**

Ellesmere Canal

car park, turn left and walk along a lane towards a roadside church.

The Church of St John the Evangelist was built in 1870 for Marion, Viscountess Brownlow in memory of her son, the second Earl Brownlow who died in 1867. The Brownlows were great land-owners in the Ellesmere district.

After a few hundred yards the lane crosses a stream by means of a stone bridge. The same stream was encountered earlier, on leaving Yellwood. The lane is also bordered by an attractive avenue of trees, including chestnut and lime. After about half a mile of lane walking, arrive at a T-junction near Lyneal School and turn left (sign-post 'Newton, Ellesmere').

The small settlement of Lyneal has a relatively modern appearance, but has one or two half-timbered buildings. The school was built in 1880, and once there were lime works near the village since it stands fairly close to the canal.

8. **At Lyneal Wharf (signed) cross the canal bridge and immediately turn left to walk down the short slope to the canal towpath. Turn left and walk under the bridge, along the left-hand side of the canal towards the next bridge.**

You have now rejoined the towpath of the Shropshire Union Canal. Immediately, you pass by Lyneal Wharf and its former (single-storey) buildings, now converted into bungalows. The entire scene has also been tastefully landscaped by Shropshire Horticultural Society to mark its centenary year.

9. Pass under a bridge and continue along the towpath. In about half a mile, a further bridge is reached. Walk under the bridge and turn immediately left, and climb a flight of steps up to a lane. Turn right and walk along a quiet country lane.

FOR THE SHORTER ROUTE.

10. Immediately after Lyneal Lodge, turn left following the fingerpost on the left. Climb a stile and enter a field to walk along its left-hand side. At the end of the field, climb a stile and enter the next field. Walk diagonally right (following yellow arrow) to climb a grassy slope. Go through a broad gateway into the next field. Walk straight ahead along a narrow field path as it skirts the lower end of the sloping field. Ignore the gap on the left and keep walking ahead. Eventually pass through another broad gap in the hedge

to enter another field. Continue along a narrow path near the bottom of a slope, and the left-hand side of some trees. Continue along the right-hand side of this field, beside hedges, go through a wide gap into the next field. Walk up this sloping field along the left-hand side of a hedge. Descend the other side of the slope towards a stile at the bottom. Climb the stile and walk diagonally right across a small field towards a wide gap in the far corner, near the main (A495) road. On emerging near the main road, turn immediate left and walk down a narrow lane which takes you back to the canal towpath at point (5).

Your return journey to Ellesmere will take you back along the canal towpath towards Blakemere and the tunnel. You could then return to the start of the walk, either by completely retracing your steps, or leaving the canal side just before the tunnel and walking alongside the main road into Ellesmere, visiting the Meres Visitor Centre and the attractive walk alongside the largest lake, called simply the Mere.

FOR THE LONGER WALK

10. Continue along the lane beyond Lyneal Lodge for about

a quarter of a mile. At the junction with the main A495 road, cross the road and turn left, walking along the pavement. Ignore the signpost 'Stocks 1 mile' and stay on the pavement as it passes the village school.

Much of Welshampton is spread along the main road. The school was built in 1848 and there has been a church here from at least the fourteenth century. The present one was built in 1863 by Sir Gilbert Scott. It stands as a memorial to Mr Charles Kynaston Mainwaring, his widow and son, who lived at nearby Oteley House. In the churchyard is the grave of Moshueshue, the son of a Basuto Chief, who died at the vicarage in Welshampton in 1863. The vicar, who had a great interest in African people, invited the young man to spend a holiday in Shropshire during a break from his studies at Canterbury. Tragically Moshueshue caught a fatal fever. For a time the village was included in Wales (part of Flintshire) hence the prefix 'Welsh' to avoid confusion with various other 'Hamptons', and there was a settlement here in Saxon times. In June 1897 a catastrophic rail crash took place here on the Cambrian line. Three hundred Sunday School members from the Oldham area were returning from a day trip to Barmouth. Just beyond the station, the train left the track; thirteen children were killed and another thirty injured.

11. Continue along the pavement for a short distance. Just after a 'School' sign, be careful to turn right and walk alongside a small red-brick farmhouse and straight through the farmyard. At the far end of the yard, join a broad farm track taking you into open countryside. At the end of the track, bear to the left of a field gate (follow yellow arrow sign) and walk up a narrow field path along the left-hand side of a hedge. At the end of this field, climb a stile into the next field. Soon pass a small pool on the left, then the path climbs gently for a short distance. At the end of the hedge on the left, turn left (follow yellow arrow) and climb towards a pair of wooden gate posts.

12. Climb a stile and enter a field, walking diagonally right (follow yellow arrow). The field path descends gradually towards a stile at the opposite edge of the field. Climb the stile and walk directly ahead across the next field (follow arrow) which

entails climbing a fairly gradual green slope. On reaching the summit, make for a stile about 100 yards ahead. Climb the stile and walk diagonally left (follow arrow) across the bottom corner of a cropfield towards the next stile. Climb the stile and turn left to join a broad track which initially runs along the left-hand side of some trees. In about 100 yards, look for and climb a stile leading into a field on the left. Bear diagonally right to climb a slight rise. At the top of the slope, you will see a stile in the fence ahead. Walk to the stile.

From the vantage point of the stile, a panorama of distant fields and hills presents itself. On the extreme right a faraway, wooded hill gives way to a flatish plain, Welsh mountains join the vista, including the long ridge over the Vale of Llangollen, Glyn Ceiriog Valley, Llanymynech Hill and a complete ribbon of hills along the horizon to the left. Nearer to hand you can see the rooftops of Ellesmere and a portion of the Mere.

13. Climb the stile and soon descend a grassy slope towards a gate. Go through the gate and walk along an unmetalled farm track, between hedges. After a few hundred yards, the track passes by an orchard on the right, then through a gateway and on past the farmhouse of Crimps Farm. Climb a stile and enter a small field. Bear diagonally right (follow arrow) walking towards a gap in the fence opposite. Go through the gap, entering the next field and bearing diagonally right towards a stile. Climb the stile and bear left up a grassy track between an avenue of young trees. At the top of a short slope, the path narrows and runs along the right-hand side of a cropfield.

The Mere, Ellesmere

Beyond the farm to your left lies the estate of Oteley House, built around 1830 in neo-Elizabethan style for Charles Kynaston Mainwaring, a member of an old Shropshire family. In the civil war, two Mainwaring brothers actually fought on opposite sides. Soon there is a glimpse of the Mere and Ellesmere Church ahead.

At the field edge, climb a stile and walk straight ahead, along the left-hand side of a hedge.

A lovely view of the Mere faces you as you descend this field path. Beyond the lake, the dominant church and a group of mature houses complete the scene.

14. At the end of the field, turn right and climb a stile. Turn left (follow arrow) and join a pathway taking you through the woodland. The pathway twists for about 100 yards then reaches a stile. Climb the stile and continue along the path which now travels close to the shore of the Mere.

The Ellesmere district is known as the lakeland of Shropshire since there are several fairly large sheets of water near or surrounding the town. The Mere is the largest of the Ellesmere lakes which are said to one of the finest groups of wetland habitats in Britain. The plant and animal life of the meres and surrounding land provide a valuable food source for a host of resident wildfowl. Like many inland British lakes, the meres also attract unusual species during wintertime, including Golden Eye, Smew, Wigeon, Pochard, Shoveller and several varieties of geese. A large heronry can be viewed in the breeding season from a telescope at the Meres Visitor Centre. The meres evolved as a direct result of the last ice age, and were probably formed as either melt water lakes left behind by the retreating ice, or as large 'kettle holes' formed when blocks of ice became detached from retreating glaciers, were submerged, then eventually melted to form meres within deep craters. Dotted around this area are large stones or 'erratics' conveyed by ice sheets from as far away as south-west Scotland, the Irish Sea, the English Lake District and North Wales.

In about 100 yards, climb another stile and walk along a broad path between trees. Stay on this path as it continues to border the lake.

You are walking through Cremorne Gardens a twelve acre spread of parkland and formal gardens donated for public use by land owner Lord Brownlow in 1953.

Stay on the path through the gardens, skirting the lake until reaching the main gates, leading you onto the roadside path.

The stretch of land separating the main road from the lake is reminiscent of a seaside promenade except that it is frequently populated with uninhibited bands of geese and ducks demonstrating their voracious appetite for tit-bits.

15. Return from the Mereside by retracing your steps in the direction of Cremorne Gardens, but this time stay on the path leading to the town. Carefully cross the road before reaching the parish church which stands on the left-hand side.

The church of St. Mary the Virgin has beckoned us intermittently during the latter portion of the walk. Now it stands loftily above the main road. The church experienced much rebuilding during the nineteenth century but numerous remnants of much earlier days have survived. The base of the tower is 700 years old, and the St Anne Chapel (also known as the Oteley Chapel) has impressive, carved roof beams which are roughly 400 years old.

Continue along the pavement of Church Street until reaching its junction with Watergate Street. Then turn left into Watergate Street (signpost 'Town Centre, Wharf Marina') eventually reach High Street. Keep straight ahead into Scotland Street and in about 50 yards, turn left into Wharf Street which soon leads you back to the car park on the wharf.

COLEMORE GREEN - RIVER SEVERN - THE BOLDINGS - ASTLEY ABBOTS - COLEMORE GREEN

✦

O.S. Map Landranger Sheet No. 138. Starting Point GR 707 973.
Parking: Roadside verge near entrance to drive leading to Colemore Farm, about one mile from Astley Abbots.
Distance: 3 miles and 6 miles.

An easy walk using field and riverside paths, and country lanes.
An historic mansion, half-timbered houses, the charm of the riverside and wooded slopes combine to provide shorter and longer walks. Stout footwear will be needed following wet weather as some parts of the riverside can become very muddy.

Colemore Green is little more than a small cluster of dwellings and a nearby, 17th century farmhouse. Its real allure is the surrounding group of open fields and attractive woodland separating the settlement from the beauty of Shropshire's most impressive river - the Severn.

1. Follow the 'Public Footpath' sign next to the farm drive and leading over a cattle-grid. Walk along an unmetalled drive towards some farm buildings ahead. Pass by some mature houses on the right, then a barn and other farm buildings on the left. Follow the drive as it curves to the right (ignore yellow arrow into field on left) Stay on the drive and in a few yards pass by some cottages on the right. 50 yards further on pass by a further row of brick cottages then immediately turn left and go through a small wooden gate. Turn right (yellow arrow) to walk along the right-hand edge of woodland. Follow the narrow curving path, over a stile, which soon descends between trees. At the bottom of the slope climb a stile and walk ahead, descending a sloping field and walking towards a further patch of woodland. On reaching a barbed wire fence at the woodland edge, turn left and walk along the left-hand side of the fence beside the woodland of Gorsty Hill.

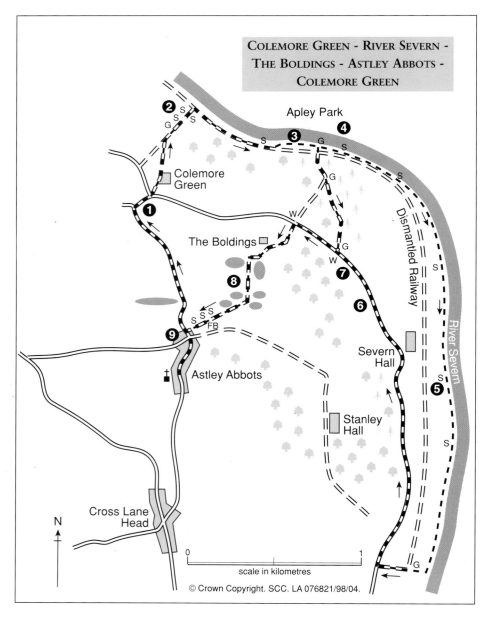

COLEMORE GREEN - RIVER SEVERN -
THE BOLDINGS - ASTLEY ABBOTS -
COLEMORE GREEN

Apley Park

Colemore
Green

The Boldings

Dismantled Railway

River Severn

Severn
Hall

Astley Abbots

Stanley
Hall

Cross Lane
Head

N

0   1
scale in kilometres

© Crown Copyright. SCC. LA 076821/98/04.

You have now reached an
enchanting part of the walk.
The route takes you through
a delightful green hollow,

bordered on either side by
woodland. Ahead to the left the
gentle folds of the wooded
landscape reach up to a plateau

66

on which stands the impressive edifice of Apley Park House. It was built in 1811 in castellated Gothic style but incorporating some remnants of an earlier 18th century house which itself had replaced a 16th century dwelling left somewhat the worse for wear by Cromwell's army in 1646.

2. In about 75 yards the track descends fairly steeply, then soon joins a wider track which curves to the right and takes you to a stile beside a wooden gate. Climb the stile and in a few yards reach an unmetalled track.

This now silent path was once a part of the track-bed of the forty mile former Great Western Line from Hartlebury in Worcestershire to Shrewsbury. It cost £13,000 per mile to build the line when work commenced in 1858. The route, which faithfully clung to the riverside for much of its scenic length fell like so many lines to Dr Beeching's axe in the 1960s. Just a few miles south of this point is the Shropshire terminal of the country's leading railway preservation society, at Bridgnorth.

Apley Park House

3. The yellow arrow on the stile just negotiated points diagonally left, and it is possible to reach the riverside by turning left and walking along the railway track-bed for about 5 yards before turning right and descending a short slope. In about 15 yards climb a stile, then turn right to walk along a path beside the river. However, the riverside path at this point can become impassable after very heavy rain. An alternative would be to turn right onto the track-bed and walk ahead for about 45 yards, then turn left and descend a short slope to a wooden fence near the riverside. Climb the fence and turn right to walk along the riverside path.

There is at this point a closer view of Apley Park House standing on its little hill on the opposite side of the river. Apley was for some centuries the ancestral home of the Whitmores, and Whitmores represented Bridgnorth in Parliament from Charles II's time until the 1870s. Thomas Charlton Whitmore spent a large sum on restoration of the house in 1811 and in 1883 Gerald Tyrwhitt (later Lord Berners) was born here. He was to distinguish himself as a composer, author, painter and, it has to be said, eccentric. In January 1962 the house became home to a boarding school, transferred from Millichope, near Craven Arms, and leased from Major General Goulburn. The school closed in August 1988.

Keep ahead along the riverside path with the railway and Chestnut coppice to the right. In places the mud may sometimes make it necessary to depart slightly from the main track.

After a few hundred yards, standing to the right is a derelict arched brick structure set into the bank. There are sandstone cliffs nearby with chambers gouged out of the rock and semblance of brick dwellings incorporated into the caves. The railway ran above the cliff-top at this point. It was constructed with the help of gangs of navvies. They tramped from site to site, sometimes with their wives and children and often constructed their own shanty hut homes, though some stayed in lodgings. It is recorded that the disused building of the Wren's Nest Forge once gave shelter to five separate households including some twenty-seven people! Perhaps the rock-dwellings at this point represented similar accommodation.

Continue for a further few hundred yards until a length of wooden fence can be seen ahead.

FOR THE SHORTER ROUTE

4. About 50 yards short of the fence, turn right and walk towards a wooden gate. Climb the gate and turn right, walking for about 12 yards back along the track-bed. Turn left and join a broad trackway which takes you gradually upwards through woodland.

The woodland is known as the Boat Coppice and this presumably refers to the ferry which used to cross the river near Chestnut coppice encountered earlier.

After about 100 yards the sometimes muddy path opens out where there is woodland on the left, and a field then a small tract of pinewood to the right. At a junction turn left and walk along a broad trackway which climbs between tall pine trees. In about 200 yards go through a narrow wooden gate to walk along the left-hand side of a hedge beside

a crop-field. After a further 200 yards go through a wide metal gate (near a 'Bridleway' fingerpost) and turn right onto a metalled lane. Continue by using instructions for the longer route starting at point 7.

FOR THE LONGER ROUTE

4. Walk in the direction of the fence and climb a stile to join a field path. This follows a bend in the river and runs along the left-hand edge of a large field. At the end of the field climb a stile and walk ahead along the left-hand edge of the next field. Climb a stile and walk ahead along the field edge near to the riverside.

Now, there are steep wooded slopes across the river to the left, while beyond the fields on the right nestle a black and white house and a batch of farm buildings. Sometimes you may also see the straight, arrow-like flight of a cormorant tracking the course of the river at this point.

5. Climb a stile and walk ahead alongside the next field, at the end of which climb another stile and walk ahead alongside yet another field. At all times, the river is your constant companion on the left. At the end of this

field ignore the stile which leads onto the Bridgnorth golf course. Instead, turn right and walk alongside a wire fence on your left-hand side, walking in the direction of a wooded hill ahead. In about 250 yards go through a wooden gate (yellow arrow) and cross the railway track-bed to join an unmetalled drive. In about 50 yards the drive takes you past a brick cottage on the left, then up to a metalled lane. Turn right and walk along this quiet country lane for about 1³/4 miles.

The river is now across fields to the right, and for a while the lane runs along a broad flat valley whose graceful flanks are tree-robed hills. In about 1/2 a mile you will pass by the black and white house and farm buildings observed earlier from the riverside path. The exceptional half-timbered house is Severn Hall, an Elizabethan pile which has seen its fair share of drama during the centuries. The Whitmores are past owners, but one tenant, John Newton who had been a Church Warden, was hanged at Shrewsbury in 1823 for murdering his wife. A copy of his doggerel verse of public confession apparently still exists at the house.

6. Immediately after the hall on the right, the lane climbs steeply beside one of the wooded slopes, known as Donelley's Bank. After the climb the lane levels out. After several hundred yards, where the lane parts company with the woodland to the left you will see Boldings farm ahead left. Ignore a fingerpost pointing into a field on the right.

7. Walk along the lane and in a short distance pass by another fingerpost pointing into a field on the right. About 50 yards further on turn left at the sign for 'Boldings Pools'. Walk down a drive towards some farm buildings. On reaching a large nissen hut turn right, and in 35 yards turn left opposite the farmhouse at Boldings Farm. Walk away from the farm buildings along a wide track. In about 200 yards pass by a fishing pool on the left. There is a further small pool nearby on the right.

You have reached Boldings Pools, a lucrative hoard of water-filled basins belonging to the owners of the farm who let them to enthusiastic anglers. The major pools are named after trees (including oak, ash and beech) and not surprisingly, lined with small tracts of woodland creating an agreeable environment. Prize catches from these waters include carp, tench and roach.

8. Ignore the path to the left and walk straight ahead along the original path which soon curves upwards and to the left. At the top of the slope you will see further pools to the right and left. 100 yards further along there is another pool on the left, and other smaller ones in the hollows to the right. Continue straight ahead along a cart track across a field. At an oak tree bearing an arrow symbol, bear right leaving the main track.

Walk alongside a row of fir trees on the right for about 70 yards to reach a second oak with an arrow symbol. Follow the arrow to bear right and in about 45 yards climb a stile. Turn left and walk along the left-hand edge of a field beside a fence. In the far left-hand

corner of the field, walk down a short slope still alongside the fence to a stile. Cross a narrow wooden footbridge over a stream then climb another stile to enter a further small field.

Walk along the left-hand side of the field, soon passing a cottage on the left. Walk through a wide gap leading onto a metalled lane. Turn left to walk immediately into the village of Astley Abbots, passing by the Post House on the left before reaching the village's main treasures; the black and white Astley Abbots House and the ancient church of St Calixtus.

The village name is thought to mean the 'East Leigh of the Abbot' (of Shrewsbury) to whom the Manor was transferred by

Houses in Astley Abbots

Roger de Montgomery. The church, built originally in 1138, is the only one in England dedicated to Calixtus, a dishonest Italian banker who much later became bishop of Rome. The church retains its original Norman font, and its chancel was rebuilt during Charles I's reign in 1633. Evocative memorials within the church include that of Colonel Billingsley, who fell at the siege of Bridgnorth, and of Hannah Phillips, who was tragically drowned crossing the river on the eve of her wedding in 1707. Her memorial consists of the maiden's garlands and gloves which hang in the north-west corner of the nave. Astley House opposite the Church is an impressive half-timbered mansion surrounded by extensive lawns and gardens.

9. Re-trace your steps out of the village again, passing by the wide gap from which you emerged onto the lane before entering the village. After several hundred yards pass by a long narrow pool on the edge of woodland on the left. In a few hundred yards pass two houses on the left. Soon the lane curves sharply right and in about 150 yards you arrive back at the start.

Melverley - River Vyrnwy - Melverley Green - Melverley - River Severn - Melverley

◆

O.S. Map 1:50,000 Landranger 126. Starting Point: GR 332 165.
Parking: Roadside verge of driveway near St Peter's Church, Melverley
just off road from Melverley Green to Crew Green.
Distance 2^1/2 miles and 3 miles.

A generally easy walk in two parts which includes appreciable stretches
of both the Vyrnwy and Severn rivers. In part two there are numerous fences
and gates to climb along the Severn which can prove rather challenging.
The area generally is prone to flooding and some paths can become muddy.

Melverley Church

Part One

The little black and white church of St Peter is undoubtedly Melverley's real treasure. It is one of only two timber-framed churches in Shropshire, composed of oak timbers both inside and out. It was probably originally built in the 15th century and some of its internal features

73

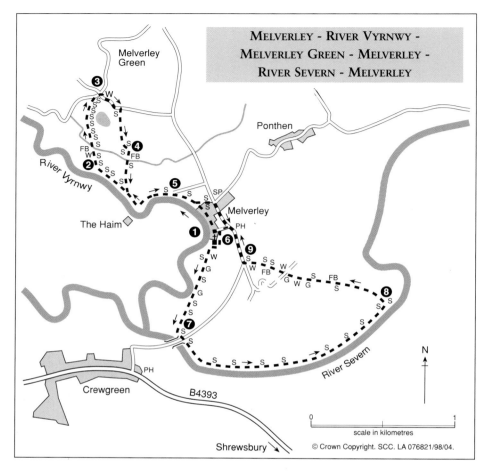

MELVERLEY - RIVER VYRNWY -
MELVERLEY GREEN - MELVERLEY -
RIVER SEVERN - MELVERLEY

© Crown Copyright. SCC. LA 076821/98/04.

include a Jacobean pulpit and a sanctuary window of red, blue and gold. The church overlooks the river Vyrnwy which swept part of the building away in the middle ages. In recent times also, the church has been under threat from the dangers of floodwater, although matters seem now to have been successfully sorted out.

1. Go through the main church gate and turn right to walk along the churchyard for about 30 yards and go through a small wooden gate. Join a wide grassy track ahead. The Vyrnwy is close by on the left. In about 150 yards climb a stile ahead.

There is a clear view of the Breidden hills in the distance to the left.

Walk along the grassy track which curves to the left and in about 250 yards reaches another stile.

You are walking on top of a length of embankment (known locally as an 'Argy'). There are several in the district and they were built mostly in the 1780's as river flood barriers. They are also able to channel floodwater from smaller water courses back into the river.

Climb the stile and walk ahead for about 50 yards to the next stile. Climb the stile and walk further along the embankment for several hundred yards. After 250 yards, pass the white-washed frontage of a small farm on the opposite bank, called the Haim. Continue along the path and eventually climb a wooden fence near a gate. Walk straight ahead and climb another wooden fence alongside a metal gate, and continue ahead. Climb a further wooden fence.

2. Walk straight ahead and in a short distance, climb yet another wooden fence before turning sharp right and descending a short grassy bank. Climb a stile then walk ahead across the field to a stile at the opposite edge.

The walk has for the time being, wandered away from the river into the flat, open countryside on the fringes of Melverley Green.

Climb the stile and cross a narrow field towards a wooden fence. Climb the fence, cross a footbridge and climb a second fence to enter another small field. Cross the field and a stile. Enter the next field and walk towards and climb a stile at the far end. Cross a narrow lane and climb the stile opposite to enter a larger field. Cross the field, bearing left towards a stile at the far side. Halfway across the field, pass by a small pool and reed-bed on the right. Climb a stile and turn immediate right in front of a corrugated shed. Cross the field which has a red brick cottage, lawns and a pool nearby on the left. Climb a stile then turn right onto a metalled lane.

3. Walk along the lane and where it turns sharp left, climb a stile opposite and follow the direction of a fingerpost.

The tree-covered Criggion and Rodney's Pillar stand in full view across the fields ahead. The rocky hill looms steep and towering over the flatter countryside beneath. The rock of

*The Haim
and the Breiddens
from the River Vyrnwy*

the Criggion is of the Ordovician period (some 492 million years old) and consists of lower shales intruded by dolerite forming the steep-sided slope so visible today.

4. At the field-edge, follow the direction arrows on wooden fences to walk along the left-hand edge of the next field. Cross a narrow footbridge then climb a stile. Follow the arrow direction across a field towards a stile on the embankment again. Climb a short grassy slope to rejoin the embankment encountered early in the walk. Climb a stile to walk above the riverside which is now down to the right.

Heron can sometimes be seen, patiently fishing along this stretch of water, while cows will often troop across the field like an exhausted army, to wade knee-deep in the Vyrnwy.

Pass by the white farm house

which stands at the opposite bank of the river. Walk for a few hundred yards along the riverside, then climb a stile and walk ahead a short distance to the next stile.

5. Climb the stile and soon leave the embankment as it curves to the right, by walking straight ahead down a slope and diagonally left across a field to a stile in the far corner. Climb the stile and turn right, walking along a metalled road soon arriving back in Melverley village. At the Tontine Inn turn right into the drive leading to the church.

Part Two

6. Just before reaching the church, turn left, as indicated by a fingerpost and walk along a broad track. In about 75 yards, climb a stile by a metal gate and bear right along

a broad trackway. Go through a wooden gate, then climb a stile and walk along the left-hand side of a hedge alongside a cropfield. At the end of the hedge, where the field opens out, walk diagonally right across a field towards a distant bridge. Eventually join an embankment and climb a metal gate and continue straight ahead. Climb a wooden fence and walk ahead between open fields to the next stile. Climb a wooden fence and walk towards a nearby bridge over the river Severn.

The Severn was joined a few hundred yards to the right of this point by the Vyrnwy which had snaked its languid way through silent meadows before finally merging its identity with that of the larger river.

7. Just before reaching the lattice-work road bridge over the river, turn left and climb a stile, then turn left onto a metalled road. In a few yards turn right, descend a short track and climb another stile on to a field path which runs close to the Severn. Beginning with the stile you have just climbed, you will need to start counting the number of stiles/fences until negotiating the tenth one.

This will be crucial to knowing how to complete the rest of the walk.

The United Kingdom's longest river, now swollen by the waters of the Vyrnwy frequently hosts parties of swan and mallard along this stretch. The bridge near which you have just walked provides a good view of the merging of the two rivers. Since the early 1960's the viaduct has been a road bridge but prior to that, it carried a branch line of one of Shropshire's most romantic light railways - the Shropshire and Montgomeryshire Railway. The line was often referred to as the 'Potts' line, since it began life in 1861 as the Potteries, Shrewsbury and North Wales Railway. Trains ran from Shrewsbury Abbey Station to Llanymynech, with a branch line between Kinnerley and Criggion via Melverley. Those early entrepreneurs were brave enough to risk building a railway to service scattered villages and flood-prone terrain. Not surprisingly the enterprise suffered a series of financial difficulties even during its earlier days. Nevertheless, the branch line was opened from Kinnerley to Criggion in 1871, mainly for the haulage of granite from the Breidden quarries. There was some passenger traffic and Melveley had its own little station. At one time the guard would have to put down a pair of steps to assist passengers in boarding the train. The original Melverley wooden viaduct collapsed in 1902 and a new one was built when the railway re-opened about ten years later. In 1932 passenger services terminated at Melverley, since the viaduct had again become unsafe. Passenger services on the entire network ceased in 1933, and goods traffic from Criggion in 1959.

The route continues now on top of another argy. Eventually, walk towards a wooden fence beside a metal gate. Climb the fence and walk towards the next fence and gate.

The Severn is nearby to the right, backed by flowing hill country. The walk continues close to the river for roughly one mile. This allows the walker ample opportunity to enjoy the pleasures of the waterside and scenic views of its accompanying wooded undulating landscape. Unfortunately, it is also necessary to climb a succession of wooden fences in order to progress along this lengthy stretch of riverside. Since hedges impede your progress at the actual waterside, you will need to use the embankment and the wooden fences to cover the route.

8. Distances between the various fences/stiles (some single, some double) vary between 120 and 270 yards, and the river is never far away. Having climbed the tenth stile/fence turn immediate left and walk along the right-hand side of a hedge. Next, walk diagonally right across a field. At the far end of the field, climb a stile and cross a footbridge leading into another field. Walk diagonally left across the field to a stile next to a wide metal gate (there is a fingerpost and 'National Rivers Authority' sign also nearby). Turn right onto a short stretch of unmetalled lane, soon passing by a second fingerpost. In a few yards leave the lane by means of a gate leading into a field. Walk diagonally right across the field. At the far end of the field, climb a stile, then a fence, then cross a footbridge leading into another field. Cross this small field by walking ahead towards a stile on the opposite

side. Climb the stile and walk ahead towards a stile and fingerpost at the field edge.

9. Climb the stile turn right on to a short stretch of lane, then right again on to the road which leads you in several hundred yards to the Tontine Hotel once again. Turn left, and walk up the drive towards Melverley church.

EXPLORING SHROPSHIRE
with Shropshire Books

BOOKS

Available Now

UNDISCOVERED SHROPSHIRE
14 Walks in North Shropshire
Eve Powell

WALKS WITH WRITERS
Gordon Dickins and
Gladys Mary Coles

GREEN WALKS FROM
OSWESTRY
Mary Hignett

WALKS AROUND TELFORD
David Gregory

TEN WALKS THAT CHANGED
THE WORLD
Walks into Shropshire's
Industrial Past
Kate and Keith Pybus

SHROPSHIRE WALKS
BY THE WATERSIDE
David Gregory

TOWN TRAILS

Available Now

Bridgnorth
Ludlow
Much Wenlock
Oswestry

LEAFLETS

Available Now

Acton Scott
Alveley
Bridgnorth
Ludlow
Much Wenlock
Oswestry
Stiperstones
Stokesay
The Jack Mytton Way
*(long distance path for walkers,
horses and cyclists)*

Forthcoming

Pontesbury
Market Drayton

CYCLE TRAILS

Available Now

Corvedale

Countryside and Woodland

The Jack Mytton Way
*(long distance path for cyclists,
horses and walkers)*

Cycling For Pleasure
in the Marches
(five leaflet pack)

◆

For further details of these and many more books on Shropshire contact:

SHROPSHIRE BOOKS
Column House, 7 London Road
SHREWSBURY SY2 6NW